Kasparov: How His Predecessors Misled Him About Chess

Tibor Károlyi and Nick Aplin

BATSFORD

First published in the United Kingdom in 2009 by

Batsford
The Old Magistrates Court
10 Southcombe Street
London
W14 0RA

An imprint of Anova Books Company Ltd

ISBN: 9781906388263

A CIP catalogue record for this book is available from the British Library.
17 16 15 14 13 12 11 10 09
10 9 8 7 6 5 4 3 2 1

Reproduction by Spectrum Colour Ltd, Ipswich

Printed and bound by Athenaeum Press Ltd., Gateshead, Tyne & Wear

This book can be ordered direct from the publisher at the website
www.anovabooks.com

Or try your local bookshop

Contents

Authors' Preface

This book is a unique reaction to a unique collection of creative work.

When Garry Kasparov, the most successful world champion, retired, he published a series of books under the title *My Great Predecessors* and it was the stimulation from reading his excellent series that prompted the present work.

After writing two books on Kasparov's astonishing career, covering his final period of active play from 1993 to 2005, we realised that there were similarities between Garry's games and some of his predecessors – and this has opened the door for a little bit of friendly leg-pulling!

Our original idea to write an article for the satirical chess magazine *Kingpin* took on greater proportions as we found more and more games resembling those of past champions.

The increasing number of examples changed the single article into a series of articles. We had originally intended to look only at the post-World War II champions but then discovered so many comparable games from earlier times that we were encouraged to write a whole book!

There was a stage during the writing of *Kasparov's Fighting Chess 1 & 2* that we briefly considered the title *The Great Successor* would be appropriate.

This present book now provides us with an obvious opportunity to introduce some humour, particularly as Kasparov – we think – subconsciously favoured some teasing of the great players and former champions more so than others. By doing so he invited others to have a joke at his expense too. Humour in chess – sometimes a rare commodity – needs to take its rightful place.

The Hungarian half of our co-authorship played in tournaments with Garry and even faced him across the board in 1980 and 1981. The 1980 World Junior Championship was particularly memorable for Tibor, because of the leisure hours he spent with Garry himself – during which time the future world champion revealed his keen sense of humour.

This characteristic is something that has not been reflected in his interviews in recent times, although there were glimpses of it when he came to write his *My Great Predecessors* books.

It goes without saying that games played by world champions can be especially interesting, entertaining and instructive. But it is also well worth looking at them from a new angle – and with a lighter touch.

The temptation is also there to look at some of Kasparov's *losses* – which are in fact well worth analysing. Anyone who manages to force resignation from the most successful chess player ever, clearly deserves due recognition for their triumph.

In no way does the present book try to erode the tremendous respect Kasparov has rightfully earned with his stunning and breathtaking performances. It just reminds everyone emphatically what a great game chess is and that even the greatest players make mistakes – and do lose sometimes! The royal game is just so complicated...

Also we consider that the *My Great Predecessors* books represent a superb contribution to chess culture and warmly recommend that both non-professionals and serious players read the whole series, as Garry's chess genius shines brightly through his deep analysis.

One of the intentions of the present book is to take a look at some lesser-known masterpieces of the champions, as well as presenting the better-known examples, with short explanations. We hope you enjoy and learn from these games.

It is great that Garry wrote his series, but if I were him I would have produced another version for reading on New Year's Eve!

Our book is designed to be light-hearted. So before we allow Garry to speak, let us emphasise that we did not contact him at all and the words are ours!! We just put our ideas into his mouth in the following way.

* * * *

My series on the world champions is entering its final phase. In these books, I have covered the development of chess culture. Thank God they sold like hot cakes. I wrote nice things about all the 12 champions, which is what they justly deserved, but I only showed the rosier side of their chess.

By now most of the books have been sold, so it is time to tell the rest of the story. My career has been the best a chessplayer has ever had and, all things considered, I am satisfied with how things went. On the other hand, I am convinced I did not achieve everything that I could have done: for example, I lost more games than was necessary. And in the present work I reveal for the first time how I came to lose quite a few important games simply because I copied the world champions. It's a pity that I didn't gain a fuller appreciation of their methods.

Almost all chessplayers read books on the world champions. I did so as well and in my childhood I even went through their games in great detail. In fact I frequently tried to memorise their games, but it is more likely that they planted themselves in the subconscious part of my brain. Their games were praised so many times and in so many places that I came to trust them implicitly.

Of course, I must also take some responsibility for my losses, but you will see that for the particular defeats shown here the world champions are mostly to blame because they misled me – sometimes seriously. After all, it was they who demonstrated the ideas in the first place.

Can you imagine how hard it has been for me to hold back my true opinions for so long? But now I cannot remain silent any longer and must show how the champions *really* played. Though I have to admit that their games are very entertaining, that can only soften, but not erase, the negative effect they had on me.

So as to underline the fact that this is not a totally serious book, I do not lay out the material in the conventional way. Instead of starting from the distant past and working my way towards the present day, I adopt a different plan based on the fact that the closer a champion was to me in time, the more energy I spent on examining his play.

So I look at the champions in reverse order, starting with Anatoly Karpov, who was crowned before me as the 12th world champion.

Anatoly Karpov the 12ᵗʰ

Anatoly Karpov was my immediate predecessor. He held the title from 1975 until 1985 and certainly had an immense effect on my chess. I played him 23 times in regular tournaments. There is nothing special about that but the 144 games in the five world championship matches we contested *is* unique in the history of chess.

Despite this large number of games, you might think they had little negative effect on my style. Of course I learned to play simple positions – there were many of them – and I improved my technique in this area.

In this book I would like to concentrate on the negative effects that I experienced from the world champions – effects which prevented me from becoming even more devastating in my play.

One idea I picked up from Karpov was to push the a- or h-pawns all the way – and win. Below are positions from Karpov's games illustrating this theme and then positions from my own games where I followed his plan.

S.Sazontiev – A.Karpov

A.Karpov – G.Kasparov

A.Karpov – P.Markland

A.Karpov – G.Kasparov

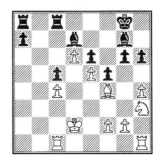

Readers note: throughout the text you will read the words *see diagram* with a reference to a certain page. It's the diagrams in the *frames* to which we refer.

First let me show you some games where Karpov employed one of his favourite concepts.

S.Sazontiev – A.Karpov
Vladimir 1964

1 d4 ♘f6 2 ♘f3 e6 3 ♗g5 d5 4 c4 ♗e7 5 ♘c3 0-0 6 e3 ♘bd7 7 ♗d3 ♖e8 8 0-0 ♘f8 9 ♘e5 c6 10 f4 ♘6d7 11 ♗xe7 ♕xe7 12 ♖f3 f6 13 ♘g4 ♘b6 14 c5 ♘bd7 15 ♖g3 ♔h8 16 ♘f2 e5 17 ♕h5 e4 18 ♗e2 g6 19 ♕h6 b6 20 b4

20...a5!

Karpov starts pushing his a-pawn. It looks like it merely undermines White's pawn chain but in fact this move represents its debut performance in a very important role.

21 b5 ♗b7 22 cxb6 ♘xb6 23 bxc6 ♗xc6

See diagram on page 9.

24 h4 ♖ec8 25 h5

25...♕g7!

To exchange the most dangerous white piece in the attack.

26 ♕xg7+ ♔xg7 27 hxg6 hxg6 28 ♖b1 ♖ab8!

Now Black turns his attention to the side where he is stronger.

29 ♗a6 ♖c7 30 ♘fd1 ♘fd7 31 ♖h3?!

White wants to transfer the rook to the queenside.

On the other hand 31 ♗e2! would have kept Black rather busy on the kingside and he would not then have had such a free hand for his queenside operations.

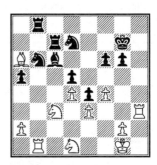

31...♗a4!

Karpov starts exchanging on the queenside so as to prepare an invasion. He follows up this plan with his customary and distinctive purposefulness.

32 ♖h2 ♗xd1 33 ♘xd1 ♘a4! 34 ♖a1 ♘c3! 35 g3 ♘xd1 36 ♖xd1 ♖c3 37 ♖e1

37...a4!

The pawn is becoming increasingly powerful.

38 ♖d2 ♖b6 39 ♗f1 ♔f7 40 ♖ee2

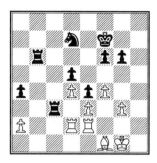

40...a3!

The pawn makes its final stride of a glorious march. It gets closer to promotion and takes control of the b2-square.

41 ♔f2 ♖b4 42 g4 ♘b6 43 ♖c2 ♖xc2 44 ♖xc2 ♖b2!

This is a poignant demonstration of the strength of the a3-pawn.

45 ♖e2 ♘a4 46 ♔e1

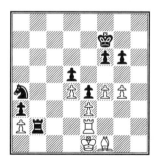

46...♘c3 47 ♖d2 ♘xa2 0-1

Finally the fixed a-pawn falls, and Black wins easily. Karpov engineered this game beautifully, yet strangely he did not include it in any books of his selected games. Maybe he did not want to alert his rivals to such an effective pawn-pushing device. Naturally, the game did not escape my attention.

A.Karpov – P.Markland

Hastings 1971/1972

1 e4 e6 2 d4 d5 3 ♘c3 ♗b4 4 e5 c5 5 a3 ♗xc3+ 6 bxc3 ♕c7 7 ♘f3 ♘e7

8 a4

I wouldn't mind betting that Karpov had not yet seen the final role this a-pawn had to play. Of course it is a well-known variation. Since that time 7 ♕g4 has taken over as the main line.

8...b6 9 ♗b5+ ♗d7 10 ♗d3 ♘bc6 11 0-0 h6 12 ♖e1 ♘a5 13 ♕d2 ♖c8 14 h4

Karpov uses his flank pawns well. Here he gains space and makes sure that ...g7-g5 is prevented.

14...0-0 15 ♕f4 f5 16 exf6 ♖xf6 17 ♕xc7 ♖xc7 18 dxc5 bxc5 19 ♘e5 ♗c8

Here 19...c4 looks better. It restricts the light-squared bishop even though that in turn grants more freedom to his dark-squared brother.

20 c4!

Karpov gets rid of the doubled pawns and opens the position for his bishops.

20...♘ac6 21 ♗b2 ♘b4

See diagram on page 9.

22 a5!?

This is a hard move to come up with. Perhaps it had been planned earlier. Had he already anticipated the role of this pawn or did he just want to prevent Black from playing a5 – a move which fixes White's a-pawn on the colour of the c8-bishop?

22...♖f8 23 ♗a3

23 h5, playing extravagantly with the other edge pawn, was also possible.

23...dxc4 24 ♘xc4 ♖f4

25 ♘d6

Karpov sacrifices a pawn to keep his opponent's rook out of the game. Here 25 ♖e4 holds on to the pawn by stopping ...♖xc4.

25...♘xd3 26 cxd3 ♖xh4 27 ♘e4 ♖h5 28 ♖ec1 ♗b7?!

After 28...♖d5 29 ♖c3 a6 Black can live with his position.

29 ♘xc5 ♗d5 30 f3 ♖f5

Black could improve his knight with 30...♘c6!?. Then 31 a6 ♘d4.

Not to be sidetracked, Karpov now plays according to a well-formulated plan. Firstly he fixes Black's a7-pawn.

31 a6! ♖f7 32 ♘e4

The a7-pawn is fixed. Karpov now brings up his bishop to place it under closer surveillance.

32...♘f5 33 ♗c5! ♖c8 34 ♗f2 ♖fc7 35 ♖xc7

Now Karpov starts to exchange pieces around the weak a7-pawn. All part of the plan.

35...♖xc7 36 ♖b1 ♘e7 37 ♖b8+ ♔h7 38 ♔h2!

This is a typical Karpovian king move. It prevents Black from delivering a check on c1, which would be followed by an attack on the a6-pawn with ♖a1.

38...♘g6?

This only helps White. He moves away a valuable piece from the area where the battle will take place.

39 ♘c5 ♖c6?

Returning the knight was better.

40 ♖d8 ♖c7

41 ♖d7!

Karpov continues to play with great purpose. He will exchange the defending rook as well.

41...♖xd7 42 ♘xd7 ♗c6 43 ♘b8 ♗b5

44 ♗xa7

Finally the ripened fruit drops quietly from the tree. White wins the pawn and so the rest is simple.

44...♘e7 45 ♗b6 ♘c8 46 ♗c5 ♔g6 47 a7 ♘xa7 48 ♗xa7 e5 49 d4 exd4 50 ♗xd4 ♔f7 51 f4 g5 52 fxg5 hxg5 53 ♔g3 ♔g6 54 ♔f3 ♔f5 55 g3 1-0

Karpov won this game in impressive style. This plan was implanted in my brain and I was just waiting for an opportune moment to carry it out in one of my own games. Quite incredibly I had my chance against Karpov himself.

A.Karpov – G.Kasparov
Game 17, World Championship
London/Leningrad 1986

1 d4 ♘f6 2 c4 g6 3 ♘c3 d5 4 ♘f3 ♗g7 5 ♕b3 dxc4 6 ♕xc4 0-0 7 e4 ♗g4 8 ♗e3 ♘fd7 9 ♖d1 ♘c6 10 ♗e2 ♘b6 11 ♕c5 ♕d6 12 e5

This was my third match against Karpov and he had prepared most diligently for it. Here he sacrifices a pawn – something he had rarely done before in this kind of situation. I think our matches forced him to increase his standard of play in the openings.

12...♕xc5 13 dxc5 ♘c8

The variation has continued to develop ever since our game. The knight can also be retreated to d7.

14 h3 ♗xf3 15 ♗xf3 ♗xe5 16 ♗xc6 bxc6 17 ♗d4

White achieves domination along the d-file – which provides compensation for the pawn deficit.

17...♗f4 18 0-0

See diagram on page 9.

18...a5?

At this moment I adopted Karpov's plan of pushing the a-pawn as far down the file as possible. And I really paid the price for this misguided decision.

A few months later Timman improved on this game with 18...e5!. Maybe he never bothered to investigate Karpov's earlier games. After 19 ♗e3 ♗xe3 20 fxe3 ♘e7 21 ♖d7 ♘f5 Timman achieved a draw against Karpov in Tilburg 1986. Black has done well in this position ever since.

19 ♖fe1 a4?!

I stuck to the plan that I had learned from Anatoly Evgenievich.

20 ♖e4 ♗h6 21 ♗e5

21...a3?

I was still playing in the spirit of Karpov, in the hope that somehow I would be able to get down to the a2-pawn. However it proves to be an illusion.

22 b3 ♘a7

This was not my day, I was unable to push either of my rook's pawns, but putting the knight on the edge was also unfortunate. 22...♗g7 was probably better.

23 ♖d7! ♗c1 24 ♖xc7 ♗b2 25 ♘a4 ♘b5 26 ♖xc6

Now White is already a pawn up.

26...♖fd8 27 ♖b6 ♖d5 28 ♗g3

28...♘c3

This is the closest I got to attacking that a2-pawn.

29 ♘xc3 ♗xc3 30 c6

The c-pawn simply kills Black.

30...♗d4 31 ♖b7 1-0

To end the misery I resigned.

A.Karpov – G.Kasparov
Game 5, World Championship,
London/Leningrad 1986

1 d4 ♘f6 2 c4 g6 3 ♘c3 d5 4 ♗f4 ♗g7 5 e3 c5 6 dxc5 ♕a5 7 ♖c1 ♘e4 8 cxd5 ♘xc3 9 ♕d2 ♕xa2 10 bxc3 ♕xd2+ 11 ♔xd2 ♘d7 12 ♗b5 0-0 13 ♗xd7 ♗xd7 14 e4 f5 15 e5 e6 16 c4 ♖fc8 17 c6 bxc6 18 d6 c5 19 h4 h6

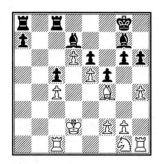

20 ♘h3!

A strong move that my team and I missed during preparation. I hoped the g7-bishop would become a powerhouse on the long diagonal, but it stayed buried all the way to the end.

20...a5?

See diagram on page 9.

Again I push the rook's pawn just like Karpov.

21 f3 a4

The plan must be pursued.

22 ♖he1!

Another strong move as it preserves the e5 pawn and makes sure the g7-bishop remains bottled up. I should have copied this aspect of Karpov's style!

22...a3

Nothing will divert me from pushing the a-pawn.

23 ♘f2

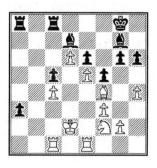

23...a2

The pawn has got this far yet it is to no avail. I was so happy to see the open road ahead but should have checked more carefully where that road would lead.

24 ♘d3 ♖a3 25 ♖a1 g5

A desperate attempt to stir things up.

26 hxg5 hxg5 27 ♗xg5 ♔f7 28 ♗f4 ♖b8 29 ♖ec1 ♗c6 30 ♖c3 ♖a5 31 ♖c2 ♖ba8 32 ♘c1 1-0

Finally White wins the a-pawn. Black spent four tempi advancing the pawn to its doom.

Here I resigned and decided that in the future I would be far more cautious about following Karpov's method of play.

Karpov contributed to one of my losses in the final of a knockout tournament I played on the internet. From the first position below he taught me that in a rook ending, with 3 pawns versus 4 on one side of the board, the game can be saved.

The second diagram shows the very similar position that I reached.

J.Piket – G.Kasparov

V.Korchnoi – A.Karpov

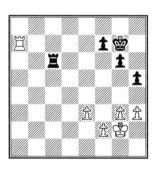

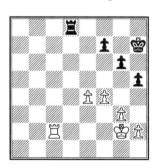

V.Korchnoi – A.Karpov
Game 5, World Championship,
Merano 1981

1 c4 e6 2 ♘c3 d5 3 d4 ♗e7 4 ♘f3 ♘f6 5 ♗g5 h6 6 ♗h4 0-0 7 ♖c1 b6

8 cxd5 ♘xd5 9 ♘xd5 exd5 10 ♗xe7 ♕xe7 11 g3 ♗a6 12 e3 c5 13 dxc5 bxc5

Two games later in the match Karpov played 13...♗b7 and drew.

14 ♗xa6 ♘xa6

15 ♕xd5

Petrosian, the specialist of this line where White delays e2-e3, did not take the pawn and went on to beat Portisch this way.

15...♘b4 16 ♕c4 ♕f6 17 ♘h4 ♕xb2 18 0-0 ♕xa2

Taking the last white queenside pawn is an achievement, yet there is no guarantee of a draw as the knights are still on the board.

19 ♕xa2 ♘xa2 20 ♖xc5 ♖fc8 21 ♖a5 ♘c1 22 ♘f5 ♖c7 23 ♘d4 ♖b8 24 ♖a1 ♘d3

Karpov is not yet ready to enter the 4 pawns against 3 rook ending. If 24...♘b3 25 ♖fb1 ♖cb7 26 ♖xb3 ♖xb3 27 ♘xb3 ♖xb3 28 ♖xa7.

25 ♖fd1 ♘e5 26 ♖a2 g6 27 ♖da1 ♖bb7 28 h3

28...h5!

This is a very useful refinement in the ensuing rook ending.

29 ♔g2 ♔g7 30 ♖a5 ♘c6

He finally agrees to defend the 4 against 3 ending. But Black was not forced to give up the pawn as 30...♔f6 was an option. This misled me and gave me the impression this it is an easy draw.

31 ♘xc6 ♖xc6 32 ♖xa7 ♖xa7 33 ♖xa7

See diagram on page 15.

33...♖c2

Karpov often pins pieces. With White's king on f2 the pawn can't go much further. I used to think it requires some effort to draw this type of position but the ease with which Karpov held this one made me think Black can't lose at all. I was wrong.

34 e4 ♖c3 35 ♖a2 ♔f6 36 f3 ♖b3 37 ♔f2 ♖c3 38 ♔e2 ♖b3 39 ♖a6+ ♔e7 40 ♖a5 ♔f6 41 ♖d5

41...♖a3 42 ♖d6+ ♔g7 43 h4 ♖b3 44 ♖d3 ♖b5 45 ♔e3 ½-½ Karpov effortlessly held this position.

J.Piket – G.Kasparov
KasparovChess Grand Prix
60 minute game, Internet 2000

1 ♘f3 ♘f6 2 c4 c5 3 ♘c3 d5 4 cxd5 ♘xd5 5 g3 ♘c6 6 ♗g2 ♘c7 7 d3 e5 8 0-0 ♗e7 9 ♘d2 ♗d7 10 ♘c4 0-0 11 ♗xc6 ♗xc6

12 ♘xe5
Piket accepts my pawn sacrifice.
12...♗e8 13 ♕b3 ♗f6 14 ♘g4 ♗d4 15 e3 ♗xc3 16 ♕xc3 b6 17 f3 ♗b5 18 ♘f2 ♕d7 19 e4 ♘e6 20 ♗e3 a5 21 ♖ad1 ♖ad8 22 ♖d2 ♕c6

According to my opponent's analysis the queen should go to b7.
23 ♖c1 ♕b7

24 a3
I also tried a6 and b5 with Black in a number of English opening games.

Would you believe what happened? You will see it in the Fischer chapter.

24...♘d4 25 ♔g2 ♖c8 26 ♖b1 ♖fd8 27 ♗xd4 ♖xd4 28 b4

In my case this plan did not work, so I was optimistic that I would do well against it.

28...axb4 29 axb4 ♕d7 30 bxc5 bxc5

Here I realised I couldn't win. But okay, no problem. It was a knockout final and I thought I would draw the next game with the white pieces.

31 ♖bb2 h6 32 ♖a2 ♔h7 33 ♖a5 ♖d8 34 ♕xc5 ♗xd3

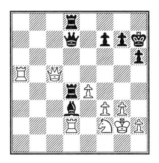

35 ♖xd3
After 35 ♖b2 ♖c8 36 ♕f5+ ♕xf5 37 ♖xf5 ♗c4 it is hard to do anything with White's pieces.

35...♖xd3 36 ♘xd3 ♕xd3 37 ♖a2 ♕b3

38 ♕c2

With queens on the board White can't really push the pawns, therefore it should be an easy draw, but I knew how easily Karpov drew with Korchnoi, so I decided to follow him. I was also aware that Karpov wasn't able to squeeze a win against Olafsson when he had an extra pawn in this kind of endgame. Even before the Karpov game I knew this position was a draw, however it was Anatoly who convinced me it was easy and made me play too casually.

38...♕xc2+ 39 ♖xc2 h5

I play just like Karpov.

40 f4 g6

See diagram on page 15.

Karpov also had his pawn on g6.

41 e5 ♖d3

I'm just following Karpov, who kept his rook on the third rank, did nothing and held easily.

42 ♔h3

Korchnoi did not try anything like this – and Korchnoi was a really strong endgame player

42...♖e3

I just keep moving like my predecessor before me.

43 ♔h4 ♔g7 44 ♔g5

Here I deviated from Karpov and removed the rook from the third rank.

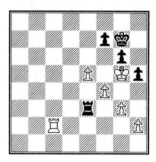

44...♖e1?

This was my independent idea – but it loses. I was short of time. Correct was 44...♖a3! 45 ♖c7 ♖a5.

45 ♖c7 ♖e2 46 ♖e7! ♖a2

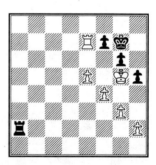

47 f5!

This is nasty indeed. I was in time pressure because it was a 1 hour game with no increment.

47...gxf5 48 e6!

Oh no.

48...h4 49 ♖xf7+ ♔g8 50 ♔f6 1-0

And I had to resign.

18

Karpov has played some very well-known games in which he moved his knight backwards to the first rank. I also know some games where he placed the knight on the rook file. Here are three of his positions – followed by three of mine.

Sadovsky – A.Karpov

G.Kamsky – G.Kasparov

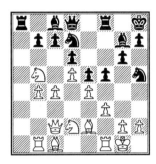

Z.Ribli – A.Karpov

Y.Nikolaevsky – G.Kasparov

J.Nunn – A.Karpov

L.Zaid – G.Kasparov

Sadovsky – A.Karpov
USSR Olympiad 1967

1 c4 ♘f6 2 ♘c3 e5 3 g3 g6 4 ♗g2 ♗g7 5 e4 d6 6 ♘ge2 ♗e6

Karpov was fairly young when he played this game.

7 d4! 0-0 8 d5 ♗d7 9 0-0 ♘h5

See diagram on page 19.

Karpov develops his knight on the edge.

10 ♗e3 f5 11 ♕d2 ♘a6

The other steed does the same thing.

12 f3 ♖f7 13 a3 ♘c5 14 ♕c2 ♕e8 15 b4 ♘a4

The third knight move to the edge.

16 c5 f4 17 ♗f2 fxg3 18 hxg3

Now the players enter a long manoeuvring phase.

18...♘xc3 19 ♘xc3 ♕e7 20 ♕d2 ♖af8 21 ♕e3 a6 22 a4 ♗f6 23 ♕d3 ♗g5 24 ♖a3 ♘g7 25 ♘e2 ♕e8 26 ♕c2 h5 27 ♗e1 ♖f6 28 ♗f2 ♔h7 29 ♗e1 ♗h6 30 ♗f2 ♗c8 31 ♖fa1?

This is overdoing a good idea. One piece too many goes to the edge. 31 ♖fb1 was correct.

31...♗g4 32 f4?! ♗xe2 33 ♕xe2 exf4 34 ♗d4 ♖6f7 35 b5 ♘f5

For a long time the knight which had been on h5 had no useful move, now it intervenes with decisive force.

36 ♗f2 fxg3 37 ♗xg3 ♘xg3 38 ♖xg3

38...♕e5

The rest is simple.

39 ♖aa3 axb5 40 cxd6 b4 41 ♖ad3 cxd6 42 ♕e1 ♖c7 43 ♖gf3 ♖xf3 44 ♗xf3 ♖c2 45 ♗g2 ♖c1 46 ♖d1 ♗e3+ 47 ♔h1 ♖xd1 48 ♕xd1 b3 49 ♕xb3 ♕g3 50 ♕xb7+ ♔h6 0-1

Z.Ribli – A.Karpov
Tilburg 1980

1 c4 e5 2 ♘c3 ♘c6 3 g3 g6 4 ♗g2 ♗g7 5 d3 d6 6 e3 ♘ge7 7 ♘ge2 0-0 8 0-0 ♗d7 9 h3 ♖b8 10 ♕d2 ♗e6

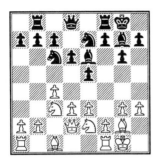 

11 ♘d5

The knights still look to the centre, but maybe this just diverts the attention of the opponent.

11...♕d7 12 ♔h2 f5 13 f4 b5 14 ♖b1 bxc4 15 dxc4 e4 16 b4? ♘a5!

See diagram on page 19.

Karpov puts his knight on the edge and wins instantly. What a lucky fellow!

17 ♘d4 ♘xc4 18 ♘xe7+ ♕xe7 19 ♕c2 ♗xd4 20 exd4 ♘b6 21 ♗b2 ♘d5 22 a3 ♘e3 23 ♕c3 ♘xf1+ 24 ♗xf1 ♗d5 25 ♗c4 ♕e6 0-1

The next game is unusual, as I was not selecting lost games from a champion, but here Karpov reached a position with two knights on the edge.

J.Nunn – A.Karpov
3rd Amber-rapid, Monte Carlo 1994

1 e4 c6 2 d4 d5 3 e5 ♗f5 4 ♘c3 e6 5 g4 ♗g6 6 ♘ge2 ♘e7 7 ♗e3 h5 8 ♘f4 hxg4 9 ♘xg6 ♘xg6 10 ♕xg4 ♘h4 11 ♗d3 g6 12 0-0-0 ♗e7 13 ♔b1 ♘d7 14 ♘e2 ♘b6 15 ♘f4 ♘a4

Karpov achieves symmetry with his knights and rooks on the two sides of the board.

16 ♘e2 b5 17 ♘c1 ♘b6 18 ♘b3 ♘c4 19 ♖hg1 a5 20 ♗c1 a4 21 ♘c5 ♗xc5 22 dxc5 ♘xe5 23 ♕g3 ♘ef3 24 ♖h1 e5 25 ♗e4 ♕f6 26 ♗xf3 ♘xf3 27 ♖d3

27...e4

Black is winning. If I wanted to be sarcastic I could say he has a winning edge (advantage) in the middle of the board.

28 ♖xf3 exf3 29 ♖e1+ ♔f8 30 ♗g5 ♕f5 31 h4 ♔g8 32 ♖e5 ♕d7 33 ♖e7 ♕f5 34 ♖e5 ♕c8 35 ♗f6 ♖h7 36 h5 ♕f8 37 a3 ♕xc5 38 ♕g1 ♖h6 39 ♕g5 ♕f8 40 hxg6 fxg6? 40...♖xg6 wins. 41 ♖e7 ♖e8 42 ♖d7 ♖h1+ 43 ♔a2 ♕h6 44 ♕g3 ♖he1 45 ♕c7 ♖1e7 46 ♖xe7 ♖xe7 47 ♕xe7 ♕f8 48 ♕e6+

21

♕f7 49 ♕xc6 d4+ 50 ♔b1 d3 51 cxd3 ♔h7 52 ♕xf3 ♖b3 53 ♕h3+ ♔g8 54 ♕h8+ ♔f7 55 ♕g7+ ♔e8 0-1

Karpov's knight on the brink was in my mind almost all the time. Let me show you one of my games from the time when I reigned as world champion and two when I was a junior player.

G.Kamsky – G.Kasparov
Dortmund 1992

1 d4 ♘f6 2 c4 g6 3 ♘c3 ♗g7 4 e4 d6 5 ♘f3 0-0 6 ♗e2 e5 7 0-0 ♘c6 8 d5 ♘e7 9 ♘d2 a5 10 a3 ♘d7

There is no chance of this knight going to h5, but with a couple of moves I manage to close the diagonal and make it possible to place the other knight in an attacking position on that square.

11 ♖b1 f5 12 b4 ♔h8 13 f3

The diagonal is now closed and it's worth spending a few tempi getting the knight where Karpov had put it.

13...♘g8 14 ♕c2 ♘gf6 15 ♘b5 axb4 16 axb4 ♘h5

Mission accomplished.

See diagram on page 19.

17 g3 ♘df6 18 c5 ♗d7 19 ♖b3 ♗h6

Against Karpov in Tilburg 1991 I played 19... ♘xg3 and the game continued 20 hxg3 ♘h5 21 f4 exf4 22 c6. I later drew the game, despite finding myself in an almost hopelessly lost position. See page 34.

20 ♖c3

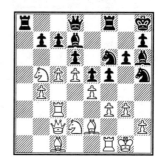

20...♗f4

This was a novelty in 1992.

21 cxd6

I was hoping for 21 gxf4?! as I could then have demonstrated some remarkable footwork along the touch line. 21...♘xf4 22 ♗c4 (22 ♘b3 ♘6xd5!) 22...♘6h5. The other knight goes there as well. Please note that all Black's moves now will be played on the flanks. 23 ♘b3 fxe4 24 fxe4 ♘h3+ 25 ♔h1 ♕h4 26 ♘xc7 ♖xf1+ 27 ♗xf1 ♖f8 and Black's subtle play has earned him a winning attack.

21...♘xg3

After 21...cxd6 22 ♘c7 ♗xg3! 23 hxg3 ♘xg3 24 ♖e1 ♘fh5 Anand produced some analysis and concluded that Black has the initiative;

Not 21...♗xb5 22 dxc7; or 21...♗xg3 22 dxc7 ♕e7 (22...♗xh2+ 23 ♔xh2 ♘g4+ 24 fxg4 ♕h4+ 25 ♖h3 wins.) 23 d6! when Black is in trouble.

22 hxg3 ♘h5

The other knight follows to h5. I did not pay due attention to the fact that Karpov had not played with such ferocity.

23 gxf4 ♘xf4

After 23...♕h4 24 ♖f2 ♘xf4 25 ♗f1 ♗xb5 26 dxc7!! wins as Anand pointed out.

24 ♗c4!

If 24 ♖f2 ♘h3+ – a common theme by now – (if 24...♕g5+ 25 ♔h1! ♕h4+ 26 ♖h2 ♕e1+ 27 ♗f1 ♗xb5 28 ♖xc7 ♘h5 – even this doesn't help – 29 ♕b2 wins.) 25 ♔f1 (25 ♔g2? ♕g5+! 26 ♔xh3 ♕g1! leads to a checkmate.) 25...♘xf2 26 ♔xf2 ♕h4+ 27 ♔g2 (27 ♔f1 ♕h1+ [27...f4 28 ♗c4!] 28 ♔f2 ♕h4+=) 27...f4 28 ♗f1 White survives the attack and wins with the extra material.

24...♘h3+

If 24...♕h4 25 ♘b3 ♘h3+ 26 ♔h1; or 24...♕g5+ 25 ♔f2 ♕h4+ 26 ♔e3.

Black gets his knight to the h-file, but does not have enough fire-power to back it up. This is rather transparent, but I also have one particularly nice memory of a surprising knight check on h3.

Here it is:

A.Grischuk – G.Kasparov
Linares 2001

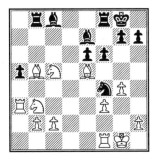

24...♘h3+!! 25 ♔g2 ♖xb5 26 ♗g3 ♘g5 27 ♗f2 ♗b7 28 ♗g1 ♖c8 29 h4 ♗xf3+ 30 ♖xf3 ♘xf3 31 ♔xf3 ♗xc5 32 ♘xc5 ♖bxc5 33 ♗xc5 ♖xc5 34 c3 h5 35 gxh5 ♖xh5 36 b4 axb4 37 cxb4 ♖xh4 0-1

Now back to my game with Kamsky:

25 ♔h1

If 25 ♔g2 ♕g5+ 26 ♔xh3? f4+ 27 ♔h2 ♕g3+ 28 ♔h1 ♕h3+ 29 ♔g1 ♕g3+=

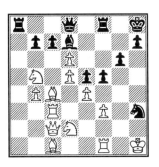

25...♕h4

This sets up a dangerous looking battery.

26 ♘b3 fxe4

After 26...♘f2+ 27 ♔g2 there is not enough juice left in the battery. 27...f4 28 ♕xf2 ♕h3+ 29 ♔g1 wins as Anand pointed out.

27 ♕h2

Not 27 fxe4?? ♘f2+ 28 ♔g2 ♗h3+ 29 ♔g1 ♕g4+ 30 ♔h2 ♕g2 mate.

27...♖f5 28 f4!

After 28 fxe4 ♖h5 (28...♕xe4+ 29 ♕g2) 29 ♖cf3 wins as well.

28...♖h5

Black's pieces are picturesquely but precariously placed on the h-file.

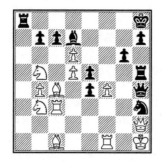

29 ♕g3 ♕xg3

This is tantamount to resignation but other moves also lose. If 29...♘xf4+ 30 ♕xh4; or 29...♕f6 30 fxe5 ♕g7 31 dxc7; or 29...♕d8 30 dxc7 ♘xf4+ 31 ♔g1 ♕f6 32 ♗xf4.

30 ♖xg3 exf4 31 ♗b2+ ♔g8 32 dxc7! ♗xb5

After 32...fxg3 33 d6+ ♗e6 34 ♗xe6 is mate.

33 ♗xb5 fxg3 34 ♔g2! ♘g5

And after 34...e3 35 ♗d7 wins.

35 d6 ♖h2+ 36 ♔xg3 ♖xb2 37 ♗c4+ ♔g7 38 d7 1-0

Y.Nikolaevsky – G.Kasparov
Moscow 1976

1 ♘f3 ♘f6 2 g3 g6 3 ♗g2 ♗g7 4 0-0 0-0 5 d4 d6 6 b3 c5 7 ♗b2 ♘c6 8 d5 ♘a5

The knight has reached its planned destination on the edge of the board fairly early in the game.

See diagram on page 19.

9 ♖e1 ♗f5

Just like Anatoly Evgenievich I am prepared to give up a tempo.

10 ♘bd2 ♕c8 11 e4

My opponent takes the free tempo, just like Karpov.

11...♗g4 12 c4

Black can build up pressure on the c4-square.

12...♘d7 13 ♗xg7 ♔xg7 14 ♕c2 ♗xf3 15 ♘xf3 ♕c7 16 ♕c3+ ♔g8 17 ♗h3 b6

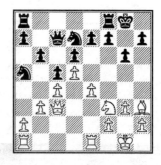

18 e5

White correctly opens the position in the centre. Now the knight is missing from the action.

18...dxe5 19 ♗xd7 ♕xd7 20 ♘xe5 ♕d6 21 ♘g4 h5 22 ♘e5 ♕f6

23 ℤe3

The e7-pawn is an obvious target.

23...ℤad8 24 ℤf3 ♕g7 25 ℤe1 ℤd6 26 b4 ♘b7 27 ♕a3 a5 28 bxa5 ♘xa5

It is a true delight that the knight can return to a5.

29 ♕a4 ♕h6 30 ℤee3?!

30 ♘d7 wins the exchange.

30...h4 31 gxh4 ♕xh4 32 ♘xf7?

An imaginative trick that wins the game, but objectively this thrust spoils White's position. 32 ♕c2 keeps an edge.

32...ℤf6?

The exploitation of the pin along the fifth rank by 32...ℤxd5!? allows many tactical possibilities, however Black almost miraculously survives in every variation. 33 ♘h6+ Going after the king achieves no more than a perpetual. (33 ♘e5 wins the exchange but leaves his king too exposed, e.g. 33...ℤxe5

34 ℤxf8+ ♔xf8 35 ℤxe5 ♕g4+ 36 ♔f1 ♕h3+ and White can do nothing with his extra exchange. White has no time to make room for his king with 33 h3 as after 33...ℤd2 34 ♘e5 ℤxf2 35 ♘xg6 ℤ2xf3 36 ♘xh4 ℤxe3 the position is equal.) 33...♔g7 34 ℤxf8 ♔xf8 35 ℤf3+ ♔g7 36 ♕e8 ♕g5+ 37 ℤg3 ℤd1+ 38 ♔g2 ♕f6 39 ♕g8+ ♔xh6 40 ℤh3+ ♔g5 41 ℤg3+.

33 ℤxf6 ♕xf6 34 ♘h6+ ♔g7 35 ♘g4 ♕d4

After 35...♕g5 36 h3 White will quickly bring his queen over to the kingside, while Black's knight has to remain on the queenside.

36 ℤxe7+

The pawn is gobbled up and Black's king remains vulnerable. Black is simply lost.

36...♔h8 37 h3 ♕c3 38 ♕d7 ♕xh3 39 ℤe8 ♕f3 40 ℤe7 ♕h3 41 ♕e6 ♕h5 42 ℤe8 ♔g7 43 ♕d7+ ℤf7 44 ♕c8 ♕h7 45 d6 g5 46 d7 ♕b1+ 47 ♔g2 1-0

L.Zaid – G.Kasparov
Leningrad 1977

1 d4 ♘f6 2 c4 g6 3 ♘f3 ♗g7 4 g3 d6 5 ♗g2 0-0 6 0-0 ♘c6 7 ♘c3 a6 8 d5 ♘a5

The knight naturally goes to the edge.
9 ♘d2 c5 10 ♕c2 ♖b8 11 b3 b5 12 ♗b2

See diagram on page 19.

12...bxc4 13 bxc4 ♗h6 14 ♘cb1 e5 15 ♗c3 ♗d7 16 ♘a3

Sad, but my opponent also knows the knight to the h- and a-file strategy.

16...♗g7 17 ♖ab1 ♕c7 18 e4 h5

I should have followed in Karpov's footsteps and played 18...♘h5.

19 f4 ♖b4 20 ♕d3 ♘b7

I wanted to leave the knight where it was, but the fact that it was undefended worried me.

21 ♘c2 ♖xb1 22 ♖xb1 h4?!

There is no time to free the h5-square for the knight. After 22...exf4 23 gxf4 ♖e8 Black is in the game.

23 fxe5 dxe5 24 ♘f3! hxg3 25 ♗xe5 gxh2+ 26 ♗xh2

White's centre is rock solid.

26...♕c8 27 ♘e3 ♘g4 28 ♘xg4 ♗xg4 29 ♘e5 ♘a5

Now White no longer attacks the a5-square. So I waste no time putting the knight back on the edge of the board.

30 ♖f1 ♗h5 31 d6 ♗xe5?

If 31...♗g4 32 ♘xg4 ♕xg4 33 ♕d5 ♗d4+ 34 ♔h1 ♕d7 Black still resists.

32 ♗xe5 ♕e6 33 ♗f6

The exposes the weak black king and the d6-pawn becomes more threatening.

33...♘c6

He must come back to hold the pawn.

34 ♕e3! ♔h7 35 ♕xc5 ♘b8

Karpov played some remarkable knight retreats during his career, for example: Karpov-Spassky, 9th game, Moscow 1974, or Karpov-Quinteros,

Malta 1980, or Bouaziz-Karpov, Hamburg 1982. Two of these were played after this game and so I hadn't seen them. In a way my retreat is more effective than Karpov's. It ends the game far more quickly, in just two moves.

36 ♗e7 ♖e8 37 ♕d5 1-0

Leaving out the analysis, here are the three retreat pearls mentioned:

A.Karpov – B.Spassky
Game 9, Candidates semi-final
Leningrad 1974

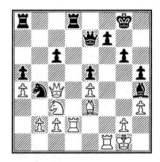

24 ♘b1!! ♕b7 25 ♔h2 ♔g7 26 c3 ♘a6 27 ♖e2 ♖f8 28 ♘d2 ♗d8 29 ♘f3 f6 30 ♖d2 ♗e7 31 ♕e6 ♖ad8 32 ♖xd8 ♗xd8 33 ♖d1 ♘b8 34 ♗c5 ♖h8 35 ♖xd8 1-0

A.Karpov – M.Quinteros
Malta Olympiad 1980

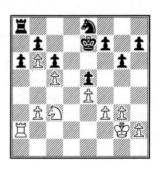

32 ♘b1! ♘g7 33 ♘d2 ♘e6 34 b4 ♖d8 35 ♘c4 ♖d4 36 ♘d6 ♖xb4 37 ♘xb7 ♖b5 38 h4 h5 39 ♔f2 ♔d7 40 ♘d6 ♖xc5 41 ♖b2 1-0

S.Bouaziz – A.Karpov
Hamburg TV 1982

25...♘b8!! 26 ♘f3 ♘d7 27 ♔g3 ♘c5 28 ♖d1 a5 29 ♔f2 ♖a6 30 ♔e2 ♘a4 31 d4 ♖b6

32 dxe5 ♖xb2+ 33 ♔f1 ♘xc3 34 exd6 cxd6 35 ♖xd6 ♖b1+ 36 ♘e1 ♔f6 37 ♖d2 b5 38 ♖c2 b4 39 ♔f2 ♖a1 40 e5+ ♔xe5 41 ♘f3+ ♔e4 42 ♘d4 ♔d3 0-1

Karpov sacrificed the e5-pawn in a sharp Sicilian against Ljubojevic. I decided to use this weapon as well.

A.Karpov – L.Ljubojevic

G.Kasparov – A.Yermolinsky

A.Karpov – L.Ljubojevic
Turin 1982

1 e4 c5 2 ♘f3 d6 3 d4 ♘f6 4 ♘c3 cxd4 5 ♘xd4 a6 6 ♗e2 e6 7 f4 ♕c7 8 0-0 b5?! 9 ♗f3 ♗b7 10 e5 dxe5 11 fxe5 ♘fd7 12 ♗f4 b4

13 ♘e4

Karpov sacrifices the pawn. This game was so convincing that the position never occurred again.

13...♘xe5

See diagram on page 27.

14 ♔h1! ♗e7

Not 14...♘bc6?? 15 ♘xc6 ♗xc6 16 ♗xe5 ♕xe5 17 ♘f6+ winning nor 14...♘bd7 15 ♘g5! and White has nice play for the pawn.

15 ♘g5! ♗xg5 16 ♗xb7! ♕xb7

If 16...♖a7 17 ♘xe6 or 16...♗xf4 17 ♗xa8 ♘g6 18 ♕e1 0-0 19 ♗e4 and White is better.

17 ♗xe5 0-0

17...♘d7 allows 18 ♗xg7 ♖g8 19 ♘xe6.

18 ♕g4 ♕e7?

After this White's advantage is decisive. Also after 18...h6? 19 ♘xe6 ♕d7 20 ♗xg7 wins. Better is 18...♘d7! 19 ♕xg5 f6 20 ♗xf6 but White is still somewhat better.

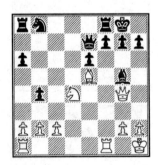

19 ♕g3! ♖c8

After 19...♖d8 20 ♖ad1!.

20 ♗d6 ♕d7

Or alternatively 20...♕d8 21 ♘xe6!

21 ♖ad1 f6

Moving the knight with 21...♘c6 22 ♕xg5 ♕xd6 23 ♘f5 ♕e5 24 ♘h6+ wins, while if 21...h6 22 h4 ♗xh4 23 ♕xh4 ♕xd6 24 ♘f5 decides.

22 ♗xb8 ♖axb8

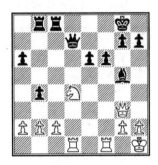

23 h4! ♗xh4

Retreating with 23...♗h6 is met by 24 ♘f5 ♕c7 25 ♘xh6+ ♔h8

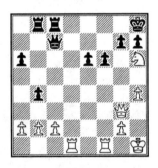

26 ♖d8+!! This lovely shot decides the game instantly.

24 ♕xh4 ♖c4 25 ♕g3 ♖bc8 26 ♘f5 ♕a7 27 ♘d6 ♖4c5 28 ♕h3 1-0

G.Kasparov – A.Yermolinsky
Leningrad 1975

1 e4 c5 2 ♘f3 d6 3 d4 cxd4 4 ♘xd4 ♘f6 5 ♘c3 ♘c6 6 ♗g5 a6 7 ♕d2 e6 8 0-0-0 ♗d7 9 f4

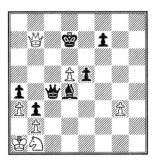

9...b5

This is a rarely played line at the top level. It leads to very exciting games.

10 ♘xc6

Karpov was nicely beaten by Torre with 10 ♕e1. Here is Torre's masterpiece. 10...♘xd4 11 ♖xd4 ♕b6 12 ♖d2 ♗e7 13 ♗d3 b4 14 ♘d1 ♗b5 15 ♘f2 h6 16 ♗h4 g5 17 fxg5 hxg5 18 ♗g3 ♘h5 19 ♘g4 ♘xg3 20 hxg3 ♖xh1 21 ♕xh1 ♖c8 22 ♔b1 ♗xd3 23 cxd3

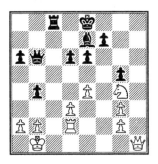

23...♕d4 24 ♕d1 a5 25 ♘h2 g4 26 ♘xg4 ♗g5 27 ♖c2 ♖xc2 28 ♔xc2 a4 29 a3 b3+ 30 ♔b1 d5 31 exd5 ♕xd5 32 ♘f2 ♕xg2 33 ♘e4 ♗e3 34 ♘c3 ♕c6 35 d4 ♕c4 36 d5 e5 37 ♕h1 ♕d3+ 38 ♔a1 ♗d4 39 ♕h8+ ♔d7 40 ♕a8 ♕f1+ 41 ♘b1 ♕c4 42 ♕b7+

42...♔d6 43 ♕b8+ ♔xd5 44 ♕d8+ ♔e6 45 ♕e8+ ♔f5 46 ♕d7+ ♔g6 47 ♕g4+ ♔f6 48 ♘c3 ♕f1+ 0-1 Karpov-Torre, Manila 1976.

Back to the game:

10...♗xc6 11 ♗d3 ♗e7 12 e5 dxe5 13 fxe5 ♘d7 14 ♗xe7 ♕xe7

15 ♗e4

29

I did not mind sacrificing the e5 pawn, hoping I would get enough play for it in return.

15...♕c5 16 ♖he1 ♖a7 17 ♗xc6 ♕xc6 18 ♕f2 ♕c5 19 ♖e3 0-0

Black has equalised by moving his king into safety.

20 ♘e4 ♕xe5

See diagram on page 27.

21 ♖g3

Karpov also allowed short castling and caught Ljubojevic's king on the kingside. I hoped my attack would bring Yermolinsky down too.

21...♖aa8 22 ♖xd7 ♕xe4 23 ♖f3 ♕g6

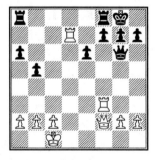

24 a3

White's heavy pieces control many files and ranks.

24...♖ac8 25 ♔b1 e5!

Keeping White busy and holding on to the pawn.

26 ♖g3 ♕e6 27 ♕d2 g6 28 ♖h3 ♕f6 29 ♕h6 ♕g7 30 ♕g5 ♖ce8 31 ♖d6 e4! 32 ♖xa6

Material equilibrium has been restored. White is still not worse, but he must play with care.

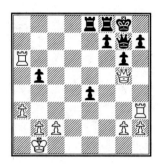

32...♖e5 33 ♕d2 ♖fe8 34 ♖e3 ♕h6 35 g3 ♕h3 36 ♖c6

36 ♖d6 is an alternative.

36...♕f5 37 ♕c3 ♕d7 38 b3 ♖f5 39 ♔b2??

White has had to play carefully for quite some time, now a losing mistake leads to disaster. The king blocks the queen. After 39 ♔a2 ♖f1 40 ♖c5 ♕d1 41 ♕b2 White is in the game.

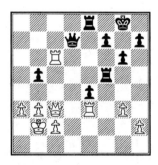

39...♖f1!!

Surprisingly catching the king on the first rank.

40 ♖f6 ♖h1 41 ♕c6 ♕d4+ 42 ♖c3 ♖f8 43 ♖xf7 ♖xf7 44 ♕xb5 ♖xh2 45 b4 ♖xc2+ 46 ♔xc2 ♖f2+ 47 ♔b3 ♕d1+ 48 ♔c4 ♕e2+ 0-1

Karpov sacrificed the b6-pawn in a hedgehog position against Garcia and went on to win.

And below is another example from my annoying predecessor, followed by my game against him where he himself took the b6-pawn.

S.Garcia Martinez – A.Karpov

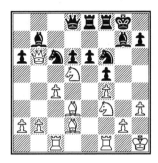

J.Saren – A.Karpov

A.Karpov – G.Kasparov

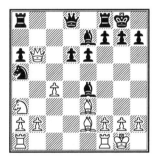

Garcia Martinez – Karpov
Madrid 1973

1 e4 c5 2 ♘f3 e6 3 d4 cxd4 4 ♘xd4 a6

Interestingly Karpov stopped playing the Paulsen pretty soon after he became world champion. Avoiding direct confrontation suits his style better.

5 ♗d3 ♘f6 6 0-0 d6 7 c4 ♕c7 8 ♕e2 g6 9 f4 ♗g7 10 ♔h1 0-0 11 ♘c3 b6 12 ♗d2 ♗b7 13 ♘f3

13...♘c6

A slightly unusual way to develop. Here Black only defends the b6-pawn with his queen. 13...♘bd7 is usual.

14 Racl Rae8 15 Wf2

This is a multi-purpose move. White can think about attacking the king with Wh4 or...

15...Ng4 16 Wg1

White keeps an eye on the b6-pawn.

16...f5 17 exf5 gxf5 18 h3?!

White diverts the knight to a better place and weakens b6 as well. He could play 18 Nd5 Wf7 19 Nxb6.

18...Nf6 19 Nd5 Wd8 20 Wxb6

See diagram on page 31.

20...Wxb6 21 Nxb6

This is the idea implemented later. Black can give up the b6-pawn in such a situation.

21...Ne4 22 Bxe4 fxe4 23 Ng5 Nd8

Karpov sacrifices a pawn and can also afford to step back with his knight. Where is it going to? To the edge of the board of course!

24 Rfe1?!

It is better to defend the f4-pawn by 24 Rce1! d5 25 cxd5 exd5 26 Nd7.

24...d5 25 Nd7

After 25 cxd5!? exd5 26 Nd7 h6 27 Nxf8 Rxf8 28 Bb4 Rxf4! 29 Be7 hxg5 30 Bxd8 Rf2 31 b3 d4 Black's central pawns are menacing. The position is hard to evaluate over the board, however White might be better here.

25...h6

26 Nxe4 dxe4 27 Nxf8 Rxf8

Black has two pieces against the rook. The position is roughly equal and the stronger player will outplay his opponent.

By the way, this game misled me in several ways. I lost twice by opting for two pieces against a rook. Once against Kappe and once against Romanishin. Here are those examples:

A.Kappe – G.Kasparov
Cagnes-sur-Mer, 1977

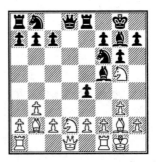

11 Ndxe4 Wxd1 12 Nxf6+ Bxf6 13 Raxd1 Bg5 14 Bxb7 Be4 15 Bxa8 Bxa8

16 h4 Be7 17 Be5 Na6 18 c3 Bc6 19 Bf4 Bf8 20 Rd2 f6 21 Rfd1 Kf7 22 Kf1 h6 23 Be3 Nc5 24 Rd8 a6 25 Rxe8 Kxe8 26 f3 Ne6 27 Kf2 h5 28 c4 Bd6 29 Rb1 a5 30 Bd2 Nd4 31 Bf4 Ke7 32 Bxd6+ Kxd6 33 Rd1

♔c5 34 ♔e3 ♘e6 35 g4 a4 36 gxh5 gxh5 37 bxa4 ♔xc4 38 ♖c1+ ♔d5 39 a5 ♗b5 40 ♖g1 ♘d4 41 ♖g8 c5 42 ♖h8 ♔c6 43 ♖xh5 ♗xe2 44 ♖h7 ♗xf3 45 a6 ♔b6 46 a7 ♗b7 47 h5 ♔xa7 48 ♖f7 ♔b8 49 ♖xf6 ♗c8 50 ♔e4 ♗e6 51 h6 ♗xa2 52 ♔e5 1-0

O.Romanishin – G.Kasparov
4-teams, Moscow 1981

26 ♖xe7 ♘b6 27 ♖b7 ♘a4 28 ♖b8+ ♗f8 29 c4 ♔g7 30 ♔g2 ♗d6 31 ♖a8 ♘b2 32 a4 ♘xc4 33 a5 ♘e5 34 ♖c8 1-0

Back to the game.

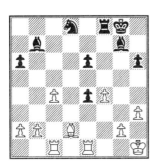

28 b4 ♗c6 29 a4 ♗xa4 30 ♖xe4 ♗c6 31 ♖e2 h5 32 ♔h2 h4 33 g3 hxg3+ 34 ♔xg3 ♔h7 35 ♗c3 ♗h6 36 ♖f1 ♖g8+ 37 ♔h2 ♘f7 38 ♗e5?!

38...♘xe5 39 fxe5 ♗g7 40 ♖f7 ♔h6 41 h4 ♔h5 42 ♔h3 ♗e8 43 ♖a7 ♗g6 44 ♖xa6 ♗d3 45 ♖f2 ♗xc4 46 ♖a3

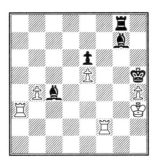

46...♗h6?
Karpov rarely misses a trick in endgames. However 46...♗xe5 was winning after 47 ♖a5 ♗d5.
47 ♖g3 ♖a8 48 ♖f7 ♖a1 49 ♖h7 ♖h1+ 50 ♔g2 ♖xh4 51 ♔g1

51...♗e2 52 ♔f2 ♗g4 53 b5 ♗f5 54 ♖h8 ♖b4 55 ♖g1 ♖b2+ 56 ♔f3 ♖b3+ 57 ♔f2 ♗e4 58 ♖g3 ♖b2+ 59 ♔g1 ♗f5 60 ♖g2 ♖xg2+ 61 ♔xg2

♗e4+ 62 ♔g3 ♔g6 63 b6 ♗d5 64 ♖b8 ♔f5 65 b7 ♔xe5

If 65...♗f4+ 66 ♔h4 ♔xe5 67 ♔g4 ♗e3 68 ♔h5 holds.

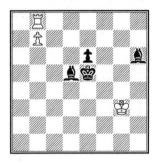

66 ♔g4?

After 66 ♖h8!! White contrives to engineer a miraculous escape. 66...♗f4+ 67 ♔g4 ♗xb7 68 ♖h5+!!

Recovering a piece, Without this move White would lose. 68...♔e4 69 ♖b5! and White wins a bishop. Luckily the position is drawish. Interestingly, it would take more time to win if Black had a knight on e6 instead of the pawn.

On the other hand in the next position against Karpov from Tilburg 1991 I did manage to salvage a draw with rook versus two knights and a bishop. People drew the conclusion from my body language that I considered my position lost at adjournment. My reaction to this? No comment!

Or should I say has any of my Predecessors had such an endgame?

A.Karpov – G.Kasparov
Tilburg 1991

111 ♘g6+ ♔g8 112 ♘e7+ ♔h8 113 ♘g5 ♖a6+ 114 ♔f7 ♖f6+! ½-½ Capturing the rook results in stalemate.

Back to the main game:

66...♗e3 67 ♔g3 ♗g5 68 ♔f2 ♗e7 0-1

Karpov sacrificed the b6-pawn not only in this game but also in an earlier one where the circumstances were very similar.

J.Saren – A.Karpov
Skopje Olympiad 1972

1 e4 c5 2 ♘f3 e6 3 d4 cxd4 4 ♘xd4 ♘c6 5 ♘b5 d6 6 c4 ♘f6 7 ♘1c3 a6 8 ♘a3 ♗e7 9 ♗e2 0-0 10 0-0 b6

11 ♗e3 ♗b7 12 f3 ♖b8 13 ♕e1 ♘d7
14 ♕f2 ♘c5 15 ♖fd1 f5 16 exf5 ♖xf5
17 ♘c2 ♗h4 18 g3 ♗e7 19 b4 ♘d7
20 f4

20...♕f8 21 b5 axb5 22 cxb5 ♘a5
23 ♗xb6 ♘xb6 24 ♕xb6 ♗d8 25 ♕a7
♖c8 26 ♕e3 e5 27 ♗g4 ♘c4 28 ♕d3
♗b6+ 29 ♔f1 ♖xf4+ 30 gxf4 ♕xf4+
0-1

I tucked this idea away safely and
prepared a novelty for my first World
Championship match. I employed it
when the score was 0:0. Let's see how
Karpov's idea worked against him.

A.Karpov – G.Kasparov
Game 3, World Championship,
Moscow 1984

**1 e4 c5 2 ♘f3 e6 3 d4 cxd4 4 ♘xd4
♘c6 5 ♘b5 d6 6 c4 ♘f6 7 ♘1c3 a6
8 ♘a3 ♗e7 9 ♗e2 0-0 10 0-0 b6
11 ♗e3 ♗b7 12 ♕b3 ♘a5**

This was my prepared novelty – you
can guess where it came from.

13 ♕xb6

See diagram on page 31.

Black's pawns have not advanced as
far as in the Garcia-Karpov game, but I
did not have to sacrifice a pawn.

**13...♘xe4 14 ♘xe4 ♗xe4 15 ♕xd8
♗xd8 16 ♖ad1 d5?!**

Maybe defending the pawn was
better, but that would be slightly
passive. An interesting psychological
echo is that 16 years later I also gave a
free pawn to my opponent in the World
Championship final when neither
player had yet scored a victory.

17 f3 ♗f5 18 cxd5

At the time, commentators thought
18 g4?! ♗g6 19 cxd5 exd5 20 ♖xd5?
was a losing move, but after 20...♖e8
21 ♖fd1! White is still a bit better.

18...exd5 19 ♖xd5 ♗e6

If 19...♖e8 20 ♔f2 ♗e6 21 ♖d6.

20 ♖d6!? ♗xa2?!

After 20...♗e7 21 ♖xa6 ♖xa6
(21...♗xa3? 22 bxa3 ♘c4 23 ♖xe6
wins.) 22 ♗xa6 ♖b8 23 ♗d4 ♘c6
24 ♗c3 ♗c5+ 25 ♔h1 ♘b4 it would be
hard to progress with White.

**21 ♖xa6 ♖b8 22 ♗c5 ♖e8 23 ♗b5!
♖e6**

Other moves were no better.

If 23...♖e5?! 24 ♗d6 ♖exb5
25 ♘xb5 ♖xb5 26 ♖a8 ♘b7 27 ♗c7
wins. If 23...♖xb5 24 ♘xb5 ♗c4
25 ♘d6!? or 25 ♖d1 ♗xb5 26 ♖xd8
♖xd8 27 ♖xa5.

24 b4 ♘b7

After 24...♖xa6 25 ♗xa6 ♘b3 26 ♖e1!?

25 ♗f2 ♗e7 26 ♘c2 ♗d5 27 ♖d1 ♗b3 28 ♖d7! ♖d8

If 28...♗xc2 29 ♖xe6 fxe6 30 ♖xe7 ♘d6 31 ♗d7 ♖xb4 32 ♗c5 ♖b1+ 33 ♔f2 wins as Taimanov pointed out.

29 ♖xe6 ♖xd7 30 ♖e1! ♖c7 31 ♗b6 1-0

A.Beliavsky – A.Karpov

Karpov won an opposite coloured bishop endgame where he had a strong light-squared bishop and a rook and won despite being a pawn down. Furthermore, to make it even more misleading, he beat a very fine player – Beliavsky.

Remembering this particular game well, I twice opted for such positions against Kramnik. In one of them *(below, left)* I was a pawn up, not down, and my opponent had no passed a-pawn and I only drew.

But this was not all in the match. In the next example *(below, right)*, I did not have a strong bishop, but the similarity is still there as my opponent was a pawn up and possessed a passed a-pawn.

Out of these two games I totalled a miserable half a point whereas Karpov scored twice as much as that from a single game. To make matters worse, this happened to me during the World Championship match against Kramnik.

V.Kramnik – G.Kasparov

V.Kramnik – G.Kasparov

A.Beliavsky – A.Karpov
USSR Championship, Moscow 1973

1 d4 ♘f6 2 c4 e6 3 ♘c3 ♗b4 4 e3 c5 5 ♗d3 0-0 6 ♘f3 d5 7 0-0 dxc4 8 ♗xc4 cxd4 9 exd4 b6

The Karpov line brought me my second loss in the Kramnik match, from there on it was hard to stage a comeback.

10 ♗g5 ♗b7 11 ♕e2 ♘bd7 12 ♖ac1 ♖c8 13 ♘e5 ♕c7 14 ♗b5 ♕d6 15 ♖fd1 ♗xc3 16 bxc3 ♕d5 17 f4 ♕d6

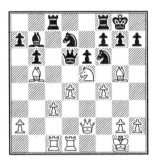

18 c4

White's centre is huge. Black should undermine that zone as the more space White has the quicker he will suffocate his opponent.

18...♕c7 19 ♗a4 a6 20 ♗c2 g6 21 ♕e1 ♔g7 22 ♗a4 h6 23 ♗h4 b5

At a cost of a pawn Karpov gets rid of the nagging bind.

24 cxb5 ♕d6 25 bxa6 ♗xa6 26 d5! ♖xc1 27 ♖xc1 ♗c8

28 ♗xd7?

Better was 28 ♘xf7! ♔xf7 (28...♖xf7 29 dxe6 ♖e7 30 ♖xc8 wins) 29 dxe6+ ♕xe6 30 ♗b3 ♘d5 31 ♕xe6+ ♔xe6 32 ♖c6+!; 28 ♘xd7 ♘xd7 29 ♕c3+ ♔h7 30 dxe6 fxe6 31 ♗g3. In both cases White's advantage is sufficient to sail home with the full point.

28...♘xd7 29 dxe6 ♕xe6 30 ♘c4 ♗a6 31 ♕xe6 fxe6

32 ♗g3?

Placing the bishop on a passive square. 32 g3 was a better way to simplify as the bishop is then far more active: 32...♖c8 33 ♖d1 ♗xc4 34 ♖xd7+ ♔f8 35 ♖a7 ♗d5 36 a4.

32...♖c8 33 ♖d1 ♗xc4 34 ♖xd7+ ♔f6

See diagram on page 36.

White has an extra pawn but no longer an advantage. But Beliavsky is a great fighter and still plays for a win.

35 a3

After 35 ♖d2 ♖a8=.

35...♗d5

36 h3?

In this case, placing the pawn on the colour of his opponent's bishop means it's going to fall in the long run.

White can force matters and move closer to a draw by 36 ♗h4+ ♔f5 37 ♖f7+ ♔e4 (37...♔g4? 38 ♗e1 and White can play for a win again.) 38 ♖f6 (38 h3 Now he makes room for the king. 38...♖c1+ 39 ♔h2 ♔e3 40 ♖f6 ♗e4 41 f5 gxf5 42 ♖xe6 ♖c2 43 ♔h1 f4 44 ♖e8 and White holds.) 38...♖c1+ 39 ♔f2 ♖c2+ 40 ♔g3 (40 ♔g1 ♔e3) 40...♔d4 41 ♔g4 ♗e4 42 ♗g3. Black's advantage is no more than symbolic.

36...♖c1+ 37 ♔f2 ♖c2+ 38 ♔e3 ♖c3+

Suddenly Karpov can start to squeeze.

39 ♔f2 ♖xa3 40 ♗h4+ g5 41 fxg5+ hxg5 42 ♗g3 ♖a2+ 43 ♔e3

43...♖xg2

From being a pawn down, Karpov reaches an endgame a pawn up!

44 ♗c7 ♖a2 45 ♖h7

45 ♗d6 avoids the immediate loss of more material. 45...♖b2 (After 45...♖a4! 46 ♔f2 it is hard to tell if Black can win.) 46 ♗d4 ♖b3? (This direct attempt to win fails. Black can maintain his edge by 46...♖e2.) 47 ♗e5+ ♔g6 48 ♖g7+ ♔h6 49 ♖g8 and White holds.

45...♖a8 46 ♔f2 ♔g6 47 ♖d7 ♖a3 48 ♖d8 ♖f3+ 49 ♔g1

49...♖xh3

Karpov once held Torre in a single rook and opposite colour bishop ending but there Torre had h- and g-pawns. Karpov's position must have been lost, but here he wins even though it takes time.

50 ♖b8 ♖c3 51 ♗d6 ♖c2 52 ♖f8 ♖c6 53 ♗e5 g4 54 ♖f6+ ♔g5 55 ♖f8 ♗f3 56 ♗f4+ ♔g6 57 ♔f2 ♖c2+

In the old days when there were adjournments the players sealed at move 56. Here Furman and the other helpers found a way to win.

58 ♔g3 ♖g2+ 59 ♔h4 ♖e2 60 ♗g3 e5

Karpov wins by pushing the e-pawn without using his king.

61 ♖b8 e4 62 ♖b5 ♖e3 63 ♖b6+ ♔f7 64 ♔g5 ♖d3 65 ♔f5 e3 66 ♖d6 ♖b3 67 ♖d7+ ♔e8 68 ♔e6 e2 69 ♖e7+ ♔f8 70 ♔f6 ♗d5 71 ♗h4 ♖f3+ 72 ♔g6 ♗f7+ 0-1

V.Kramnik – G.Kasparov
Game 8, World Championship,
London 2000

1 d4 ♘f6 2 c4 e6 3 ♘c3 ♗b4 4 ♕c2 0-0 5 a3 ♗xc3+ 6 ♕xc3 b6 7 ♗g5

♗b7 8 f3 h6 9 ♗h4 d5 10 e3 ♘bd7 11 cxd5 ♘xd5 12 ♗xd8 ♘xc3 13 ♗h4 ♘d5 14 ♗f2 c5 15 ♗b5 ♖fd8 16 e4

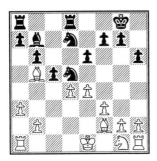

16...♘c7!!

At the time this was a very important novelty. We had already played a few games in which I accepted a weakness or a material deficit for better development.

17 ♗xd7 ♖xd7 18 dxc5 f5! 19 cxb6 axb6 20 ♘e2

Giving back the pawn at once with 20 ♖d1!? would lead to an equal game. For example: 20...♖xd1+ 21 ♔xd1 fxe4 22 fxe4 ♗xe4 23 ♘f3.

20...fxe4 21 fxe4 ♗xe4

22 0-0?

After 22 ♘c3 ♗xg2 23 ♖g1 ♗f3 24 ♖g3 ♖d3 25 ♗xb6 ♘d5 26 ♘xd5 exd5 we could say it's a balanced yet fighting game.

22...♖d2 23 ♘c3 ♗b7

The g2-pawn is weak and the bishop can target it, just as in the Karpov game.

24 b4 ♖f8 25 ♖a2 ♖xa2 26 ♘xa2 ♘d5 27 ♗d4 ♖a8

28 ♘c3

After 28 ♖f3 g5! (28...♘xb4? 29 ♖g3) 29 ♘c3 ♘f4 Black has the upper hand. If 28 ♗b2 ♘e3 29 ♖c1 ♖d8 (29...♗d5 30 ♘c3 ♘c4 31 ♖c2! Probably Black has no win here, because he can get the a- and the b-pawn in exchange for the e-pawn, reaching a rook ending a pawn up but which I evaluated as slightly better for Black only.) 30 ♖c7 ♗e4! (30...♖d2 31 ♖xg7+ ♔f8 32 ♗c3 holds.) 31 ♗c1 (31 ♖xg7+? ♔f8 32 ♗c3 ♗b1 33 ♖g3 ♘f5 34 ♖f3 ♖d1+ 35 ♔f2 h5 wins.) 31...♖d1+ 32 ♔f2 ♘g4+ (32...♖d5? 33 ♘c3=) 33 ♔g3 ♘f6 34 ♗e3 ♖d8! Black keeps his winning prospects as I pointed out in some analysis in *Informant*.

28...♘xc3 29 ♗xc3 ♖xa3 30 ♗d4 b5

See diagram on page 36.

31 ♖f4

31...♖d3

I was a pawn up whereas Karpov was a pawn down. He won, so it made me too complacent and I missed a chance...

After 31...h5! 32 g4 h4 33 g5 ♖a2 34 ♖xh4 ♖g2+ 35 ♔f1 ♖xg5 the situation is almost identical to the Beliavsky-Karpov game. The extra b-pawns must increase the stronger side's chances.

32 ♖g4 g5 33 h4!

Now White holds.

33...♔f7 34 hxg5 hxg5 35 ♔f2 ♖d2+ 36 ♔e3

36...♖xg2

I win the g2-pawn as well, but sadly it only leads to a draw since my passed pawns are too close to one another. A gap of one rank is usually not enough.

37 ♖xg2 ♗xg2 38 ♗e5 ½-½

V.Kramnik – G.Kasparov
Game 2, World Chess Championship
London 2000

1 d4 ♘f6 2 c4 g6 3 ♘c3 d5

Against Kramnik, I had quite a few draws in the Grünfeld during the second half of the 1990s. Some were very close, maybe I should have sensed that sooner or later I would lose one.

4 cxd5 ♘xd5 5 e4 ♘xc3 6 bxc3 ♗g7 7 ♘f3 c5 8 ♗e3 ♕a5 9 ♕d2 ♗g4 10 ♖b1

10...a6

Later I said I just gave up a pawn here. I had already visualised the ensuing opposite coloured bishops position.

11 ♖xb7 ♗xf3 12 gxf3 ♘c6 13 ♗c4 0-0 14 0-0 cxd4 15 cxd4 ♗xd4 16 ♗d5 ♗c3

Not 16...♗xe3? 17 ♕xe3 ♖ac8 18 ♖c1 ♘b4 19 ♖xc8 ♖xc8 20 ♕d2 ♕d8 and Black must suffer in this position a pawn down. If 20...e6? 21 ♗xe6 wins.

17 ♕c1! ♘d4 18 ♗xd4 ♗xd4

I was not particularly unhappy here.

19 ♖xe7 ♖a7 20 ♖xa7 ♗xa7

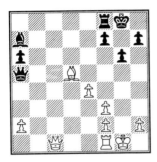

21 f4! ♕d8 22 ♕c3 ♗b8

If 22...♕h4 23 ♕g3.

23 ♕f3 ♕h4 24 e5 g5 25 ♖e1 ♕xf4

If 25...gxf4 26 e6 fxe6 27 ♖xe6. Later, in my second loss in this match, I did not mind a battery when Kramnik moved a rook to e6. 27...♕g5+ 28 ♕g2 ♕xg2+ 29 ♔xg2 ♔g7 30 ♖xa6. White is a tempo up compared with that game.

26 ♕xf4 gxf4 27 e6 fxe6 28 ♖xe6 ♔g7

Even 28...a5 is possible, but it leads to a miserable defence.

29 ♖xa6

See diagram on page 36.

29...♖f5

Karpov still had to take the g2-pawn, which did not even exist here. The a-pawn never assumed a role in that game – and I was hoping for the same. I knew in a match Kramnik would not be careless and lose as Beliavsky did, but if Karpov won his game I should have at least made a draw.

After 29...♖f6 30 ♖a8 (30 ♖a5!?) 30...♖b6 31 a4 ♖b2 32 a5 ♗d6 33 ♖c8 White is likely to win. Indeed 33...♖b5 34 a6 ♖xd5 35 a7 f3 36 ♖g8+ ♔f6 37 ♔h1 is decisive in a nice line shown by Kramnik.

30 ♗e4 ♖e5

Upon 30...♖b5!? 31 ♔g2 ♖b2 32 a4 ♗e5 33 ♖c6!? ♗d4 34 ♗c2 ♖a2

35 ♖c4 White retains decent winning chances.

31 f3 ♖e7

If 31...♖b5 32 a4 ♖b2 33 h4!?

32 a4

32...♖a7

After 32...♗a7+!? 33 ♔g2 ♗e3 Kramnik suggests several plans to convert the pawn advantage. Here are two of them. 34 ♔h3! (or 34 ♖c6!? ♖a7 35 ♗c2) 34...♖e5! (34...♖a7? 35 ♖xa7+ ♗xa7 36 ♔g4 ♗e3 37 a5 h6 38 ♔f5 wins.) 35 ♔g4 h5+ 36 ♔h4 ♗f2+ 37 ♔h3. It's difficult to tell which one was the best, but in all lines Black must suffer.

33 ♖b6 ♗e5

Maybe I should have tried to defend with 33...♗c7 34 ♖b4 ♗d6! 35 ♖c4 ♖a5.

34 ♖b4 ♖d7 35 ♔g2 ♖d2+ 36 ♔h3 h5 37 ♖b5 ♔f6 38 a5 ♖a2 39 ♖b6+

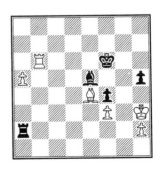

39...♔e7??

This loses a piece in one move. However, the position is lost anyway.

Even after 39...♔g7 40 a6 ♗d4 41 ♖g6+ ♔f8 42 ♗b7! is winning. Here are Kramnik's lines. 42...♖a5 (42...♗e3 43 ♖g5 h4 44 ♖g4 ♔e7 45 ♖xh4 ♗g1 46 ♔g4 wins.) 43 ♖d6 ♗g1 44 ♖d1! ♗e3 (44...♖g5 45 ♖xg1)

45 ♖d5 White loses the opposite colour bishop ending as he drops a second pawn or else allows White's king to invade on the queenside. 45...♖xd5 (45...♖a2 46 ♖xh5 ♗g1 47 ♔g4) 46 ♗xd5 ♔g7 (46...♗f2 47 ♔g2 ♗a7 48 h4) 47 ♔g2 h4 (47...♔f6 48 h4) 48 ♔h3 ♗f2 49 ♔g4.

40 ♗d5 1-0

I should not have lost the title match against Kramnik. My first loss was related to Karpov while in the second – as you will see in the Alekhine chapter – I followed the fourth world champion. See page 215. Why do my countrymen have such an adverse effect on me – forcing me to lose my title? Fortunately the crown at least remained in Mother Russia.

The last kind of position that influenced me from Karpov's games had also occurred twice in my match with Kramnik. Karpov's contribution to the loss of my title was considerable.

The 12th world champion won a game where he had a sole extra c-pawn on the queenside and both sides had four pawns on the kingside. He also won another game like this against Van Wely.

A.Karpov – P.Nikolic

L. van Wely – A.Karpov

Having shown you the positions Karpov went on to win, I'll show you mine against Kramnik. I spoiled my position and only drew – and ended up not winning a single game in the match.

Quite incredibly the structure occurred once again in the same match – only that there were additional a-pawns in each camp and there were no minor pieces on the board.

V.Kramnik – G.Kasparov

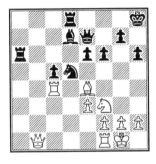

V.Kramnik – G.Kasparov

Karpov also had a game against Antunes which was very similar to my second game against Kramnik and I thought that this time I would make it as Karpov won the position despite not even being a pawn up (his opponent had a doubled pawn), but again I could not convert the material advantage.

A.Antunes – A.Karpov

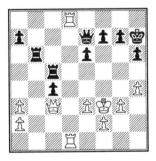

A.Karpov – P.Nikolic
Tilburg, 1988

1 d4 ♘f6 2 c4 e6 3 ♘f3 b6 4 g3
A quick look in the database shows that Karpov has had this position with White 100 times in regular and rapid games and lost only twice.
4...♗a6 5 b3 ♗b7 6 ♗g2 ♗b4+ 7 ♗d2 a5 8 0-0 0-0

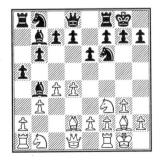

43

9 ♕c2

The start of a long manoeuvring phase.

9...c5 10 ♖d1 ♘a6 11 ♗e3 a4 12 ♘c3 axb3 13 axb3 d5?! 14 ♘a4!

Nicely applying pressure on the queenside.

14...h6 15 ♕b2 ♖e8 16 ♘e5 ♖b8 17 ♘d3! dxc4 18 ♗xb7 ♖xb7 19 bxc4 ♕e7?

This loses a pawn.

20 ♘axc5! bxc5 21 ♖xa6 ♘g4 22 ♕c1 cxd4 23 ♗xd4

See diagram on page 42.

White wins a pawn and steadily converts his advantage.

23...e5

Predrag looks for counterplay. Waiting passively with 23...♖c8!? may have prolonged the game.

24 ♗a1 e4 25 ♘xb4 ♖xb4 26 c5 ♖b5 27 ♖ad6 ♕g5

Trying to fish in muddy waters. 27...e3 28 f3 ♘f2 29 ♖1d5 was also hopeless.

28 h3! ♘xf2

This is a hacking sacrifice. Karpov easily neutralises the ploy and wins.

29 ♔xf2 e3+ 30 ♔g2 ♖xc5 31 ♕b1 ♖b5 32 h4 ♕h5 33 ♕d3 ♖f5 34 ♖f1 ♖xf1 35 ♔xf1 ♕g4 36 ♔g2 1-0

Karpov had another game like this and won it as well.

L. van Wely – A.Karpov
European Rapid 30 minute
Championship, Cap d'Agde, 1996

1 d4 ♘f6 2 c4 e6 3 ♘f3 b6 4 g3 ♗a6 5 b3 ♗b4+ 6 ♗d2 ♗e7 7 ♗g2 c6 8 ♗c3 d5 9 ♘e5 ♘fd7 10 ♘xd7 ♘xd7 11 ♘d2 0-0 12 0-0 ♘f6 13 ♖e1 c5 14 e4 cxd4 15 ♗xd4 dxc4 16 ♘xc4

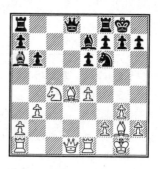

16...♗xc4

Karpov creates a weakness.

17 bxc4 ♖c8 18 ♖c1 ♗c5 19 ♗xc5

♖xc5 20 ♕a4? ♕c7 21 e5 ♘d7 22 f4 b5!

Winning a pawn.

23 ♕a3 bxc4

See diagram on page 42.

24 ♖ed1 ♘b6 25 ♖c3 g6 26 ♖d6

Waiting passively did not offer much hope either.

26...♖c8 27 h4 ♘d5 28 ♖c2 ♖a5 29 ♕f3 ♕c5+ 30 ♔h2 ♘e3 31 ♖cd2

31...c3

The c-pawn makes its decisive advance.

32 ♖d8+ ♔g7 33 ♖xc8 ♕xc8 34 ♖c2 ♘xc2 0-1

V.Kramnik – G.Kasparov

Game 12, World Championship, London 2000

1 d4 ♘f6 2 c4 e6 3 ♘c3 ♗b4 4 e3 0-0 5 ♗d3 d5 6 ♘f3 c5 7 0-0 dxc4 8 ♗xc4 ♘bd7 9 a3 cxd4 10 axb4 dxc3 11 bxc3 ♕c7 12 ♗e2!?

12...♕xc3

I was two points behind and had to try to win, even with Black.

13 ♗a3 ♘d5! 14 ♕b1 ♕f6 15 ♗d3 h6

If 15...♕h6?! 16 b5.

16 b5 ♖d8 17 ♗b2 ♕e7 18 ♖a4?!

This is both imaginative and risky.

If 18 ♗a3! ♕f6. The alternative 18...♘c5?! is a risky way to play for a win. 19 ♗h7+ ♔h8 20 ♘e5. Now 19 ♗b2=.

18...♘c5 19 ♗h7+

Not 19 ♗a3? ♘c3.

19...♔h8

20 ♖h4

Kramnik moves against the king. Kramnik could play on the c-file with 20 ♖c4 but 20...♗d7 followed by ♗e8 keeps Black in the game. Going after the king on the g-file with 20 ♖g4!? might have led to some very exciting tactics. 20...e5! 21 ♖g3

21...e4!! (21...♘f6 22 ♘xe5! [22 ♗xe5 ♘h5] 22...♖d5 23 f4 ♘xh7 24 ♘c6 ♕f8 25 ♗xg7+ and Kramnik prefers White in his *Informant* analysis.) 22 ♘e5! (22 ♘d2 ♘a4!!) 22...♘f6 (22...♔xh7? 23 ♘c6) 23 ♗g6! ♗e6 24 f3! with an unclear position.

20...f6

Not 20...♘f6? 21 ♗xf6 ♕xf6 22 ♖f4.

21 ♖c4!

Vladimir wisely returns to the queenside.

21...♗d7 22 ♗a3?!

A trip to the edge of the board with 22 ♘h4! would have kept the position balanced. White has enough play for the pawn.

22...b6 23 ♗e4

If 23 ♖fc1 ♗xb5!

23...a6!

After 23...♖ac8 24 ♘d4! ♗e8 25 ♖fc1 it is a matter of personal taste which colour you prefer.

24 bxa6?

This is a serious mistake as it allows the rook to come into play. After 24 ♘h4 ♗e8; or 24 ♖fc1 axb5 25 ♗xc5 bxc5 26 ♖xc5 and White has just enough to hold.

24...♖xa6 25 ♗xc5

Here 25 ♗xd5 ♖xa3! 26 ♘h4 (26 ♕xb6? ♘a4) 26...♗e8 27 ♗c6 and it is difficult to tell whether or not there is enough in the position to win.

25...bxc5 26 ♖fc1 ♖a5!

See diagram on page 43.

Black is a safe pawn up and as Karpov had won so convincingly with the same structure, perhaps I became a little too casual.

27 ♕b2

If 27 ♕b7 ♕d6; or 27 ♘h4 ♕d6!

27...♖b5 28 ♕a3 ♘b6

Karpov exchanged this at once. I did not have the opportunity to follow suit, so I had to think about alternatives. 28...♘b4!? was promising. Placing the bishop on the long diagonal, just as Karpov had done, looks reasonable. Then 29 ♗b1 (29 ♕a7 ♕d6) 29...♗c6 30 e4, intending ♕e3.

29 ♖4c3

Not 29 ♖xc5? when ♗c6!! wins; nor 29 ♖d4!? ♖c8.

29...♖b4! 30 ♘d2

Nor 30 ♗b1?? when ...♖a8 wins. And if 30 ♕a5 ♘a4.

30...f5?

This is too hasty. Also 30...♘a4?! allows 31 ♖xc5. However Kramnik points out the beautiful 30...♗c6!?, (...♖c8 is a good move as well) 31 ♖xc5 (31 ♗xc6 ♖xd2) 31...♖xe4 32 ♕a5 ♖xd2 33 ♕xd2 ♗d7 with excellent winning chances.

I beat Vladimir from a very similar position in the 2001 Botvinnik Memorial, my first rapidplay match.

V.Kramnik – G.Kasparov
Botvinnik Memorial rapidplay
Moscow 2001

33 罩a8+ ♞f8 34 ♛c2 g6 35 g3 ♚g7
36 ♚g2 e5 37 罩a4 ♛d6 38 ♛c4 ♞e6
39 ♛d5 ♛b8 40 罩a8 ♛b2 41 罩a2 ♛c3
42 ♛d2 ♛b3 43 ♛d5 ♛b8 44 罩a8 ♛c7
45 罩a6 ♝d4 46 ♛c6 ♛e7 47 罩a8 ♛f6
48 ♛c2 ♞g5 49 罩a3 ♛e6 50 h4 ♛h3+
51 ♚g1 ♞e6 52 罩b3 ♛g4 53 ♛d3 ♞c5
54 ♛f3 ♛xf3 0-1.

Back to the game

31 ♝f3?
Having little time left White misses
the drawish simplification 31 罩xc5!.
Then 31...罩xe4 (31...罩b5 32 ♝f3 ♝e8
33 ♞b1!; 31...罩a4 32 ♛b2) 32 ♞xe4
fxe4 33 ♛b4! and White wins the
e4-pawn, which is enough to hold on.
33...♞a4 (33...♛d6 34 ♛xe4=)
34 罩5c4 ♛xb4 35 罩xb4.

31...♞a4?
But Black blunders the pawn back,
after which his dream of winning is
gone. If 31...♝c6? 32 罩xc5=. Best was
31...罩c8 which keeps the extra pawn
and retains some chances of winning.
Kramnik mentions this move, but also
31...c4 looks promising.

32 罩xc5! 罩b2
If 32...罩bb8 33 罩5c3.
33 ♞c4 ♛xc5 ½-½

All the queenside pawns are gone
and there is nothing left to play for. If
33...罩xf2? 34 罩c8.

A.Antunes – A.Karpov
Tilburg 1994

1 ♞f3 ♞f6 2 c4 e6 3 g3 d5 4 ♝g2
♝e7 5 0-0 0-0 6 d4 dxc4 7 ♞e5 ♞c6
8 ♞xc6 bxc6 9 ♞a3 ♝xa3

10 bxa3

This somewhat awkward pawn structure often occurs in the Catalan opening.

10...♗a6 11 ♗g5?!

Taking the pawn is the main line and is more natural.

11...h6 12 ♗xf6 ♕xf6 13 ♗xc6 ♖ab8 14 ♕a4 ♖b6 15 ♖fd1 ♖d8 16 ♗f3 c6 17 ♔g2 ♕e7 18 e3 ♖c8 19 h4 ♗b5 20 ♕b4 c5 21 dxc5

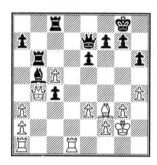

21...♖xc5

Karpov creates a passed c-pawn.

22 ♖d8+ ♔h7 23 ♖ad1 ♗c6 24 ♕c3 ♗xf3+ 25 ♔xf3

See diagram on page 43.

25...♖f5+

If 25...♕b7+!? 26 e4 ♖b2.

26 ♔g2 ♕b7+ 27 ♔g1 ♕f3 28 ♖f1

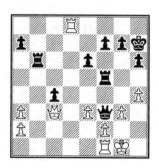

28...♖c6?

Though this wins this game, he misses a clearer path to victory by 28...♖b1!! 29 ♖xb1 (29 ♕c2 ♖xf1+ 30 ♔xf1 ♕h1+ 31 ♔e2 ♕g2 wins.) 29...♕xf2+ 30 ♔h1 ♕xg3.

29 ♖d4 ♕e2 30 ♖d2 ♕f3 31 ♖d4 ♕e2 32 ♖d2 ♕h5

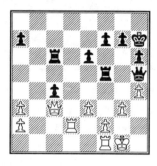

33 ♖b1 ♖d5

Black's advantage has by no means evaporated.

34 ♕c2+ ♕g6 35 ♕xg6+ ♔xg6 36 ♖c2 ♖d3 37 a4 ♖a3 38 ♖b4 c3 39 ♔f1 ♖a6

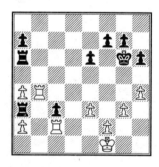

40 ♖b3

40 ♖g4+!! would be an interesting check that gives better chances as it drives the king further away from the centre. 40...♔h7! (40...♔f6 41 ♖f4+ ♔e7 42 ♖c4 ♖6xa4 43 ♖2xc3 ♖xa2 [on 43...♖xc3 44 ♖xa4! and White holds]

44 ♖c7+ ♔f6 45 ♖b7 Black has no time to defend f7 therefore White gets away with it.) 41 ♖c4 (41 ♔e2 ♖3xa4 42 ♖xa4 ♖xa4 43 ♔d3 ♖a3) 41...♖6xa4 42 ♖2xc3 ♖xa2 43 ♖c7 ♔g6 44 h5+ ♔xh5 45 ♖xf7 and White probably holds.

40...♖3xa4 41 ♖cxc3 ♖xa2 42 ♖b7 ♖b6

43 ♖xb6 axb6 44 ♖b3 ♖a6 45 e4 ♔f6 46 f4 ♔e7 47 ♔e2 ♔d6 48 g4 ♖a2+ 49 ♔e3 ♔c6 50 ♖c3+ ♔b7 51 ♖d3 ♖c2 52 h5 b5

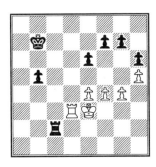

53 e5?

53 ♖d7+ would have produced a better fight. 53...♖c7 54 ♖d8 ♔b6 55 g5 b4 56 ♖g8 ♔b7 57 ♖d8 and White still has chances of holding the game (57 ♖xg7?? b3!).

53...♔c7 54 ♖a3 ♔b6 55 ♖a8 ♖c3+ 56 ♔d4 ♖c4+ 57 ♔e3 ♖c3+ 58 ♔d4 ♖c4+ 59 ♔e3 ♖c7

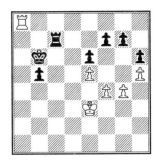

60 ♖g8?!

The subtle intermediate check 60 ♖b8+!! would at least force Karpov to fight hard for the point. 60...♔a5 (after 60...♖b7 61 ♖g8 b4 62 ♔d2 ♖c7 63 g5 b3 64 ♖b8+ ♖b7 65 ♖g8 I think White draws – by the way there is no beautiful win by 65 ♖xb7+ ♔xb7 66 f5 exf5 67 g6 as after ...fxg6 Black's king is close enough to stop the e-pawn.) 61 ♖g8 b4 62 ♖xg7 b3 63 ♖g8 ♖b7 64 ♔d2 and White can hold as the b-pawn can't be pushed because the rook check on a8 saves White.

60...b4 61 ♔d3?!

With 61 ♔d2! White has more chances of getting behind the b-pawn. 61...♔a7! (Karpov should play differently from the game. After 61...b3? 62 ♖b8+ ♔b7 63 ♖c8 ♔a6 64 ♔c1 White has decent drawing chances.) 62 ♖d8 b3 63 ♖d3 b2 64 ♖b3 ♖b7 65 ♖xb7+ ♔xb7 66 ♔c2 ♔c6 and Black wins.

61...b3 62 ♖b8+ ♖b7 63 ♖c8 ♔a7 64 ♖c1

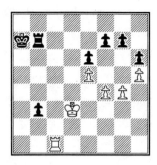

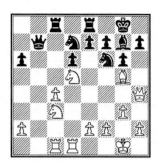

64...♖b5!

Karpov's subtle play has provided his king with a path to invade the kingside.

65 ♖b1 ♔b6 66 ♔c3 ♔c5 67 ♔b2 ♖b4 68 ♖f1 ♔d5 69 ♖f3 ♔e4 70 ♖f1 ♖b7 71 ♖f2 ♔e3 72 ♖f1 ♔e2 73 ♖g1 ♔f2 0-1

V.Kramnik – G.Kasparov
Game 12, World Championship,
London 2000

1 ♘f3 ♘f6 2 c4 b6 3 g3 c5 4 ♗g2 ♗b7 5 0-0 g6

Once I drew a very important game against Karpov with this variation. This was in the 23rd game of our third match when I needed a draw to hold on to my title – and I achieved my objective with this particular English opening.

6 ♘c3 ♗g7 7 d4 cxd4 8 ♕xd4 d6 9 ♖d1 ♘bd7 10 ♗e3 ♖c8 11 ♖ac1 0-0 12 ♕h4 a6 13 ♘e1?! ♗xg2 14 ♘xg2 ♖e8! 15 b3

If 15 ♗g5 ♖c5! to prepare 16...h6. Then after 16 b4 ♖e5! 17 f4 ♖e6 Black is okay.

15...♕c7 16 ♗g5 ♕b7 17 ♘e3 b5 18 ♘ed5 bxc4 19 bxc4

Black has at least equalised by isolating White's c-pawn.

19...h5 20 ♕f4 ♕c6 21 ♗xf6! ♘xf6 22 ♘xf6+

After 22 ♕e3 ♘xd5 23 cxd5 ♕c5.

22...♗xf6 23 ♘d5 ♗b2 24 ♖b1 ♗g7 25 ♕g5 ♔f8 26 ♖dc1 e6 27 ♘f6 ♖ed8 28 h4!

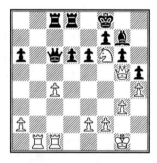

28...♕a8!

If 28...♕c5 29 ♖b7!

29 c5!

Kramnik prefers to sacrifice the c-pawn rather than let my rook get to c5.

29...♖xc5!

If 29...dxc5 30 ♖xc5 ♗xf6 31 ♖xc8=.

30 ♖xc5 ♗xf6 31 ♕xf6 dxc5

See diagram on page 43.

Almost the same pawn structure has occurred in the match again. This time

50

I decided not to give the pawn back.

32 &h2! &g8

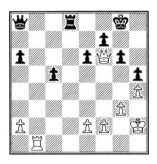

33 &b6!

This is a nasty move, White now threatens simultaneously to take on a6 and e6.

33...&e8

a) If 33...c4 34 &xe6 &d1 35 &c6 holds.

b) Alternatively 33...&b8 34 &f3! &a7 35 &c6 &b7 36 a4 &c8 37 &xc5! as Kramnik pointed out.

c) If Black tries to go after White's king with 33...&d1 there is a draw. Kramnik shows some remarkable lines. 34 e4 &c8 35 &e5! &d8 36 &g2!? c4 37 g4! hxg4

c1) 37...c3 38 gxh5= c2? 39 h6 wins.

c2) 37...&h7 38 gxh5 (38 &f6 &d7) 38...&g8 39 hxg6+ &xg6+ 40 &h3; 38 h5 gxh5 (38...&h7?! 39 &f6) 39 &g5+ (39 &b7? f6!) 39...&f8 40 &xa6! and Black's king is too exposed to do anything.

34 &f3?

After 34 &e5? &d5. But 34 &c3!, blocking the c pawn earlier, was stronger. 34...&c8 (34...&e4 35 &d3) 35 &c4 &d5 (35...&c6 36 &e4; 35...a5 36 &xe6!) 36 &xa6! &a8 37 &b5 c4 38 a4 and White gets away with it.

34...&xf3

Not 34...&c8? 35 &c6=

35 exf3 &c8 36 &xa6 c4 37 &d6

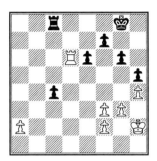

37...c3?

Pushing the pawn too far. 37...&f8! would have put much more of an obstacle in White's path. White has chances to survive but he must play very carefully. I show Kramnik's line. 38 &g2 &e7 39 &d1 &a8 (39...e5!? 40 a4!? &a8! 41 &a1 &d6 42 a5 [42 &f1 &c5 43 &e2 &b4 44 &b1+ &c3 wins] 42...&a6!? [42...&c5 43 a6 &b6 44 &b1+ &xa6 45 &f1] 43 &f1 &c5 44 &e2 &b4 and White has a really difficult task.) 40 &d4 (40 &c1 &a4) 40...c3 (40...&a4 41 f4) 41 &c4 (41 a4 &c8 42 &d1 c2 43 &c1 &d6 44 &f1 &d5 45 &e2 &c3!) 41...&a3 42 &f1 &d6 43 &e2 (43 &c8 &d5 44 &e2 e5! [44...&d4 45 &d8+] 45 &e3 f5) 43...&xa2+ (43...&d5 44 &c7 &d4 45 &d7+) 44 &e3 &a3 45 f4 and maybe this position can be held.

38 &d1 &a8

After 38...&g7 39 &g2 &f6 40 f4! &f5 41 &f3 c2 (41...&a8 42 &c1 &a3 43 &c2) 42 &c1 &c3+ 43 &e2 &e4 44 &d2 &f3 45 &e2=

39 &c1

39...♖xa2

I had to allow the proud c-pawn to fall after all. From here on the position is drawish. After 39...♖a3 40 ♔g2 ♔g7 41 f4 ♔f6 42 ♖c2 e5 43 ♔f3=.

40 ♖xc3

If 40 ♔g2? ♖a3 41 ♔f1 ♔g7 42 ♔e2 ♔f6 43 ♖c2 ♔f5 44 ♔d3 e5 45 ♖xc3 (45 ♔e3 ♖b3 46 ♔d3 ♖b2 wins) 45...♖xc3+ 46 ♔xc3 e4 47 fxe4+ ♔xe4 48 ♔d2 ♔f3 49 ♔e1 f5 wins according to Illescas.

40...♖xf2+ 41 ♔g1 ♖a2

42 ♖c7

42 f4! looks dodgy because of the isolated king, however Black still can't win. 42...♔g7 43 ♖c5 ♔f6 44 ♔f1 ♖d2 45 ♖a5 ♖d5 46 ♖a7 ♔f5 47 ♖xf7+ ♔g4 48 ♖f6 ♔f3 49 ♔g1=.

42...♔f8

If 42...e5 43 ♖c5 f6 44 ♖c7 ♔f8 45 ♔f1 ♖d2 46 ♖a7 ♖d8 47 ♔e2 ♖e8 48 ♔e3 ♖e7 49 ♖a4 ♔f7 50 f4.

43 ♖b7 ♔e8 44 ♖b8+ ♔e7 45 ♖b7+ ♔f6 46 ♔f1

Better was 46 f4!

46...e5 47 ♖b6+ ♔f5 48 ♖b7 ♔e6 49 ♖b6+ ♔f5 50 ♖b7 f6

51 ♖g7

Unnecessarily providing Black with another chance. 51 ♖f7! was called for.

51...g5

If 51...♖d2 52 ♖g8.

52 hxg5 fxg5 53 ♖g8 g4

After 53...h4 54 ♖f8+ ♔g6 55 ♖g8+ ♔f6 56 gxh4 gxh4 57 ♖g4 h3 58 ♔g1 h2+ 59 ♔h1 ♖f2 60 ♖f4+ White holds with the help of the stalemate motif.

54 ♖f8+ ♔e6 55 ♖e8+

55...♔f5

This was just not my World Championship match. With 55...♔f6!? I could still have created problems. However White can save the game with precise play. 56 ♖g8! gxf3 57 ♖f8+

♔g5 (57...♚e6 58 ♖xf3 ♚d5 [58...e4 59 ♖b3] 59 ♖f5=) 58 ♖xf3 ♚g4 (58...e4 59 ♖f4) 59 ♖e3; or 55...♚d5!? 56 ♖d8+ (56 f4 e4) 56...♚c4 (56...♚c5 57 fxg4 hxg4 58 ♖g8 ♖a4 59 ♚e2=) 57 fxg4 hxg4 58 ♖g8 ♚d3 59 ♖xg4 and though the position is equal, White still has to be careful.

56 ♖f8+ ♚g6? 57 ♖g8+ ♚f5

This allows a threefold repetition. After 57...♚f7 58 ♖g5 ♚f6 59 f4 exf4 60 gxf4 ♖h2 61 ♚g1 ♖h3 62 ♚g2 ♚e6 63 ♚f2=.

58 ♖f8+ ½-½

This was my last game with the Black pieces as the reigning world champion.

Tal said once that Karpov was the honoured trainer of Azerbaijan. Yes, Tal has a point as I improved during my matches with Karpov. On the other hand you can see I lost games because of him. Had I won these two games the aggregate score in our five World Championship matches would not have been 21 wins 19 losses for me, but 23 wins and 17 losses in my favour.

Robert James Fischer the 11th

Fischer won the title at the end of the 1969-1972 cycle. On his way to the final he beat Taimanov and Larsen 6-0 and Petrosian 6½-2½. In the world title match he dethroned Spassky 12½-8½ which ended a 24 year-long Soviet dominance of the World Championship, which began in 1948.

It was only natural that I should have investigated Fischer's games deeply, and the effect can be seen in my repertoire with the Black pieces, especially as we both played the Najdorf most of the time. Bobby also had an opening repertoire which was ahead of his time.

Intriguingly, he actually helped me indirectly by not playing against Karpov – whose name in English means 'carp' and this darting fish eluded the reluctant fisherman! – as he would have strengthened Anatoly with the experience of additional match-play. Karpov would have had an even better chance to defeat me in our matches.

Fischer's influence included bringing more money into the game which also was beneficial for me. However as you will see from the following examples I may have had even better results if I had not followed his games so closely.

Let's see one of his games which is well known and a focal point for me later when I played against Karpov. Fischer had a strong e-pawn, Black had a good queenside. Below you see his position first and then my own:

R.Fischer – L.Stein
Sousse Interzonal 1967

1 e4 e5 2 ♘f3 ♘c6 3 ♗b5 a6 4 ♗a4 ♘f6 5 0-0 ♗e7 6 ♖e1 b5 7 ♗b3 d6 8 c3 0-0 9 h3 ♗b7 10 d4 ♘a5 11 ♗c2 ♘c4 12 b3 ♘b6 13 ♘bd2 ♘bd7 14 b4

White intends to transfer his knight to a5.

A typically occurring situation in the main Ruy Lopez: White has a strong e-pawn, kingside majority and central advantage – and Black a good queenside.

R.Fischer – L.Stein

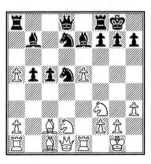

G.Kasparov – A.Karpov

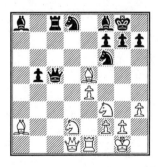

14...exd4 15 cxd4 a5

Black starts to undermine the centre.

16 bxa5 c5 17 e5

Fischer pins his hopes on the idea that the e5-pawn provides space in the centre and opens the way for White's pieces to irritate Black's king. In my Predecessors book 17 ♗b2 was recommended.

17...dxe5 18 dxe5

In one of my later games I also adopted the idea of having an e-pawn like this.

18...♞d5

See diagram on page 54.

19 ♞e4

White has to act quickly since if Black gets to an endgame his chances are encouraging as he possesses a pawn majority on the queenside.

19...♞b4

After 19...♖xa5 20 ♞eg5 h6 21 ♕d3 g6, I showed that the tactical shot 22 ♞xf7 wins. (Fischer's 22 ♞e6 is not so convincing because of 22...♞b4!) 22...♖xf7 23 ♕xg6+ ♖g7 24 ♕e6+ ♔h8 25 ♕xh6+ ♔g8 26 e6 ♞f8 27 ♖e5 and White has a winning attack. And if 19...c4 20 ♗g5!

20 ♗b1 ♖xa5 21 ♕e2

Keres' suggestion was 21 ♞eg5.

Then 21...♗xf3! 22 ♞xf3 c4 23 ♞d4 ♗c5 24 ♗b2 ♕b6 and it is not easy to attack with White.

21...♞b6?

With his last three moves Stein has strengthened the queenside but neglected to take precautions on the other flank. 21...♖e8 followed by ♞f8 ensures a playable position.

22 ♞fg5!

Fischer starts operations against Black's king.

22...♗xe4

If 22...h6 23 ♞h7 wins.

23 ♕xe4 g6 24 ♕h4!

No more preparatory work is needed and Fischer forces matters with direct threats.

24...h5 25 ♕g3! ♞c4

Not 25...♕d4? 26 ♞xf7 ♖xf7 27 ♗xg6 when White has a devastating attack.

26 ♞f3?

Fischer's move is slow. He could land a potentially lethal harpoon by 26 e6!? f5 27 ♞f7 ♖xf7 28 exf7+ ♔xf7 29 ♗xf5 gxf5 30 ♕f3 ♔g6 31 g4 generating a strong attack. Even more deadly however is the sacrifice 26 ♞xf7! which leads to a win after 26...♖xf7 27 ♗xg6 ♖g7 28 ♗h6 ♕f8

55

29 ♗xg7 ♕xg7 30 e6 h4 31 ♕b8+ ♕f8 32. ♗f7+ ♔g7 33 ♕f4.

26...♔g7

Upon 26...♘d3 comes 27 ♖d1 ♘xc1 28 ♖xc1.

27 ♕f4 ♖h8

28 e6!

White has to hurry with his operations against the black king.

28...f5

After 28...♗f6 29 exf7 ♗xa1 30 f8=♕+ ♕xf8 31 ♕c7+ ♔g8 32 ♗xg6 ♘d5 33 ♕b7 ♘f6 34 ♖e6 ♖a8 35 ♕xb5 ♘d6 36 ♕b1 ♗d4 37 ♘xd4 cxd4 38 ♕b3 ♖b8 39 ♕g3 h4 40 ♕g5 ♖b5 41 ♗f7+ wins as I pointed out in the Predecessors book.

29 ♗xf5!

White demolishes the pawn chain around the black king.

29...♕f8

Stein settles for an endgame a pawn down which, however, still requires special skill to win. If 29...♕b8 30 ♘e5! (Hübner). Alternatively 29...gxf5 30 ♕g3+ (30 ♕xf5 ♕e8 31 ♘e5 ♕xe5 32 ♕xe5+ ♗f6 33 ♕g3+ ♔h7 34 ♕c7+ ♕e7 35 ♕xa5 ♗xa1 36 ♕xb5 looks better for White.) 30...♔h7 31 ♘g5+ ♗xg5 32 ♗xg5 ♖a3! 33 ♕f4 ♕f8 34 ♖ad1 ♖d3 (34...♘d3 35 ♕g3)

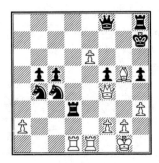

35 a4!! ♘b2 36 ♖b1 ♘xa4 37 ♕e5 ♕e8 38 e7 White has a winning attack.

30 ♗e4?

Sacrificing the knight with 30 ♘h4! would have finished off Black. 30...♗xh4 31 ♕xh4 ♕xf5 (31...♕f6 32 ♕g3 ♖e8 33 ♗b1 ♖a7 34 ♗g5 ♕xa1 35 ♗h6+ wins so nicely.) 32 ♕e7+ 33 ♕d8+ ♔g7 34 ♕c7+ ♔g8 35 e7 wins as Fischer pointed out.

30...♕xf4 31 ♗xf4 ♖e8?

This time another queenside move was required. Better was 31...♖xa2! 32 ♖xa2 ♘xa2 33 ♘e5 g5 34 ♗g3 ♘b4 35 ♘xc4 bxc4 36 ♗e5+ ♗f6 37 ♗d6 ♖e8 38 ♗xc5 ♘d3 39 ♗xd3 cxd3 and Black can simplify to a tenable endgame.

32 ♖ad1 ♖a6

Regaining the extra pawn with 32...♖xa2 does not solve Black's problem. After 33 ♖d7 ♖a6 34 ♗b1 ♘c6 35 ♗g5 White is better.

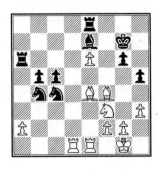

33 ♖d7! ♖xe6 34 ♘g5 ♖f6 35 ♗f3!

The most artistic way to win was with 35 a3. Then 35...♘xa3 36 ♗e5 ♘c4 37 ♗a1! ♘b6 38 ♖b7 ♘c8 39 ♗b1!

35...♖xf4 36 ♘e6+

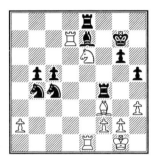

36...♔f6

With an exchange sacrifice Black stabilises his position and prolongs the game considerably. To convert White's advantage requires the technique that Fischer possesses.

37 ♘xf4 ♘e5 38 ♖b7 ♗d6 39 ♔f1 ♘c2 40 ♖e4 ♘d4 41 ♖b6 ♖d8 42 ♘d5+ ♔f5

43 ♘e3+

Fischer sealed this move.

43...♔e6 44 ♗e2 ♔d7 45 ♗xb5+ ♘xb5 46 ♖xb5 ♔c6 47 a4 ♗c7 48 ♔e2 g5 49 g3 ♖a8 50 ♖b2 ♖f8 51 f4 gxf4 52 gxf4 ♘f7 53 ♖e6+ ♘d6 54 f5 ♖a8 55 ♖d2 ♖xa4 56 f6 1-0

In the next game I constructed very much the same Spanish centre as Fischer did against Stein. But, to put it mildly, I should not have done this.

G.Kasparov – A.Karpov
Game 5, World Championship,
Moscow 1985

1 e4 e5 2 ♘f3 ♘c6 3 ♗b5 a6 4 ♗a4 ♘f6 5 0-0 ♗e7 6 ♖e1 b5 7 ♗b3 d6 8 c3 0-0 9 h3 ♗b7 10 d4 ♖e8 11 ♘bd2 ♗f8 12 a4 ♕d7 13 axb5 axb5 14 ♖xa8 ♗xa8 15 d5 ♘a5 16 ♗a2 c6 17 b4 ♘b7 18 c4 ♖c8 19 dxc6

After 19 ♕e2 ♘d8 20 ♗b2 bxc4 21 ♘xc4 ♕a7! 22 ♖a1 cxd5 23 exd5 ♗xd5 24 ♘xd6 ♗xd6 25 ♗xd5 ♕xa1+ Black has compensation.

19...♕xc6

20 c5?!

Just as in the Fischer game the developing move 20 ♗b2 was stronger.

20...♘d8 21 ♗b2 dxc5 22 bxc5 ♕xc5 23 ♗xe5

See diagram on page 54.

When I captured the pawn I was inspired by the Fischer game. Here, just like the American champion, I had an extra pawn in the centre while Black had an extra pawn on the queenside. I was hoping to create an attack on Karpov's king and even dared to think that I would conduct the attack without any mistakes. Maybe this distracted me from the reality of the game.

23...♘d7 24 ♗b2 ♕b4!

This intermediate move is undoubtedly strong as it allows White no time to build up an attack on the king. However I was still relaxed because another famous Fischer game sprung to mind – one which was very similar to the present one. Here it is:

R.Fischer – B.Spassky
Game 10, World Championship,
Reykjavik 1972

26 ♗b3 axb5 27 ♕f4 ♖d7 28 ♘e5 ♕c7 29 ♖bd1 ♖e7 30 ♗xf7+ ♖xf7 31 ♕xf7+ ♕xf7 32 ♘xf7 ♗xe4 33 ♖xe4 ♔xf7 34 ♖d7+ ♔f6 35 ♖b7 ♖a1+ 36 ♔h2 ♗d6+ 37 g3 b4 38 ♔g2 h5 39 ♖b6 ♖d1 40 ♔f3 ♔f7 41 ♔e2 ♖d5 42 f4 g6 43 g4 hxg4 44 hxg4 g5 45 f5 ♗e5 46 ♖b5 ♔f6 47 ♖exb4 ♗d4 48 ♖b6+ ♔e5 49 ♔f3 ♖d8 50 ♖b8 ♖d7 51 ♖4b7 ♖d6 52 ♖b6 ♖d7 53 ♖g6 ♔d5 54 ♖xg5 ♗e5 55 f6 ♔d4 56 ♖b1 1-0

25 ♘b3?!

By defending one piece and attacking another, you might think this kills two

birds with one stone. But the catapult is pointing backwards. The queen should have gone to the diagonal with 25 ♕b1 as happens later in the game.

25...♘c5!

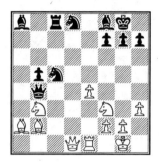

26 ♗a1

I gave up material in order to ensure play against the black king. It was possible to hang on to the pawn by 26 ♘xc5 and then defend passively – but I did not like to do that as after 26...♕xb2 27 ♖e2 ♕c3 28 ♘d3 Black stands rather better with his two bishops and distant passed pawn.

26...♗xe4 27 ♘fd4 ♘db7 28 ♕e2 ♘d6

Karpov should have pinned my queen to the defence of the a2-bishop by 28...♖a8!? His extra pawn would probably then be decisive.

29 ♘xc5 ♕xc5

30 ♕g4

Just like Fischer I create some play against the king. However, in my case this proves to be insufficient.

30...♖e8 31 ♖d1

If 31 ♕f4 ♗d5!

31...♗g6!

White no longer has any realistic attacking chances against the king.

32 ♕f4 ♕b4

Karpov likes to restrict his opponents and often does so with a pin.

33 ♕c1 ♗e4 34 ♖e1 ♕a5 35 ♗b3 ♕a8!? 36 ♕b2 b4

Karpov takes no risks and declines the pawn on g2.

37 ♖e3 ♗g6 38 ♖xe8 ♕xe8 39 ♕c1 ♘e4 40 ♗d5 ♘c5 41 ♘b3 ♘d3 0-1

White has nothing for the pawn, which is why I resigned.

Let's continue with another even more famous Fischer game – or should I say endgame. This example of domination by the bishop in endgames is often taught to young players. Here the opponent's pawns are fixed and the pawns are positioned on both wings. My game which follows has similarities.

R.Fischer – M.Taimanov

G.Kasparov – N. de Firmian

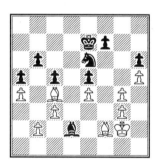

R.Fischer – M.Taimanov
Game 4, Candidates match,
Vancouver 1971

1 e4 c5 2 ♘f3 ♘c6 3 d4 cxd4 4 ♘xd4 ♕c7 5 ♘c3 e6 6 g3 a6 7 ♗g2 ♘f6 8 0-0 ♘xd4 9 ♕xd4 ♗c5 10 ♗f4 d6 11 ♕d2 h6 12 ♖ad1 e5 13 ♗e3 ♗g4 14 ♗xc5 dxc5 15 f3 ♗e6 16 f4 ♖d8 17 ♘d5 ♗xd5 18 exd5 e4 19 ♖fe1 ♖xd5 20 ♖xe4+ ♔d8 21 ♕e2 ♖xd1+ 22 ♕xd1+ ♕d7 23 ♕xd7+ ♔xd7 24 ♖e5 b6 25 ♗f1 a5 26 ♗c4 ♖f8 27 ♔g2 ♔d6 28 ♔f3 ♘d7 29 ♖e3 ♘b8 30 ♖d3+ ♔c7 31 c3 ♘c6 32 ♖e3 ♔d6

33 a4 ♘e7 34 h3 ♘c6 35 h4 h5 36 ♖d3+ ♔c7 37 ♖d5 f5 38 ♖d2 ♖f6 39 ♖e2 ♔d7 40 ♖e3 g6 41 ♗b5 ♖d6 42 ♔e2 ♔d8

43 ♖d3!

Fischer exchanges rooks, after which the bishop's domination over the knight will be even more potent.

43...♔c7 44 ♖xd6 ♔xd6 45 ♔d3

See diagram on page 59.

White has a winning advantage as Black's kingside pawns are fixed on the same colour square as the bishop and he has a route for a queenside invasion.

45...♘e7 46 ♗e8 ♔d5 47 ♗f7+ ♔d6 48 ♔c4 ♔c6 49 ♗e8+ ♔b7

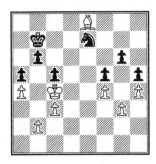

50 ♔b5

The way Fischer improves his position is quite beautiful.

50...♘c8 51 ♗c6+ ♔c7 52 ♗d5 ♘e7 53 ♗f7 ♔b7 54 ♗b3 ♔a7 55 ♗d1 ♔b7 56 ♗f3+ ♔c7

57 ♔a6

The white king invades.

57...♘g8 58 ♗d5 ♘e7 59 ♗c4 ♘c6 60 ♗f7 ♘e7 61 ♗e8 ♔d8

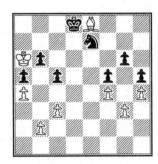

62 ♗xg6!

White's passed pawn will be decisive.

62...♘xg6 63 ♔xb6 ♔d7 64 ♔xc5 ♘e7 65 b4 axb4 66 cxb4 ♘c8 67 a5 ♘d6 68 b5 ♘e4+ 69 ♔b6 ♔c8 70 ♔c6 ♔b8 71 b6 1-0

Fischer played the entire endgame very powerfully.

Now let's have a look at an endgame with a very similar queenside pawn structure – just like the famous Fischer-Taimanov encounter.

G.Kasparov – N. De Firmian
PCA/Intel-Grand Prix, New York 1995

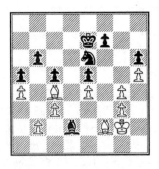

34 ♗xe6!

My pawn structure is very similar to the Fischer example. In that game Bobby swapped rooks. I knew the bishop was not the same piece but I followed his exchanging idea to invade.

34...♔xe6 35 ♔f3 ♔d6

Closing the queenside with 35...♗c1 would be clever, but White is not obliged to allow that. 36 ♔e2 ♗xb2 37 ♔d2 ♗a3 38 ♗e3 White wins.

36 ♔e2 ♗c1

37 ♔d3

I stopped short of exchanging; luckily it did not spoil anything.

After 37 ♗e3 the pawn ending was simply winning. 37...♗xe3 38 ♔xe3 f6 (on 38...c4 39 g5! White soon promotes the pawn to a lady.) 39 ♔d3 ♔d7 40 ♔c4 ♔c6 41 b3 (White has a lot of spare moves to lose a tempo.) 41...♔d6 42 ♔b5 ♔c7 43 ♔a6 (White has to be careful; he can't do whatever he wants, e.g. 43 g5? fxg5 44 g4 [44 ♔a6 g4] 44...♔b7 and Black holds.) 43...♔c6 (43...c4 44 bxc4 ♔c6 45 ♔a7 ♔c7 46 c5 bxc5 47 ♔a6 ♔c6 48 ♔xa5 and White wins.)

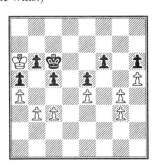

44 c4 Black is in zugzwang and White still has a spare tempo at his disposal. 44...♔c7 45 ♔a7 ♔c6 46 ♔b8 and White invades.

37...♔c6 38 ♗e1 ♗g5 39 ♔c4 ♗e3

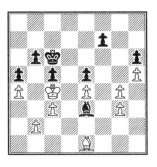

40 b4!

Aiming to open the position for invasion. As Black is in zugzwang the game continuation is forced.

40...cxb4 41 cxb4 axb4 42 ♗xb4 ♗c1 43 ♗f8 ♗g5 44 ♗g7

As often happens in same coloured bishop endings, the weaker side is caught by a zugzwang.

44...f6

A sad necessity. Black has to put one more pawn on the same colour as the opponent's bishop. 44...♔d6 was not any better. 45 ♔b5 ♗e3 46 ♗f6.

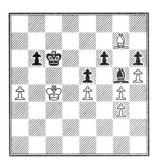

45 ♗h8!

I was lucky to have an extra square available on the diagonal.

45...♔d6 46 ♔b5 ♔c7 47 ♗g7

The bishop's objective is to get to d8 in order to net a pawn.

47...♔b7 48 ♗f8

Transferring the bishop to d8.

48...♔c7 49 ♗e7 ♔d7 50 ♗b4 ♗e3

If 50...♔c7 51 ♗e1 ♗e3 only temporarily prevents the bishop from invading. 52 g5! fxg5 53 g4 ♗c5 (53...♗d4 54 ♗b4 White wins.) 54 a5 ♔b7 55 axb6 (55 a6+ ♔a7 56 ♗c3 ♗d6 57 ♗b2 and Black is in zugzwang.) 55...♗f8 – setting up a fortress can sometimes save an identical coloured bishop ending. Though this time it is ineffective, such a device can sometimes rescue the weaker side. (55...♗xb6 56 ♗b4 wins.) On 56 ♗c3 ♗d6 57 ♗b2 Black is in zugzwang.

51 g5!!

This is a very nice and instructive breakthrough. Black's pieces are overloaded.

51...fxg5 52 g4 ♔e6 53 ♔c6

The simplest option. Taking on b6 wins more quickly than going after the h6-pawn. 53 ♗f8 would be winning as well, since after 53...♔f6 54 ♗xh6 ♔f7 55 ♔c6 ♗d2 56 ♔d5 ♗f4 57 ♔d6 Black is in zugzwang.

53...♗d4 54 ♗d6 1-0

I followed Fischer. It was a close call but nevertheless I won!

In general I am not going to compare the champion's effectiveness at damaging my career. Maybe this 'lucky' win makes Fischer's effect on me less negative.

Before I show the games in which I emulated Fischer's play, I would like to present one game on a topic already discussed in the Karpov section. This game was also planted in my mind as well as Karpov's.

R.Fischer – M.Taimanov
Palma de Mallorca Interzonal 1970

1 e4 c5 2 ♘f3 ♘c6 3 d4 cxd4 4 ♘xd4 e6 5 ♘b5 d6 6 c4 a6 7 ♘5c3 ♘f6 8 ♗e2 ♗e7 9 0-0 0-0 10 ♘a3 b6 11 ♗e3

So far the players have followed main line theory. Now the Russian grandmaster deviates from the most common 11...♗b7.

11...♗d7 12 ♖c1 ♕b8 13 f3 ♖a7 14 ♘c2 ♖d8 15 ♕e1 ♗e8

Black plays for b5. In the main line they play for d5 or even ♔h8 and ♖g8 with g5.

16 ♕f2 ♖b7 17 a4

This stops b5 once and for all.

17...a5 18 ♘d4 ♘xd4 19 ♗xd4 ♘d7

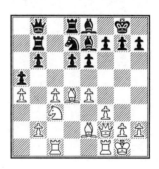

20 ♕g3

I usually play on the queenside against the hedgehog set-up.

20...♗f6 21 ♗xf6 ♘xf6 22 ♖fd1 e5

Black has obtained a fully playable game.

23 ♕h4 h6 24 ♖d2 ♘d7 25 ♗d1 ♘c5 26 f4 exf4 27 ♕xf4 ♘e6

According to Vasiukov the position is equal after 27...♖e7! 28 ♗c2 ♖e5.

28 ♕g3 ♕c7 29 ♘d5 ♕c5+ 30 ♔h1 ♗c6 31 ♖c3 ♘g5 32 ♗c2 ♗xd5

White is just a little better after 32...♖e8 33 h4! ♘h7 34 ♘e3 ♖e6 35 ♘f5 ♖g6 36 ♕e3.

33 ♖xd5 ♕c7?!

This blocks the b7-rook. Better is 33...♕c6! 34 e5 (34 b3 ♖e7) 34...♖bd7 35 ♗f5 ♘e6 when Black is safe.

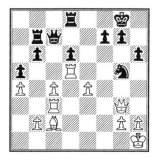

34 e5!

The more the position opens up, the more the bishop has a chance to dominate the knight.

34...dxe5 35 ♕xe5 ♖db8?!

Vasiukov's move 35...♘e6 is more natural.

36 ♗f5 ♕xe5 37 ♖xe5 g6 38 h4 ♘h7

After 38...f6 Black could exchange the light pieces. Four-rook endings tend to give considerable drawing chances.

39 ♗g4 ♘f6

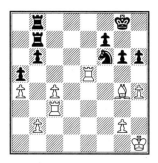

40 ♗f3!

The bishop is very nicely placed on the diagonal. If White creates a passed a-pawn it will get tremendous support from the long diagonal bishop. This is what I wanted to do against Karpov, but the circumstances there were far less fortunate than in Bobby's game.

40...♖d7

Black can live with his position after 40...♖c7! 41 ♖b5 ♖c5.

41 ♖b5 ♖d4?

This wins a pawn but allows White to open the queenside. Better was 41...♖dd8.

42 c5! ♖xh4+ 43 ♔g1 ♖b4 44 ♖xb4 axb4 45 ♖c4 bxc5

Or 45...♘d7 46 c6.

46 ♖xc5

Now the bishop is a real powerhouse.

46...♔g7 47 a5 ♖e8 48 ♖c1! ♖e5 49 ♖a1 ♖e7 50 ♔f2!

The a-pawn and the bishop are indeed strong, however they still need the help of the king.

50...♘e8 51 a6 ♖a7 52 ♔e3 ♘c7
53 ♗b7

White buries the rook.

53...♘e6 54 ♖a5! ♔f6 55 ♔d3 ♔e7
56 ♔c4 ♔d6

57 ♖d5+ ♔c7 58 ♔b5 1-0

The king soon invades on b6 as well and this decides the outcome of the game.

In the next game Fischer had a negative effect on my play like no other champion.

V.Akopian – G.Kasparov
Russia v The World, Moscow 2002

1 e4 c5 2 ♘f3 ♘c6 3 ♗b5 e6 4 0-0
♘ge7 5 b3 a6 6 ♗xc6 ♘xc6 7 ♗b2 b5
8 c4 bxc4 9 bxc4 ♖b8 10 ♗c3 d6
11 ♘a3! e5 12 ♘c2 ♗e7 13 ♘e3 0-0
14 d3 ♕e8 15 ♖b1 ♖xb1 16 ♕xb1

16...♗d8?

This move was inspired by one of Fischer's ideas – Random Chess. At the start of the game the pieces are positioned on the first rank in irregular or random positions. Somehow I must have thought we were playing his brand of chess, so I started to arrange my pieces on the first rank in an unorthodox manner.

17 ♘d2 g6

Of course the knight can't retreat to b8 but ♘e7-g6-h8 would have given a most exciting Fischer Random position. Black would then only have to transfer the c8-bishop to a8.

18 ♘d5 f5 19 exf5

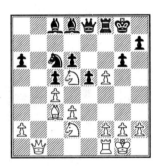

19...gxf5?

Preoccupied with thoughts of Fischer Random Chess, I just wanted to keep my pieces on the back rank. But better was 19...♗xf5.

20 f4!

Akopian puts pressure on the centre and the king.

20...♖f7 21 ♕e1 ♖g7 22 ♘f3 ♕g6
23 g3

Here it dawned on me that we were playing ordinary chess and that I was now simply lost.

23...♖f7

23...e4 was no better. 24 ♗xg7 ♔xg7
25 dxe4 fxe4 26 ♘d2 ♗a5 27 ♕a1+
♔f7 28 f5 wins.

24 fxe5 f4

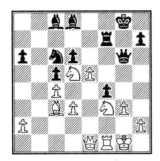

25 exd6

I had to resign here, because White has a decisive battery: 25...fxg3 26 ♕e8+ ♖f8 27 ♕xf8+ 1-0

A most unfortunate encounter.

Incidentally Karpov himself also got caught by the Fischer Random virus. Here is his position:

A.Karpov – G.Kasparov
Linares 1993

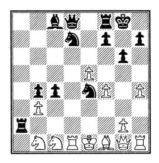

22...c3 23 ♘xa2 c2 24 ♕d4 cxd1=♕+ 25 ♔xd1 ♘dc5 26 ♕xd8 ♖xd8+ 27 ♔c2 ♘f2 0-1

After this effort my games against Karpov were far less regular than they had been previously...

Fischer won a game in a 1 c4 c5 English type position, where his opponent had a c4-pawn, while he himself had a d6-pawn and undermined White's pawn structure with ...a6 and ...b5 and went on to win.

I played ...b5 under very similar conditions in three games, losing all three, against Romanishin *(below)*, Shneider and Anand *(next page)*.

M.Aaron – R.Fischer

O.Romanishin – G.Kasparov

A.Shneider – G.Kasparov

V.Anand – G.Kasparov

M.Aaron – R.Fischer
Stockholm Interzonal 1962

**1 d4 ♞f6 2 c4 g6 3 ♞c3 ♝g7 4 e4 d6
5 f3 0-0 6 ♝e3 ♞bd7 7 ♕d2 c5 8 ♞ge2
a6 9 ♞g3?! cxd4 10 ♝xd4 ♞e5
11 ♝e2 ♝e6 12 ♞d5 b5!**

See diagram on page 65.

Fischer undermines Black's pawn structure.

13 cxb5 axb5

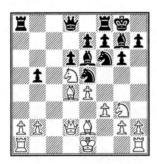

14 ♝xb5

White could not have gone a pawn up by 14 ♞xf6+ since after 14...♝xf6 15 ♝xb5 comes the lovely tactical shot 15 ... ♞xf3+! 16 gxf3 ♝xd4 17 ♕xd4 ♕a5+.

14...♞xd5

14...♝xd5!? 15 exd5 ♝h6 16 ♕xh6 ♕a5+ 17 ♕d2 ♕xb5 leaves Black slightly better.

**15 exd5 ♝xd5 16 a4 e6 17 0-0 ♕h4
18 ♞e2 ♖fc8 19 ♝e3**

It would be more appropriate not to give up the two bishops by 19 ♖fc1. Then after 19...♝h6 20 ♖xc8+ ♖xc8 21 ♕e1 ♕g5 22 ♕g3 ♕f5 the position would be unclear.

**19...♞c4 20 ♝xc4 ♕xc4 21 ♖fc1
♕a6 22 ♖xc8+ ♖xc8 23 ♞c3 ♝c4
24 f4**

After 24 ♝d4 ♝xd4+ 25 ♕xd4 e5 26 ♕d2 (26 ♕e3 ♖b8) 26...♕b6+ 27 ♔h1 d5 it is easier to play Black's position.

24...d5 25 ♗d4 ♗xd4+ 26 ♕xd4 ♕b7!

Fischer improves his position with strong, natural moves.

27 ♕f2?! ♗a6 28 ♖d1 ♖c4

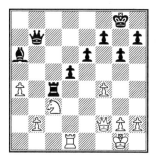

29 ♖d2?

A bad blunder in a tough position.

29...♖xc3 0-1

This was a convincing game, so I decided to give the a6/b5 plan a try:

O.Romanishin – G.Kasparov
Moscow-4-teams 1981

1 ♘f3 g6 2 d4 ♗g7 3 g3 ♘f6 4 ♗g2 0-0 5 c4 c5 6 0-0 cxd4 7 ♘xd4 ♘c6 8 ♘c3

I had a few irregular games against Kramnik in this variation. Once he drew after playing an early d6 and ♗d7 instead of castling – and once when I withdrew my knight to c2.

8...♘xd4

I beat him in the Kosmos 1998 blitz match with 8...♘g4.

9 ♕xd4 d6 10 ♕d3 a6 11 ♗e3 ♗d7 12 ♗d4 ♗c6 13 e4 ♖e8 14 ♖fe1 ♖c8 15 ♖ad1 ♕a5 16 a3 b5

See diagram on page 65.

I also undermine the centre.

17 cxb5 axb5

18 e5!

It's a smart idea to weaken the b5-pawn.

18...dxe5 19 ♗xc6 exd4!

I planned this exchange sacrifice. Unlike the Fischer game, here the b5-pawn is really weak after 19...♖xc6 20 ♖xe5.

20 ♗xe8 dxc3

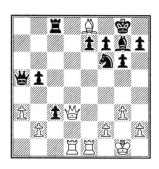

21 ♗d7!

This subtle intermediate move forces the rook to a less effective square.

21...♖d8

Black has nothing for the exchange after 21...♖b8 22 ♕xc3. If 21...♖c7 Black can exchange all of White's queenside pawns, but only just – and it requires very precise calculation. But there is no point entering into this when there is a more comfortable line in 22 b4! ♕xa3 23 ♗xb5

23...♗f8!! (After 23...♖c8 24 ♗a6 White is better.) 24 ♕d8 (24 ♖b1 ♕a2 25 ♖e2 [25 ♕d8 ♘e4 26 ♖f1 ♘xf2! 27 ♖a1 ♘h3+ 28 ♔h1 ♕e6 29 ♖ae1 ♕a2 and White is unable to take the rook, so Black is not worse.] 25...c2 26 ♖c1 ♘d5! Black wins the b-pawn and survives. 27 ♖exc2 ♘xb4 and Black gets away with it.) 24...♖a7 25 ♕d4 e5! 26 ♕xe5

26...♔g7!! 27 g4 (27 ♕d4 ♖b7 [27...♗xb4] 28 ♖a1 ♕xb4 29 ♕xb4 ♗xb4 30 ♗d3 ♗c5 and Black holds

despite being the exchange down.) 27...h6 28 h4 c2 (28...♕xb4 29 ♖d4 [29 g5 ♕g4+=] 29...♗e7 30 ♖xb4 ♖xe5 31 ♖xe5 ♗xb4 32 ♗a4 [32 f3?? c2] 32...♗d6) 29 ♖a1 (29 g5 cxd1=♕=) 29...♕xa1 30 ♕xa1 (30 ♖xa1

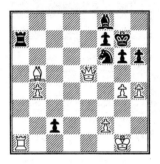

30...♗d6!! 31 ♕xf6+ ♔xf6 32 ♖c1 ♖c7 Black is safe.) 30...♖xa1 31 ♖xa1 ♘d5 (Black can also draw by 31...♗xb4 as well as White has no time to keep all his kingside pawns. 32 ♖c1 ♘xg4 33 ♖xc2 h5) 32 ♗a4 ♘xb4 33 ♖c1 ♗d6 and Black has no problem at all.

22 ♕xb5

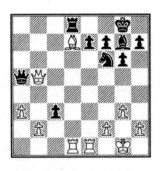

22...♕c7?

After 22...♕xb5 23 ♗xb5 ♖b8 24 bxc3 (upon 24 a4 cxb2 the pawn on b2 is really strong and compensates for the exchange. After 25 ♖e2 ♘d5 White's advantage is symbolic.) 24...♖xb5 25 ♖xe7 Now one can see why my text move was a big mistake. Black still has the rook to hold the queenside pawns until his minor pieces come over to help.

23 bxc3 ♖xd7 24 ♖xd7 ♕xd7 25 ♕xd7 ♘xd7

26 ♖xe7

Black has no pieces on the queenside to hold back White's pawns.

26...♘b6

After 26...♘c5 27 ♖e8+ ♗f8 28 ♖a8 ♘e4 29 a4 Black is in trouble as well.

27 ♖b7 ♘a4 28 ♖b8+ ♗f8 29 c4 ♔g7 30 ♔g2 ♗d6 31 ♖a8 ♘b2

32 a4 ♘xc4 33 a5 ♘e5?

Taking the pawn was possible, but it offers no chances of holding the game. I had virtually the same position against Speelman in Graz 1981 and easily converted my advantage. However, if White's pawn were on h4 and Black had one on h5 that might be a draw.

34 ♖c8!

Now I can't even sacrifice a single one of my pieces.

1-0

A.Shneider – G.Kasparov
EU Cup, Lyon 1994

1 d4 ♘f6 2 c4 g6 3 ♘f3 ♗g7 4 g3 c5 5 ♗g2 cxd4 6 ♘xd4 0-0 7 0-0 ♘c6 8 ♘c3 ♘xd4 9 ♕xd4 d6

10 ♕d3

I knew that Fischer had beaten Spassky in the 8ᵗʰ game of their 1972 match but had an idea I wanted to try out to combat Fischer's plan. I must admit that those games where two champions played each other always gave me such a headache. Which champion to follow? When I began to realise that they could also be inaccurate even when they won, then it became even more confusing.

10...a6 11 ♗d2 ♖b8 12 ♖ac1 b5

See diagram on page 66.

13 b3

Oops, what to do now – they took on b5 in the previous examples.

13...♗f5

I wanted to close the diagonal, thinking it was worth a tempo.

14 e4 ♗d7 15 h3!?

This stops ...♘g4.

15...bxc4 16 ♕xc4 ♕a5

16...♕b6 is less provocative.

17 ♕d3 ♕a3?

18 ♖c2! ♗b5?

It may seem weird but perhaps retreating with the queen was objectively stronger than this move. Not 18...♖fc8? when 19 ♘b1! traps the queen.

19 ♘xb5 axb5 20 ♖c7 e6 21 ♗e3! ♖bc8

Other moves were miserable as well.

a) 21...♕xa2? 22 ♖a7 ♕b2 23 ♗d4 wins.

b) 21...♖a8 22 ♖fc1 ♕xa2 23 e5 hurts.

c) 21...♖fc8 22 ♖a7 (22 ♖fc1 ♖xc7 23 ♖xc7 ♘e8 (or 23...♕xa2 24 ♖a7 ♕b2 25 ♕xd6) 24 ♖a7 ♕b2) 22...♕b4 23 ♖d1 ♘e8 and Black is passive.

22 ♖a7 ♕b4

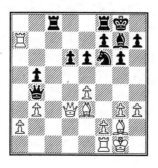

23 ♖d1 ♘e8

Here 23...♖fd8 24 ♗b6 (24 a3 ♕c3 25 ♕xb5 ♖b8 26 ♖xd6 wins prettily.) 24...♖d7 25 a3 ♕c3 26 ♕xc3 ♖xc3 27 ♖a8+ ♗f8 28 ♗d4 and Black must resign.

24 a3 ♕c3 25 ♕xb5 ♕b2 26 ♕d3

Simpler is 26 b4.

26...♖c3 27 ♕b1 ♕xb3 28 ♕xb3 ♖xb3

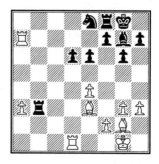

29 a4

In Fischer's game the queenside pawns played no role. My opponent, unlike Fischer's, opened the back rank, so there was no real hope.

29...h5 30 a5 ♖a3 31 a6 ♗e5 32 ♗h6 ♗g7 33 ♗g5 ♗f6 34 ♗xf6 ♘xf6 35 ♖xd6 ♖a1+ 36 ♔h2 ♖a2 37 e5 ♘h7 38 ♖ad7 ♖xf2 39 ♖d2 1-0

V.Anand – G.Kasparov
PCA/Intel-Grand Prix, Moscow 1995

1 e4 c5 2 ♘f3 d6 3 d4 cxd4 4 ♕xd4

In 1999 Peter Svidler tried this line against me. That time I won.

4...♗d7 5 c4 ♘c6 6 ♕d2 g6 7 ♗e2!?

Anand now stops 7...♗h6, as 8 ♕c3 is then possible.

7...♗g7 8 0-0 ♘f6 9 ♘c3 0-0 10 ♖b1 a6 11 b3 ♕a5 12 ♗b2 ♖fc8 13 ♖fd1

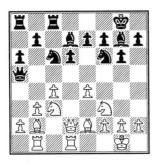

13...♗g4

Perhaps it is would be more efficient to prepare b5, e.g. by 13...♖ab8 14 h3 b5.

14 ♕e3 ♘d7 15 ♘d5 ♗xb2 16 ♖xb2 ♗xf3 17 ♗xf3 e6 18 ♘c3

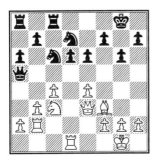

18...♖d8?

This is too passive. Usually playing a dynamic move like 18...b5!? would come naturally to me. Fischer also did not move his centre much, maybe that is why I postponed it. 19 ♖xd6 ♘ce5 20 ♗e2 (20 ♖bd2 ♘f6 21 c5 ♕a3) 20...bxc4 21 b4 ♕a3 22 ♕d2 a5 23 b5 ♘d3 and Black is in the game.

19 ♖bd2!?

When the rook took on b2, it was simultaneously building up White's position. Suddenly the d6-pawn is vulnerable.

19...♘de5 20 ♗e2 ♘b4 21 h4 b5??

See diagram on page 66.

In the preceding game (against Shneider) White did not take and that led to trouble. Maybe it was primarily because of that game that I subconsciously did not expect my opponent to capture here. It was better to stop the h-pawn with 21...h5.

22 cxb5

Taking the b5-pawn simply wins. Black doesn't lose just one pawn, but two.

22...axb5 23 ♘xb5 ♘bc6 24 a3 d5 25 exd5 ♖xd5 26 ♖xd5 exd5 27 b4 ♕a4

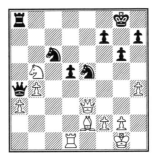

28 ♖xd5 1-0

There are many elements to Fischer's contributions to chess culture, some of which are quite complex. However, in pure chess terms, perhaps his contribution to his own pet opening – the Najdorf – is the biggest. He adopted it in almost all his games when faced with 1 e4. I employed some other variations at times but the Najdorf was my most common response.

Fischer was so good at taking pawns and calculating precisely. I also took the e5-pawn once... but let's start with Fischer's game.

B.Larsen – R.Fischer

Fischer took the centre pawn on e5 with his knight and calculated precisely to win.

So I decided I would try the same thing.

H.Lehmann – R.Fischer

Velibekov – G.Kasparov

H.Lehmann – R.Fischer
Capablanca Memorial, Havana 1965

1 e4 c5 2 ♘f3 d6 3 d4 cxd4 4 ♘xd4 ♘f6 5 ♘c3 a6 6 ♗e2 ♘bd7 7 0-0

I had a nice and in my opinion very instructive win against 7 a4, as played by Short in the Moscow Olympiad 1994. White should try to follow my plan despite the different move order.

G.Kasparov – N.Short
Moscow Olympiad 1994

1 e4 c5 2 ♘f3 d6 3 d4 cxd4 4 ♘xd4 ♘f6 5 ♘c3 a6 6 ♗e2 e6 7 f4 ♗e7 8 0-0 ♕c7 9 ♕e1 ♘bd7 10 ♗f3 0-0

11 ♔h1 ♔h8 12 a4 ♖b8 13 g4 b6 14 g5 ♘e8 15 ♗g2 ♗b7 16 b3 ♕d8 17 h4 g6 18 ♗b2

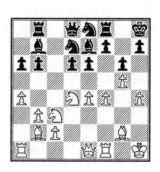

18...♘g7 19 ♖d1 ♖c8 20 f5 e5 21 f6 exd4 22 fxe7 ♕xe7 23 ♖xd4 f6 24 ♕d2 fxg5 25 ♖xf8+ ♖xf8 26 ♖xd6 ♘e5

27 Rxb6 gxh4 28 Nd5 Bxd5 29 Wxd5 Re8 30 Bh3 Wc7 31 Re6 Rxe6 32 Bxe6 Nc6 33 Wg5 Wd6 34 Bd5 Nb4 35 Wf6 Wxf6 36 Bxf6 Nxc2 37 Bc3 h6 38 b4 Kh7 39 b5 axb5 40 axb5 Nh5 41 b6 Ng3+ 42 Kh2 1-0.

Back to the Fischer game.

7...e6 8 f4 b5 9 Bf3 Bb7

10 e5

White feels like forcing the issue without delay.

10...Bxf3 11 Nxf3 dxe5 12 fxe5 Ng4 13 We2 b4 14 Ne4

White scores well without sacrificing the e5-pawn. He could opt for 14 Na4.

14...Ngxe5 15 Nxe5 Nxe5

See diagram on page 72.

16 Ng5

White has to react quickly since if Black castles then that's it.

16...Wb6+ 17 Kh1

17...Wb5!

Gaining an important tempo.

18 We1 Be7 19 b3 0-0

Fischer has survived and the win was just a matter of time.

20 a4 Wc5 21 We2 Rac8 22 c4 bxc3 23 Ba3 Wc7 24 Bxe7 Wxe7 25 Wxe5 Rc5

Fischer calculated so well.

26 We2 Rxg5 27 Wxa6 Wb4 28 Rfb1 Rd8 29 a5 h6 30 Wc4 Wxc4 31 bxc4 c2 32 Rc1 0-1

B.Larsen – R.Fischer
Game 6, Candidates match,
Denver 1971

1 f4 c5 2 Nf3 g6 3 e4 Bg7 4 Be2 Nc6 5 0-0 d6 6 d3 e6 7 Na3 Nge7 8 c3 0-0 9 Be3 a6 10 d4 cxd4 11 Nxd4 b5 12 Nxc6

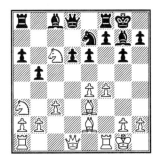

12...Nxc6

Black has equalised effortlessly.

13 Wd2 Wc7 14 Rad1 Rd8 15 Nc2 Rb8 16 a3 Na5 17 e5

At this point the match stood at 5-0 – such a shock for Larsen. Nevertheless, he presses on as he has nothing really to lose.

17...Bf8 18 b4 Nc6 19 Nd4 dxe5 20 fxe5 Nxe5

See diagram on page 72.

Fischer again takes the e5-pawn in a Sicilian.

21 ♗g5 ♖d5 22 ♕f4 ♗g7 23 h4 ♖b7?!

Alternatively, 23...♕xc3! and White has almost nothing for the sacrificed material.

24 ♗f6? ♗xf6 25 ♕xf6

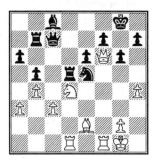

25...♕xc3 26 h5 gxh5

After 26...♖xd4 27 ♕xe5 ♖d3 28 ♕f4 ♖xd1 29 ♖xd1 ♗d7 30 ♖d3 White has compensation.

27 ♔h1

27 ♘xe6 simplifies to an equal position after 27...♗xe6 (27...♕e3+ 28 ♔h2 ♗xe6 29 ♖xd5 ♗xd5 30 ♕d8+) 28 ♖xd5 ♗xd5 29 ♕d8+.

27...♘g4 28 ♗xg4 hxg4 29 ♕h6 ♗d7

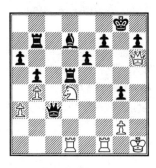

30 ♖f4

Larsen refuses to force a perpetual, still hoping to break his duck.

30 ♖xf7 is one way to draw. Then 30...♔xf7 31 ♖f1+ ♖f5 32 ♕xh7+.

30 ♘xe6 is another. Then after 30...♗xe6 31 ♖xd5 ♗xd5 32 ♕g5+.

30...f5 31 ♕f6??

Larsen finally cracks. How else to explain why a world-class player makes a losing move like this.

31 ♔h2 allows the knight to move. 31...♕c7 (31...♗c8?? 32 ♘xe6 wins.) 32 ♕g5+ ♔f7 33 ♕h5+ and there is another perpetual.

After 31 ♕g5+ ♔f7 32 ♕h5+ Black's king should not try to run away from the checks by 32...♔e7 33 ♕g5+ ♔d6?

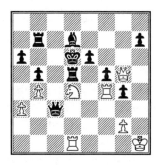

...as 34 ♖xf5!! and suddenly Black's king is under fire.

31...♗c8 32 ♖ff1

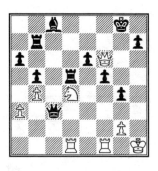

32...♖f7

It's all over now.

33 ♕h6 ♗b7 34 ♘xe6 ♕f6 35 ♕e3 ♖e7 36 ♖de1 ♖d6 37 ♕g5+ ♕xg5

38 ♘xg5 ♖xe1 39 ♖xe1 ♗d5 40 ♖e8+ ♔g7 0-1

Karpov also took an e5-pawn and went on to win.

V.Ivanchuk – A.Karpov
Sicilian tournament,
Buenos Aires 1994

1 e4 c5 2 ♘f3 e6 3 d4 cxd4 4 ♘xd4 ♘c6 5 ♘c3 ♕c7 6 ♗e2 a6 7 0-0 ♘f6 8 ♔h1 ♗e7 9 f4 d6 10 ♗e3 0-0 11 ♕e1 ♗d7 12 ♕g3 ♔h8 13 ♖ad1 ♖ac8 14 ♘f3 ♘b4 15 ♘e1 b5 16 a3 ♘c6 17 e5 dxe5 18 fxe5 ♕xe5

19 ♗f4 ♕c5 20 ♗e3 ♕e5 21 ♖xf6 ♕xg3 22 hxg3 ♗xf6 23 ♖xd7 ♔g8 24 ♘d1 ♖fd8 25 ♖xd8+ ♖xd8

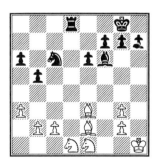

26 ♘f3 It is hard to imagine how Karpov can win this endgame against

such a good player. 26...h5 27 ♔g1 ♘e7 28 ♗d3 ♘d5 29 ♗d2 ♗e7 30 ♔f2 ♗c5+ 31 ♔e2 ♗d6 32 c4 bxc4 33 ♗xc4 ♗xg3 34 ♗xa6 ♘f4+ 35 ♗xf4 ♗xf4 36 ♘e3 g5 37 ♘d2 f5 38 a4 ♔f7 39 ♘dc4 ♖b8 40 ♘c2 g4 41 ♘d4 h4 42 ♘c6 ♖a8 43 ♗b5

43...h3 44 gxh3 gxh3 45 ♘6e5+ ♔f6 46 ♘d7+ ♔e7 47 ♘db6 ♖h8 48 ♗c6 h2 49 a5 ♗b8 50 a6 ♔d8 51 ♗h1 ♖g8 52 ♘e5 ♔c7 0-1

Of course I too developed an appetite for swallowing the e5-pawn in the Sicilian.

Velibekov – G.Kasparov
USSR 1976

1 e4 c5 2 ♘f3 e6 3 d4 cxd4 4 ♘xd4 ♘f6 5 ♘c3 d6 6 ♗e2 a6 7 0-0 ♘bd7 8 f4 b5 9 ♗f3 ♗b7 10 a3

My opponent may have known the Fischer game.

10...♕c7 11 ♔h1

It would also be nice to know whether he was aware of the following game between two former champions. After 11 ♕e1 ♗e7 12 ♔h1 ♖b8 13 b3 0-0 14 ♗b2 ♖fe8 15 ♕g3 ♗f8

75

16 ♖ae1 e5 17 ♘f5 ♔h8 18 ♕h4 exf4 19 ♕xf4 ♘e5 20 ♖e3 g6 21 ♘h6 ♗g7 22 ♘d5 ♘xd5 23 exd5 f6 24 ♗e4 g5 25 ♕f5 ♗xh6 26 ♕xf6+ ♗g7 27 ♕f5 ♘g6 28 ♖h3

28...♗xb2 Black is winning. 29 ♕xg6 ♖e7 30 ♖h6 ♖g8 31 ♕f5 ♗c8 32 ♕f3 g4 33 ♕d3 ♗e5 34 c4 bxc4 35 bxc4 ♖eg7 36 c5 dxc5 37 d6 ♕a7 38 ♗d5 ♖d8 39 ♕e4 ♗d4 40 ♕f4

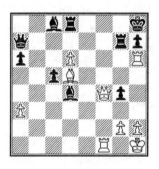

40...♖gd7?? (40...♕d7 was winning.) 41 ♖f6! 1-0 Tal-Smyslov, Candidates,

Yugoslavia 1959. What a hacking game.

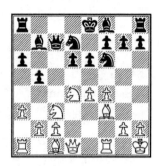

11...h5?!

This is a risky move!

12 ♗e3 ♘c5 13 e5 dxe5 14 fxe5 ♘g4 15 ♗xb7 ♕xb7 16 ♗g5 ♘xe5

I took the pawn – just as Fischer liked to do.

17 ♕e2 ♘cd7 18 ♖ad1 ♗e7 19 ♘e4

See diagram on page 72.

Suddenly Black has difficulty in finding a continuation.

19...♕c7 20 ♗xe7 ♔xe7

Steinitz didn't mind placing his king in the centre.

21 ♘g5 ♖af8 22 ♕e1

22...♘c5??

This is a dreadful mistake. I came to the conclusion that it is not as simple to take the e5-pawn as one may think.

23 ♕xe5! 1-0

When the King's Indian becomes a Benko Gambit...

M.Cuellar – R.Fischer

V.Ivanchuk – G.Kasparov

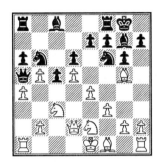

The Najdorf was my pet opening, whereas the Benko Gambit was a rare choice. I played it only a few times. I should clarify that the Benko type of position in the King's Indian sometimes transposes to the Benko and then a similar pawn sacrifice occurs.

M.Cuellar – R.Fischer
Stockholm Interzonal 1962

1 d4 ♘f6 2 c4 g6 3 g3 ♗g7 4 ♗g2 0-0 5 ♘f3 d6 6 0-0 ♘c6 7 ♘c3 ♗f5 8 d5 ♘a5 9 ♘d4 ♗d7 10 ♕d3 c5 11 ♘b3 ♘g4 12 f4

12...b5
This pawn sacrifice is rather a surprise as the knight can capture as

well. On the other hand, I already hinted that a Benko type pawn sacrifice might occur.

13 ♘xa5 ♕xa5 14 ♘xb5 ♗xb5 15 cxb5 ♖fb8 16 ♗f3 ♘f6 17 a4 a6

See diagram above!

18 bxa6
After 18 ♗d2!? ♕b6 19 e3.

18...♕xa6
For players who do not know the Benko, it comes as a small surprise that Black exchanges pieces when he is a pawn down. But the idea has its logic. Black exchanges in order to clear squares for an invasion by his well-positioned pieces. Black has no need to fear the endgame.

19 ♖a3 ♕xd3 20 exd3 ♖b4 21 a5

21 b3!? keeps the pawn, but Fischer would have compensation anyway.

21...♖b5

22 ♗d2 ♖xb2

Black recovers the pawn which makes him feel more comfortable, however he is not yet better as the white a-pawn stymies him and his opponent's position is not loose enough to invade.

23 ♗c3 ♖b7 24 ♖e1 ♘e8 25 ♗d2

This defends a5 but allows Black's dark-squared bishop to assume a dominating role.

25...♔f8 26 ♗d1 ♖b2 27 ♗c1 ♗d4+ 28 ♔h1 ♖f2

White has the usual problem in the Benko of keeping his position together.

29 ♗g4 ♘f6 30 ♗h3 ♖c2 31 a6 ♖a7 32 ♗c8

If 32 ♗g2 ♘g4.

32...♘xd5

Black moves ahead in material and White's position deteriorates very quickly.

33 ♖b3 ♘b4 34 f5 gxf5 35 ♗g5 e6 36 ♗d8 ♖a8 37 ♗b6 ♖xc8 0-1

I beat Bareev with the Benko at Linares 1994 and in the last round of the Dubai Olympiad I defeated Schmidt when the Soviet Union needed to win 4-0. Evgeny took the pawn whereas Schmidt kept the position closed. Despite these pleasant memories, when I think of the Benko Gambit it is the Fischer effect that is the most pronounced and it really hurts. The next defeat helped Karpov to win another Linares tournament.

V.Ivanchuk – G.Kasparov
Linares 1997

1 d4 ♘f6 2 c4 g6 3 ♘c3 ♗g7 4 e4 d6 5 f3 0-0 6 ♗g5 a6 7 ♕d2 c5 8 d5 b5 9 cxb5 ♘bd7 10 a4 ♕a5 11 ♘ge2 ♘b6

See diagram on page 77.

12 ♘c1 axb5 13 ♗xb5 ♗a6 14 ♘1a2

If 14 ♗xa6 ♕xa6!

14...♗xb5

15 axb5

The pawn formation is slightly different from that in the Fischer game.

15...♘h5

Black could try swapping pieces on the queenside with 15...♘a4!?

16 ♖b1

After 16 0-0 ♗d4+ 17 ♔h1 ♗xc3 18 bxc3 f6 19 ♗h6 ♖fb8 Black has compensation in an unusual form.

16...♗d4

I also manage to put my bishop on the dominating d4-square.

17 ♗h6

17...♖fe8

Bobby put his rook here too. Of course he was defending the e7-pawn whereas I was looking for dynamic play, but his rook move affected me and played a negative role in my decision making.

Maybe the simplest way was to exert pressure on the queenside with 17...♖fb8!? and try to gobble up the b5-pawn. 18 b3 ♘d7 19 ♗e3 (19 b4 ♕a3; 19 ♔e2 ♘e5) 19...♗xe3 20 ♕xe3 ♖xb5 and Black is better. I also suggested the dynamic attempt 17...f5? sacrificing the exchange. Then 18 ♗xf8 ♖xf8 19 b3 (19 b4!? ♕a7 and Black has nice play for the material.) 19...fxe4 20 ♘xe4 (20 fxe4 ♖f2 21 ♕xf2 ♗xf2+

22 ♔xf2 c4 23 b4 ♕a7 is unpleasant for White) 20...♕xb5 21 ♘ac3 ♕a6 is lovely for Black.

18 b3 e6 19 dxe6 ♖xe6!?

After 19...fxe6!? comes 20 ♗e3.

20 ♗e3 ♗xe3 21 ♕xe3 d5

22 b4

Not 22 ♕xc5? ♘f4 23 0-0 d4! 24 ♕xd4 ♕xa2 25 ♖f2 (25 ♘xa2?? ♘e2+) 25...♕a5 and this time the three pawns are not enough for the piece.

22...♕a3?!

After 22...cxb4 23 ♘xb4 dxe4 24 0-0 exf3 25 ♕xf3 Black should be able to live with his small disadvantage.

23 bxc5 ♘c4

If 23...dxe4 24 0-0 exf3 25 ♕d4 fxg2 26 ♖f2 ♘a4 27 c6 White's passed pawns are menacing.

24 ♕d4 ♘f4

25 0-0!

Ivanchuk simply sacrifices a knight to neutralise Black's play and get his passed pawns rolling.

25...♕xa2 26 ♖f2!

Not 26 ♘xa2? because of ♘e2+.

26...♕a3

27 ♘xd5

White's connected passed pawns can't be contained and he has a completely winning position.

27...♕d3 28 ♕xd3 ♘xd3 29 ♖c2 ♘a3 30 ♖a2 ♘xc5

After 30...♘xb1 31 ♖xa8+ ♔g7 32 c6 wins.

31 ♖ba1 f5 32 ♘c7 ♖e5 33 ♘xa8 ♘xb5 34 exf5 gxf5 35 ♘b6 ♘c3 36 ♖c2 1-0

And here I lost on time.

Boris Spassky the 10th

The tenth world champion reigned from 1969 to 1972. He defeated Tigran Petrosian at the second time of asking. Beating the Armenian world champion was in itself a great achievement, but winning the Candidates matches twice was also great. In the second half of the 60s he was probably the strongest player. From 1970 Fischer took over that mantle, and in 1972 won the title. Spassky, like Capablanca, Euwe, Smyslov, Tal, Fischer and Topalov never successfully defended the title. Of these, Fischer was the only one who did not actually try to do so. I wrote in the Predecessors book that Spassky's style was more attacking than universal.

I copied a positional idea from Spassky, but it did not pay off. He used to create many problems for Black in queenless variations of the Queen's Gambit Accepted. The pawn structure is symmetrical and yet Spassky managed to inject power into the proceedings. I also tried the idea of pressing in a symmetrical queenless opening. Here are the positions:

B.Spassky – R.Fischer

G.Kasparov – P.Leko

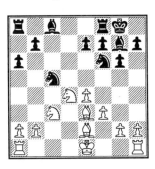

Let's start with a game by two world champions.

B.Spassky – R.Fischer
Game 4, St Stefan/Belgrade match
1992

1 d4 d5 2 c4 dxc4 3 ♘f3 ♘f6 4 e3 e6 5 ♗xc4 c5 6 0-0 a6 7 dxc5!?

This is one of Spassky's pet lines. He managed to breathe life into this seemingly dead boring variation and after his return match with Fischer the line caught on. Kramnik tried it against me as well. Now we understand this position much better than before Fischer-Spassky 1992.

7...♕xd1

In a match, players tend to be happy with a draw. For a long time people did not understand how many pitfalls there were in this variation.

8 ♖xd1 ♗xc5

Despite its symmetrical nature, this endgame provides White with more opportunities to fight for an advantage than was at first thought.

9 b3

Spassky tried this move three times against Fischer in the match.

In the fourth and final occurrence of the line Boris changed over to another plan with 9 ♘bd2. By this time Fischer had learned how to neutralise the endgame advantage. 9...0-0 10 a3 b5 11 ♗e2 ♗b7 12 b4 ♗e7 13 ♗b2 ♘bd7 14 ♖ac1 ♖fc8 This way of developing looks very convincing for Black and he has equalised the position. 15 ♘b3 ♖xc1 16 ♖xc1 ♖c8 17 ♖xc8+ ♗xc8 18 ♘fd4 ♘b8 19 ♗f3 ♔f8 20 ♘a5 ♗d6 21 ♘db3 e5 22 ♘c5 ♔e7 23 h3 ♘fd7 24 ♘d3 f6 25 ♗e4 g6 26 f4 exf4 27 exf4 ♘b6 28 ♘b7 ♗c7 29 ♘bc5 ♘c4 30 ♗c1 ♘d7 31 ♔f1 ♘xc5 32 ♘xc5 ♗b6 33 ♗d3 ♗xc5 34 bxc5 ♗e6 35 ♔f2 ♔d7 36 ♗xc4 ♗xc4 ½-½ Spassky-Fischer, Belgrade 1992.

9...♘bd7 10 ♗b2 b6

This was Fischer's first reaction to the problem. He holds back b5 as he doesn't want the queenside to be attacked by a4.

On the next two occasions the American no longer rejected the tempo-gaining 10...b5 and after 11 ♗e2 ♗b7 12 ♘bd2 Fischer castled when he faced the line for the third time. 12...0-0. Interestingly, castling has an unusual advantage compared to what happened in his second attempt at this variation. Here the king defends the g7-pawn. The more natural king move 12...♔e7 was Fischer's choice upon facing the line for the second time, when play continued 13 a4 bxa4 14 ♖xa4 ♖hb8 15 ♖c1 ♗d5 16 ♘e5 ♗d6 17 ♘xd7 ♘xd7 18 ♖xa6 ♖xa6 19 ♗xa6 f6 20 ♗c4 ♗xc4 21 ♖xc4 ♘c5 22 ♖c3 f5 23 ♗a3 ♘e4 24 ♖c7+ ♔d8 25 ♗xd6 ♘xd2

And after 26 ♖xg7 Bobby survived this lost position.

It may have affected me in some games, but I have not worked out yet in which one. 26...♖xb3 27 h4 h5 28 ♗f4 ♔e8 29 ♔h2 ♖b2 30 ♔h3 ♘e4 31 f3 ♘f2+ 32 ♔g3 ♘d3 33 ♗g5 e5 34 ♔h3 ♘f2+ 35 ♔h2 ♘d3 36 ♗h6 ♘e1 37 ♔g1 ♘d3 38 ♗g5 ♖b1+ 39 ♔h2

♜b2 40 ♜e7+ ♚f8 41 ♜e6 ♚g7 42 ♚h3 ♜e2 43 ♜d6 ♞e1 44 ♝f6+ ♚g8 45 ♝xe5 ♜xe3 46 ♝f4 ♜e2 47 ♜g6+ ♚f7 48 ♜g5 ♚e6 49 ♝c7 ♜a2 50 ♝b6 ♞d3 51 ♚h2 ♞e1 52 ♚h3 ♞d3 53 ♝c7 ♜c2 54 ♝b6 ♜a2 55 ♚g3 ♞e1 56 ♜xh5 ♜xg2+ 57 ♚f4 ♞d3+ 58 ♚e3 ♞e5 59 ♜h6+ ♚d5 60 ♝c7 ♜g7 61 ♝xe5 ♚xe5 ½-½ Spassky-Fischer, Belgrade 1992) 13 ♜ac1 ♜fc8 14 h3 ♚f8 (Fischer still returns to the centre.) 15 ♚f1 ♚e7 16 ♞e1 ♝d6 17 a4

17...♝c6 (Black defends the queenside in a different way.) 18 axb5 axb5 19 ♜c2 ♜c7 20 ♜dc1 ♜ac8 21 ♝f3 ♝xf3 22 ♞dxf3 e5 23 ♜xc7 ♜xc7 24 ♜xc7 ♝xc7 25 ♞c2 ♞e4 26 ♞a3 b4 27 ♞c4 f6 28 ♞e1 ♞dc5 29 ♞c2 ♞xb3 30 ♞xb4 ♞bd2+ 31 ♞xd2 ♞xd2+ 32 ♚e2 ♞c4 ½-½ Spassky-Fischer, Belgrade 1992.

11 ♞c3

This was Boris' deviation from one of his earlier games.

11...♝b7 12 ♜ac1 ♝e7

After 12...h6 comes 13 ♞a4! which is the point of White's 11th move. Then 13...♝e7 14 ♝xf6 ♝xf6 15 ♜xd7! and Black loses a pawn.

13 ♞d4 ♜c8

Not 13...0-0? 14 ♞xe6!

14 f3!?

I also won a few games by freezing a b7 bishop, for example against Karpov in the second game of our 1990 World Championship match. However, as you will probably guess, this plan is not as sparkling as it looks.

14...b5 15 ♝e2 ♝c5! 16 ♚f1! ♚e7

17 e4

This is the position that confused me. The outcome of the game and the pressure Boris managed to exert in this line prompted the idea of going for a position with a similar pawn structure.

See diagram on page 81.

17...g5

Bringing the h8-rook to the queenside was playable for Black.

18 ♞b1 g4 19 ♝a3 b4?

Taking on a3 was better.

20 ♜xc5!

The exchange sacrifice brings Fischer into an eternal pin.

20...♘xc5 21 ♗xb4 ♖hd8?!

This turns out to be a loss of tempo. Better was 21...♘fd7.

22 ♘a3!

A subtle way of developing the knight.

22...gxf3 23 gxf3 ♘fd7

After 23...♘e8 24 ♘c4 (or 24 ♖c1 ♖xd4 25 ♗xc5+ ♔d7 26 ♖c2 and Black has nothing for the pawn.) 24...♘d6 25 ♘b6 ♖c7 26 ♖c1 White wins.

24 ♘c4

It is remarkable that the knight on c4 actually blocks the c-file, thus helping Black to defend the c5-knight. Yet it paralyses Black's position. Fischer may have underestimated the move.

24...♗a8 25 ♔f2 ♖g8 26 h4 ♖c7 27 ♘c2 ♖b8?!

After 27...♔f6 28 ♗a5 ♖b7 29 ♗d2 ♔e7 30 ♘d4 White has nice play for the exchange.

28 ♗a3! h5?

Giving up the g-file turns out to be a huge mistake. After 28...♖g8 29 b4 ♘a4 30 b5+ ♔d8 31 b6 ♖c8 32 ♘2e3 Black is in trouble.

29 ♖g1 ♔f6 30 ♔e3

30 ♖g5 is met by 30...♗xe4!

30...a5 31 ♖g5 a4?! 32 b4 ♘b7 33 b5

If 33 ♗d3 ♖bc8 34 e5+ ♔e7 35 b5+ ♘bc5 36 ♘b4 ♗b7 (36...♖h8 37 ♘a6 wins.) 37 b6 wins. 33 f4 wins as well.

33...♘bc5 34 ♘d4 e5

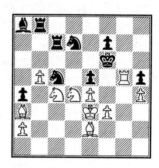

35 ♘xe5!

After 35 ♘f5! ♖xb5 36 ♖xh5 wins, as Ftacnik pointed out.

35...♘xe5 36 ♖f5+ ♔g7 37 ♖xe5

White has obtained a winning position.

37...♘xe4 38 ♗d3!

If 38 fxe4 ♖c3+.

38...♖c3

If 38...♘c3 39 ♗d6 wins.

39 ♗b4 ♖xd3+

Giving back the exchange in order to prolong the game but really it changes nothing else in the position.

40 ♔xd3 ♘f6 41 ♗d6 ♖c8 42 ♖g5+ ♔h7 43 ♗e5 ♘e8 44 ♖xh5+ ♔g6 45 ♖g5+ ♔h7 46 ♗f4 f6 47 ♖f5 ♔g6 48 b6 ♖d8 49 ♖a5 ♗xf3

50 h5+! 1-0

Black resigned as White can soon play b7 which wins.

It's time to look at the games in which Spassky's 'instructive' play affected me. We start with his strategy in the symmetrical Queens Gambit Accepted pawn structure.

G.Kasparov – P.Leko
Fujitsu-Siemens Giants,
Frankfurt 2000

1 d4 ♘f6 2 ♘f3 g6 3 c4 ♗g7 4 ♘c3 d5 5 ♕b3 dxc4 6 ♕xc4 0-0 7 e4 a6

The Hungarian variation, played by a Hungarian grandmaster.

8 ♕b3

White makes a third move with the queen. This subtle move order is the result of experience.

8...c5 9 dxc5 ♕a5 10 ♕b6 ♕xb6 11 cxb6 ♘bd7 12 ♗e2 ♘xb6 13 ♗e3 ♘bd7

14 ♘d4!

An endgame has arisen which greatly resembles that mastered by Boris Spassky in the Queens Gambit Accepted. I follow Spassky's strategy. Let's see where it led me!

14...♘c5?!

This is not the best despite the fact that piece play is fully in the spirit of the Grünfeld Defence.

14...b5 looks more natural but my opponent may have been worried that I had analysed it all previously at home. Then 15 f3, Spassky's idea to cut off the b7-bishop in this pawn structure, (other moves can be met satisfactorily, e.g. 15 a4 b4; 15 ♗f3 ♘e5; 15 ♘c6 ♗b7) 15...♗b7 16 ♘b3 and White has a small edge as the knight soon reaches a5. But then it will be difficult to decide which small advantage to go for as any of them might prove to be more significant than expected. Alternatively 14...b6!? deserved some consideration. Pushing the b-pawn only one square allows him to control more squares.

15 f3

In the queenless middlegame I am building up my pawn structure in the same way that Spassky did. In my case it did not bring the same result.

See diagram on page 81.

15...e5

Or 15...♘e6 to get rid of the dominating d4-knight and develop his bishop on e6. Then 16 ♘b3! and Black is still under pressure. His queenside is vulnerable and he must also reckon with e5. 16...♗d7 (16...b5 17 ♔f2 ♗d7 [or 17...♗b7 18 ♘a5] 18 ♖hd1 and White has an edge.) 17 f4 ♗c6 18 ♗f3 ♗h6 19 g3 ♖fd8 20 ♔e2. White's space advantage in the centre makes Black's game difficult.

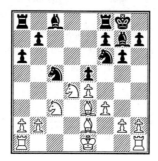

16 ♘c6!

This is the only jump that causes headaches for Black – otherwise Black will just complete his development. After 16 ♘f5 gxf5 17 ♗xc5 ♖d8 18 ♗b6 ♖e8 19 ♖d1 ♗e6 and Black is doing all right.

If 16 ♘c2 ♘e6 17 0-0-0 b5 18 ♘d5 ♗b7 the position is safe for Black.

16...bxc6

Leko takes on a pawn weakness. On the other hand the move considerably loosens White's grip.

Black could think of sacrificing a pawn instead with 16...♘e6. Then 17 ♘xe5! (17 ♘e7+ ♔h8 18 ♘a4!?) 17...♘xe4 18 ♘xg6 hxg6 (18...♘xc3 19 ♘xf8 ♔xf8 20 bxc3 ♗xc3+ 21 ♔f2 ♗xa1 22 ♖xa1 and the endgame is not attractive for Black.) 19 fxe4 ♘d4 and Black has some counterplay, though he is a pawn down.

17 ♗xc5 ♖d8

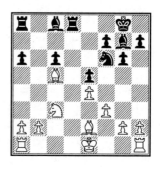

18 ♔f2?!

At least an inaccuracy as it allows the c8-bishop to move to e6. 18 ♗c4! is a better move as it hampers the opponent's bishop. Having the king on e2 would be better and even queenside castling might be possible. Another try is 18 ♗b6!? which would create some confusion in Black's camp.

18...♗e6 19 ♖hd1

19 ♖hc1!? looks better. Then 19...♖d2 (19...♘d7 20 ♗e3 a5 [20...f5 21 ♘a4] 21 ♘a4 ♖dc8 22 ♗c4 and defending c6 is not going to be fun.) 20 b3 ♗h6 21 ♗e3 ♗xe3+ 22 ♔xe3 and Black's rook is active on d2 but may soon come under pressure.

19...♘d7! 20 ♗e3 ♗f8! 21 ♖d2 f5! 22 ♖ad1 ♗e7! 23 g3

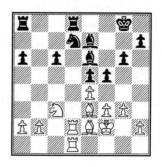

23...♔f7!

Black has improved his pieces. Now he has play of his own.

24 b3 a5 25 ♖c2 ♘f6!

Black has certainly played very purposefully over the last six moves and managed to equalise.

26 ♖xd8 ♖xd8 27 exf5

Defending the e4-pawn would not leave White very much scope for action.

27...gxf5 28 ♘a4 ♗d5 29 ♗b6 ♖a8 30 ♗c5 ♘d7 31 ♗xe7 ♔xe7 32 ♔e3 ♔d6

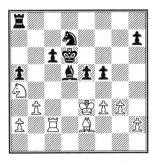

33 ♗d3?!

I had to win to have a chance of catching up with Anand who was leading the event. Of course White does not stand at all worse after 33 ♘c3.

33...f4+!

Black seizes his chance to take the initiative.

34 gxf4 exf4+ 35 ♔xf4 ♖f8+ 36 ♔g5 ♘e5 37 ♗xh7

After 37 ♗e4 ♘xf3+ 38 ♗xf3 ♖xf3 39 ♘c3 ♔e5 Black's king is somewhat troublesome, yet White should be able to live with it.

37...♘xf3+ 38 ♔h6 ♖f4!

39 ♖e2??

After 39 ♗g6? ♖h4+ 40 ♔g7 ♖g4 the pin is lethal.

Or 39 ♖f2 ♖h4+ 40 ♔g7 ♖xh2 41 ♖xh2 ♘xh2 42 ♔f6 and White achieves a draw.

39...♖h4+ 40 ♔g7 ♘xh2

The intermediate 40...♘d4! was winning at once, e.g. 41 ♖e8 ♘e6+.

41 ♘c3 ♘f3 42 ♘e4+ ♔c7 43 ♘f6 ♘d4 44 ♘xd5+ cxd5 45 ♖d2 ♔d6 46 ♗d3?

I was already short of time in this rapid game. After the text my bishop lands in a losing pin. Maybe I was angry that the strategy did not work as well for me as it had done for Spassky and that affected my concentration. Black could try playing on but White can probably hold with 46 ♗b1.

46...♘e6+ 47 ♔f6 ♖f4+ 0-1

White resigned as after 48 ♔g6 ♖d4 Black wins.

B.Larsen – B.Spassky

We now look at how Spassky used the h-file as a stunning avenue for attack.

I knew these games and wanted to hammer my opponents in the same way along the h-file.

B.Spassky – J. van Oosterom

G.Kasparov – V.Anand

It is worth seeing Spassky's games.

B.Spassky – J. van Oosterom
Junior World Championship,
Antwerp 1955

1 d4 ♘f6 2 c4 g6 3 ♘c3 ♗g7 4 e4 d6 5 f3 0-0 6 ♗e3 e5 7 ♘ge2 ♘c6 8 ♕d2 ♘d7

Black opens the diagonal for his bishop. In fact this move is still played competitively.

9 0-0-0 a6 10 d5 ♘a7

10...♘e7 looks more natural than putting the knight on the edge.

11 g4 b5

Black doesn't get enough play on the queenside and wastes time on the other flank. The alternative 11...f6 12 h4 ♔f7 is depressing for Black but he can at least last longer than in the game.

12 ♘g3 bxc4

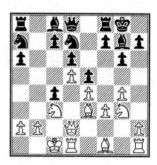

13 h4

Spassky commences operations on the h-file.

13...f6?

This buries the g7-bishop. After 13...♞b5!? 14 ♗xc4 ♞d4 15 ♕f2 White should do well – nevertheless Black is still alive and kicking.

14 h5 ♕e7?

Black played 13...f6 to make an escape route for the king, but now he blocks the path with this natural-looking yet losing move. Better resistance was offered by 14...♖f7.

15 hxg6 hxg6

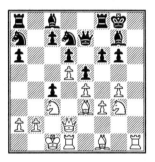

16 ♕h2!

So natural. And what makes it even nicer is that it wins directly.

16...♔f7

After 16...♞b6 17 ♕h7+ ♔f7 18 ♖h6 g5 19 ♕g6+ wins.

17 ♞f5!!

I also made a similar knight sacrifice in my game against Chiburdanidze.

17...gxf5 18 ♕h5+ ♔g8 19 gxf5 ♖f7 20 ♗e2 ♞c5?!

This allows a forced checkmate, but Black is completely lost anyway. If 20...♔f8 21 ♖dg1 ♕e8 (21...♔e8 22 ♖xg7; 21...♞b5 22 ♕h8+ and White delivers a nice checkmate.) 22 ♕h7! ♞b5 23 ♖xg7 (Capturing with the queen would be more elegant but this is far more decisive.) 23...♖xg7 24 ♗h6 wins.

21 ♖dg1 ♕d7?!

Other moves would have lasted longer but it's all the same now.

22 ♕h8 mate

The next game is probably Spassky's most famous masterpiece and of course I knew it well.

B.Larsen – B.Spassky
USSR v Rest of the World,
Belgrade 1970

1 b3 e5 2 ♗b2 ♞c6 3 c4 ♞f6 4 ♞f3?! e4 5 ♞d4 ♗c5 6 ♞xc6 dxc6 7 e3 ♗f5 8 ♕c2 ♕e7 9 ♗e2 0-0-0 10 f4?

Black is ahead in development, so White has no time for this.

10...♘g4!

Spassky acts at once, before White can bring his pieces into the game.

11 g3 h5!

To open the kingside.

12 h3?

White allows the opening of the kingside. After 12 h4 f6 Black stands better anyway.

12...h4!

Black opens the h-file at the cost of a piece – which turns out to be a low priced but highly fruitful investment.

13 hxg4 hxg3 14 ♖g1

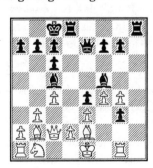

14...♖h1!!

See diagram on page 88.

Black sacrifices a whole rook for a decisive tempo.

15 ♖xh1 g2 16 ♖f1?!

In a hopelessly lost position White walks into a checkmate. But if 16 ♖g1 ♕h4+ 17 ♔d1 ♕h1 wins.

16...♕h4+

Spassky's queen invades on the h-file and checkmates White.

17 ♔d1 gxf1=♕+ 1-0

White could make only three more moves.

We saw how effectively Spassky used the h-file for attack. I was not careful enough when I tried to emulate his play. This game was unfortunate indeed!

G.Kasparov – V.Anand
Reggio Emilia 1992

1 e4 e6 2 d4 d5 3 ♘d2 c5 4 exd5 ♕xd5 5 dxc5

The first sign that White may castle queenside.

5...♗xc5 6 ♘gf3 ♘f6 7 ♗d3 0-0 8 ♕e2

White persists with his idea of castling long.

8...♘bd7 9 ♘e4 b6!

Black would rather give up the two bishops than fall behind in development.

10 ♘xc5 ♕xc5! 11 ♗e3 ♕c7 12 ♗d4 ♗b7

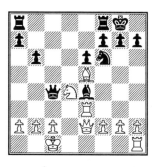

13 0-0-0

It has taken some effort but at last White can consider launching a snap attack on the kingside.

13...♘c5! 14 ♗e5

After 14 ♗xf6 White can't double Black's pawns because of 14...♘xd3+ 15 ♖xd3 ♕f4+.

14...♘xd3+ 15 ♖xd3?! ♕c4!

Grabbing a counettrattacking chance, offered by the unprotected state of the a2-pawn.

16 ♘d4?!

Going for a slightly worse but tenable ending with 16 ♗xf6 was White's best option. After 16...♕f4+ 17 ♔b1 ♕xf6 White can live with this position. But not 16 ♔b1?! ♗e4 17 ♖e3 ♕xe2 18 ♖xe2 ♗xf3 and the doubled pawns make it a really tough endgame for White.

16...♗e4

After 16...♕xa2 17 ♗xf6 gxf6 18 ♕g4+ ♔h8 19 ♕h4 ♕a1+ 20 ♔d2 ♕a5+ 21 ♖c3 ♕g5+ 22 ♕xg5 fxg5 23 ♖c7 White has some compensation for the pawn.

17 ♖e3

17...♕xa2!

Black is confident that he has got his bearings right in this complicated position.

18 ♗xf6

If 18 ♖xe4? ♘xe4 19 ♕xe4 ♕a1+ 20 ♔d2 ♕xh1 21 ♕g4 f6 wins.

18...♗g6!

Black can't win the rook with 18...♕a1+? as White's attack has grown too strong. 19 ♔d2 ♕xh1 20 ♖xe4 gxf6 21 ♕g4+ ♔h8 22 ♕h4 ♖g8 23 ♕xf6+ ♖g7 24 ♖g4 ♖ag8 25 ♘f3 and quite incredibly Black is defenceless.

19 ♖a3 ♕d5 20 h4

After 20 ♗e5 f6 21 ♗g3! ♕xd4 22 ♕xe6+ the position is equal according to Ernst.

20...gxf6 21 h5 ♕xd4 22 hxg6 hxg6

23 ♖ah3

See diagram on page 88.

This is the position I was hoping for. Spassky's raids on the h-file were very much the models I had in my mind. He succeeded with this theme several times.

23...f5 24 ♖h4

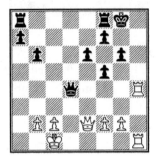

24...f4!

Black correctly keeps his queen in the centre where it can easily deny its counterpart access via the h-file. If instead 24...♕f6 25 ♕e3!? ♖fd8 26 ♕h3 ♔f8 27 ♖h8+ ♔e7 28 ♕a3+ ♔d7 29 ♖d1+ and White has an attack.

25 ♕f3 ♖ac8 26 ♖xf4

The queen can reach the h-file with 26 ♕h3, but it would all be in vain. 26...♕xf2! 27 ♖h8+ ♔g7 28 ♖h7+ (28 ♕h6+ ♔f6) 28...♔f6 29 c3 ♕e3+ and Black wins.

26...♕c5 27 c3 ♔g7

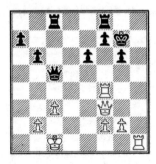

28 ♖hh4

A sad moment for White, who gives up his hopes of creating an effective attack on the h-file.

28...♕e5 29 g3 ♕e1+ 30 ♔c2 ♖cd8 31 ♖d4 ♕e5 32 ♖hf4 ♕c7 33 ♕e3 e5! 34 ♖xd8 ♖xd8 35 ♖e4

35 ♖h4 would allow no more than a check on the h-file. Black replies 35...♕d6.

35...♖d5

Black gradually makes progress with his extra pawn.

36 g4 b5 37 g5 ♕d6 38 f3

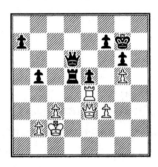

38...a5!

Now he starts opening up White's king.

39 ♕e2 ♕e6 40 ♕h2

A useless demonstration on the h-file.

40...♕f5 41 ♕g3 ♕d7 42 ♕e1 b4 43 cxb4

Upon 43 ♖xe5 ♕a4+ 44 ♔c1 bxc3! wins.

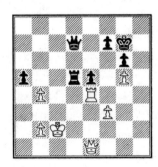

43...♕a4+

This is particularly annoying as it is Black who creates a winning attack from an edge file. This was exactly what I wanted to do to my opponent and now I get checkmated in the same way. So not only Spassky but also Anand gets it right – just not me!

44 b3

After 44 ♔c3 Ernst gives 44...♕c6+ 45 ♖c4 axb4+ 46 ♔xb4 ♖b5+ 47 ♔c3 ♕xf3+ wins.

44...♕a2+ 45 ♔c3 a4 46 bxa4 ♕a3+ 47 ♔c2 ♕xa4+ 48 ♔c3 ♕a3+ 49 ♔c2 ♖d3 0-1

Tigran Petrosian the 9th

Petrosian's wish came true in 1963 when he defeated Botvinnik. The first Soviet world champion was not afforded the privilege of a rematch, so Petrosian enjoyed a complete three year cycle as Champion before being challenged. Tigran is in many ways the closest to me, as he is from a Caucasus republic. He spent his childhood in Tbilisi, Georgia, just a few hundred kilometres away from Baku where I grew up.

In which particular way did Tigran Vartanovich affect me? He is known for his exchange sacrifices. I also tried them a few times.

Here are a couple of his exchange sacrifices which I had in mind when I made my own.

S.Reshevsky – T.Petrosian

25...Шe6!!

A.Yusupov – G.Kasparov

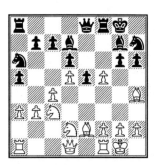

14... gxf5 15 Дh5 Шc8 16 Дe7 Шe8

M.Tal – T.Petrosian

31...Шf4!!

J.Timman – G.Kasparov

16...Шb4

94

J. Van der Wiel – G.Kasparov

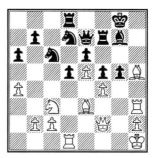

I lost all these games after sacrificing the exchange.

Let's look deeper into them and see what went wrong!

24...g4

S.Reshevsky – T.Petrosian
Candidates tournament,
Zurich 1953

1 d4 ♘f6 2 c4 e6 3 ♘c3 ♗b4 4 e3 0-0 5 ♗d3 d5 6 ♘f3 c5 7 0-0 ♘c6 8 a3 ♗xc3 9 bxc3 b6

This is a relatively rarely played line. Petrosian adopted it four times in 1953 and 1954, then he stopped using it. Before him, Keres was the only great player to employ this line. For example, he drew against Alekhine with it in 1938. Petrosian used this move for the first time in this game.

10 cxd5 exd5 11 ♗b2

At the 1953 Candidates tournament in Switzerland, Petrosian played the line twice more. In the first two games the bishop move was played. In a third game at Zurich, Taimanov beat him after 11 ♘e5 when, interestingly, Petrosian tried a similar exchange sacrifice but this time it didn't work – just as in my games! 11...♕c7 12 ♘xc6 ♕xc6 13 f3 ♗e6 (after 13...a5

14 ♕e2 c4 15 ♗c2 b5 16 e4 ♗e6 17 ♕e1 ♘d7 18 ♕g3 f6 19 ♗f4 ♖f7 20 ♖fe1 ♘f8 21 ♗d6 ♖d8 22 ♗c5 ½-½ Rabar-Petrosian, Belgrade 1954. White obtained some advantage and probably convinced Petrosian that he should switch to another Nimzo-Indian line.) 14 ♕e1 ♘d7 15 e4 c4 16 ♗c2 f5 17 e5 ♖f7 18 a4 a5 19 f4 b5 20 axb5 ♕xb5 21 ♗a3 ♘b6 22 ♕h4 ♕e8 23 ♖f3 ♘c8 24 ♗a4

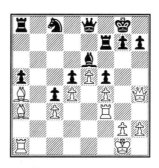

24...♖d7 (24...♗d7 25 e6 wins.) 25 ♖b1 ♕d8 26 ♗xd7 ♕xd7 27 ♖g3 ♘a7 28 ♗e7 ♗f7 29 ♕g5 ♗g6 30 h4 ♘c6 31 ♗a3 ♘d8 32 h5 ♘e6 33 ♕h4 ♗f7 34 h6 g6 35 ♕f6 ♕d8 36 ♗e7

95

♛c7 37 ♖xg6+ hxg6 38 h7+ ♚xh7 39 ♕xf7+ ♘g7 40 ♚f2 1-0 Taimanov-Petrosian, Zurich 1953

11...c4 12 ♗c2 ♗g4

Reshevsky played 12...♘e7 in a match against Najdorf the same year. He drew one and lost one out of these games.

13 ♕e1 ♘e4 14 ♘d2 ♘xd2

A Soviet player Ababkarov played 14...♗f5 twice in 1957, interestingly he won both games.

15 ♕xd2 ♗h5 16 f3 ♗g6 17 e4 ♕d7 18 ♖ae1 dxe4

A couple of rounds later Petrosian diverged and played what was perhaps his most famous game. Against Smyslov he went 18...f5 and the game continued 19 exd5 ♕xd5 20 a4 ♖fe8 21 ♕g5 ♕f7 22 ♗a3 h6 23 ♕g3 ♖xe1 24 ♖xe1 ♖e8 25 ♖xe8+ ♕xe8 26 ♚f2 ♘a5 27 ♕f4 ♘b3 28 ♗xf5 ♗xf5 29 ♕xf5 ♕xa4 30 ♕c8+ ♚h7 31 ♕f5+ ♚g8 32 ♕e6+ ♚h7 33 ♕e4+ ♚g8 34 ♕a8+ ♚h7 35 ♕e4+ ♚g8 36 ♕d5+ ♚h7 37 ♗e7 ♘c1 38 ♕f5+ ♚g8 39 ♕f8+ ♚h7 40 ♕f5+ ♚g8 41 d5 ♕a2+ 42 ♚g3 ♕d2 43 d6 ♕e1+ 44 ♚g4 ♘d3 45 ♕d5+ ♚h7 46 d7 ♕e5 47 ♕xd3+ cxd3 48 d8=♕ ½-½ Smyslov-Petrosian, Zurich 1953.

19 fxe4 ♖fe8 20 ♕f4 b5 21 ♗d1 ♖e7

22 ♗g4

By inserting this move he announces his intention of pushing the e-pawn. Alternatives were 22 h4!? and 22 ♖e3!?

22...♕e8 23 e5

This is menacing since White can open up the position with e6. However it gives up the d5-square and the bishop on b2 is out of play.

23...a5 24 ♖e3 ♖d8 25 ♖fe1

Crouch recommends 25 ♖ef3 as it prevents 25...f6.

See diagram on page 94.

25...♖e6!!

Black blocks the e6-thrust, and at the same time Petrosian clears the e7-square.

26 a4?!

In the Predecessor series I indicated a preference for the immediate capture 26 ♗xe6. Then 26...♕xe6! (26...fxe6 27 ♖g3 ♘e7 28 ♖f1 ♘d5 29 ♕g5 ♕e7 [29...♖d7 30 h4] 30 ♗c1 ♕xg5 31 ♗xg5 ♖b8 32 ♗d2 and White has an advantage in the endgame.) 27 ♖g3 ♘e7 28 h4 ♘d5 29 ♕g5 ♖d7 30 h5 h6 31 ♕h4 ♗d3 and Black has a reasonable fortress. If 32 ♗c1 ♘xc3.

26...♘e7!

Tigran Vartanovich radically improves the position of his knight.

27 ♗xe6 fxe6 28 ♕f1

After 28 ♖f3 b4! 29 ♖ef1 ♘d5 30 ♕g5 ♖b8 Black stands well as I pointed out in the above-mentioned analysis.

28...♘d5!

There are no open files for the rooks and both Black's minor pieces have wonderful play.

29 ♖f3 ♗d3 30 ♖xd3

White gives back the exchange, but Black's knight remains very strong and easily compensates for the pawn deficit.

30...cxd3 31 ♕xd3 b4 32 cxb4

If 32 c4 ♘b6.

32...axb4 33 a5

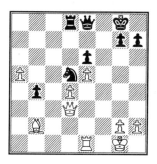

33...♖a8

Even though he is a pawn down, Black does not even stand worse.

34 ♖a1 ♕c6 35 ♗c1 ♕c7 36 a6 ♕b6 37 ♗d2

If 37 h3 ♘c7 picks up the pawn, as pointed out by Crouch.

37...b3 38 ♕c4 h6 39 h3 b2 40 ♖b1 ♔h8 41 ♗e1 ½-½

M.Tal – T.Petrosian
USSR 1958

1 e4 e5 2 ♘f3 ♘c6 3 ♗b5 a6 4 ♗a4 ♘f6 5 0-0 ♗e7 6 ♖e1 b5 7 ♗b3 0-0

8 c3 d6 9 h3 ♘a5 10 ♗c2 c5 11 d4 ♕c7 12 ♘bd2 ♗d7

Petrosian played this line seven times, holding three world champions. Both Karpov and I were unable to hurt him.

13 ♘f1 ♘c4 14 ♘e3

14 b3 is the main line.

14...♘xe3 15 ♗xe3 ♗e6?!

Players no longer put the bishop on e6 – nowadays it's c6. Tigran drew against Karpov in Milan 1975 with 15...♖fc8.

16 ♘d2 ♖fe8 17 f4 ♖ad8 18 fxe5

If 18 f5 exd4! or 18 d5 exf4.

18...dxe5 19 d5 ♗d7 20 c4 ♖b8 21 a4 b4

22 a5!

Tal wants to exchange the light-squared bishop in order to remove an important defensive piece.

22...♖f8 23 ♗a4 ♗xa4 24 ♖xa4

24...♖bd8!

Black improves the rook, but his position remains troublesome.

25 ♕f3 ♖d6 26 ♘b3 ♘d7 27 ♖aa1 ♖g6 28 ♖f1 ♗d6 29 h4 ♕d8 30 h5 ♖f6 31 ♕g4

See diagram on page 94.

31...♖f4!!

A great saving concept, Petrosian sacrifices the exchange for a blockade.

32 ♗xf4?!

Even such a broad-minded player as Tal could not resist taking the exchange. Tal could have retained an advantage by playing 32 ♖xf4. Then 32...exf4 33 ♗xf4 ♕e7 (After other moves White will stand clearly better, e.g. 33...♗xf4 34 ♕xf4 ♕e7 35 h6 g6 36 ♖f1; 33...♘f6 34 ♕f3 ♗xf4 35 ♕xf4 ♘xh5 36 ♕e3; 33...♘e5 34 ♕g3 ♖e8 35 h6 g6 36 ♖c1 ♕c7) and Black can either try to blockade or break out. There might follow 34 h6 g6 35 ♕g3 ♗xf4 36 ♕xf4 f5 37 ♖e1.

32...exf4 33 ♘d2 ♘e5 34 ♕xf4?

White had two moves to obtain the better prospects. Either 34 ♕h3 ♕g5, or 34 ♕f5 g6 35 ♕h3.

34...♘xc4 35 e5 ♘xe5 36 ♘e4

If 36 h6 f5.

36...h6 37 ♖ae1?

After 37 b3!? c4 38 ♘xd6 (38 bxc4 ♗b8) 38...♕xd6 39 ♖ae1 f6 40 bxc4 ♖c8 41 ♖e4 ♕c5+ 42 ♔h2 ♕xa5 43 ♕f5 the position is unclear.

37...♗b8 38 ♖d1

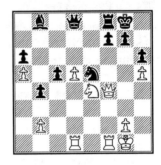

38...c4 39 d6 ♘d3 40 ♕g4?

Better was 40 ♕e3! f5 (40...♘xb2 41 ♖d5! ♕d7 42 ♘c5 ♕c6 43 ♖ff5!) 41 ♕d4 with a still unclear position.

40...♗a7+ 41 ♔h1 f5 42 ♘f6+! ♔h8 43 ♕xc4 ♘xb2 44 ♕xa6 ♘xd1 45 ♕xa7

Tal was not yet prepared to defend passively with 45 ♖xd1!?, but maybe it was the better option as after 45...♗b8 46 ♘d5 ♗xd6 47 ♘e7 ♕xe7 48 ♕xd6 ♕xd6 49 ♖xd6 ♖a8 50 ♖b6 ♖xa5 51 ♖xb4 White probably holds.

45...♕xd6?

Petrosian misses a win. Black can force the issue after 45...♘c3! 46 ♕e7 gxf6 47 ♖xf5 ♕xe7 48 dxe7 ♖e8 49 ♖xf6 ♔g7 50 ♖b6 (50 ♖g6+ ♔f7 51 ♖xh6 ♘a4!! wins.) 50...♖xe7 51 ♖xb4 ♖e5 52 g4 ♖xa5 53 ♖b7+ ♔f6 54 ♖b6+ ♔g5 55 ♔g2 ♘e4!

46 ♕d7 ♕xf6

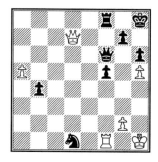

47 ♕xd1 ♖b8 48 ♖f3?

He should play 48 ♕d3 b3 49 a6.

48...♖a8?

After 48...♖b5 49 ♕e1 ♔h7 50 ♖b3 ♖xa5 51 ♕xb4 ♖a1+ 52 ♔h2 ♖f1 wins.

49 ♕e1 ♖xa5 50 ♕xb4 ♖e5 51 ♕f4 ♔h7 52 ♔h2 ♖d5 53 ♖f1 ♔g5 54 ♕f3 ♖e5 55 ♔g1 ♖c5 56 ♕f2 ♖e5 57 ♕f3 ♖a5 58 ♔h2 ♔h8 59 ♔g1 ♖a2 60 ♕d5?

60...♖c2?

60...♕e3+!! would have been decisive. Then 61 ♔h2 ♖a4 62 ♕d8+ ♔h7 63 ♖xf5 ♖d4 64 ♖d5 ♔g4 65 ♖d3 ♕e5+ 66 ♔g1 ♕e1+ (66...♕e4 67 ♕d5 ♖xg2+ 68 ♔h1 ♕xd5 69 ♖xd5 ♔g5 Black wins.) 67 ♔h2 ♖h4+ 68 ♖h3 ♕e5+ 69 ♔g1 ♖d4 and Black catches White's king.

61 ♕a8+ ♔h7 62 ♕f3 ♖c1 63 ♖xc1 ♕xc1+ 64 ♔h2 ♕c7+ 65 ♔h3 ♕e5 66 g4 fxg4+ 67 ♔xg4 ♕g5+ 68 ♔h3

♕f6 69 ♕e4+ ♔g8 70 ♕e8+ ♕f8 71 ♕xf8+ ♔xf8 72 ♔g4 ♔f7 73 ♔f5 ½-½

Here is my game against Timman.

J.Timman – G.Kasparov
Tilburg 1981

1 d4 ♘f6 2 c4 g6 3 g3 ♗g7 4 ♗g2 0-0 5 ♘f3 d6 6 0-0 c5 7 ♘c3 ♘c6 8 d5 ♘a5 9 ♘d2 a6 10 ♕c2 ♖b8

A deviation from this line with 10...e5 resulted in Tigran's Vartanovich's most beautiful and most famous combination from the 1966 World Championship final match against Spassky. Here is how that game went: 11 b3 ♘g4 12 e4 f5 13 exf5 gxf5 14 ♘d1 b5 15 f3 e4 16 ♗b2 exf3 17 ♗xf3 ♗xb2 18 ♕xb2 ♘e5 19 ♗e2 f4 20 gxf4 ♗h3 21 ♘e3 ♗xf1 22 ♖xf1 ♘g6 23 ♗g4 ♘xf4 24 ♖xf4 ♖xf4 25 ♗e6+ ♖f7 26 ♘e4 ♕h4 27 ♘xd6 ♕g5+ 28 ♔h1 ♖aa7 29 ♗xf7+ ♖xf7

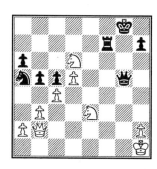

30 ♕h8+!! 1-0 Petrosian-Spassky, Moscow 1966.

11 b3 b5 12 ♗b2 bxc4 13 bxc4 ♗h6

In the databases Donner is credited with playing this for the first time against Botvinnik, way back in 1958.

14 ♘cb1

According to the database this move was introduced by Udovcic. It was then seen regularly, although it has never been played as often as 14 f4. Petrosian tried 14 f4 unsuccessfully with White against his problem opponent in the sixties. 14...e5 15 ♖ae1 (Petrosian deviated from Portisch's play when he faced the young Chiburdanidze by playing 15 dxe6 fxe6 16 ♖ab1 ♗g7 17 ♘ce4 ♖xb2 18 ♖xb2 ♘g4 19 ♖bb1 ♗d4+ 20 ♔h1 ♘e3 21 ♕c1 ♗b7 22 ♗f3 ♘xf1 23 ♕xf1 ♗xe4 24 ♘xe4 ♕e7 25 ♘g5 ♔h8 26 ♕h3 e5 27 ♘e6 ♖e8 28 ♗d5 exf4 29 ♘xf4 ♕f6 30 ♕d7 ♕d8 31 ♕xd8 ♖xd8 32 ♖b6 ♗c3 33 ♘e6 1-0 Petrosian-Chiburdanidze, Vilnius 1978) 15...exf4 16 gxf4 ♘h5 17 e3 ♖e8 18 ♘ce4 ♗f5 19 ♘c3 ♘b7 20 ♕a4 a5 21 ♖b1 ♕e7 22 ♖fe1 ♗d7 23 ♕c2 ♗f5 24 ♕a4 ♔f8 25 ♖b6 ♖bd8 26 ♕b3 ♗c8 27 ♘f1 ♖d7 28 ♘fg3 ♘xg3 29 hxg3 ♗g7 30 ♕b2 f5 31 ♗xg7+ ♕xg7 32 ♘f6 1-0 Portisch-Petrosian, Santa Monica 1966.

14...e5

In the debut game, Suetin preferred 14...♗d7 which then became routine.

15 ♗c3 ♗d7 16 ♘a3

See diagram on page 94.

16...♖b4

I got excited when I read about exchange sacrifices in a chapter in Petrosian's book. What advantages does Black accrue with this exchange? The position is closed so the rooks do not work well. In addition the c5-square is firmly under Black's control and he has an outside passed pawn. I did not pay attention to the interesting fact that Petrosian himself had opted for this position. In my younger days I

did not offer this exchange sacrifice at once. I lost a game against Zaid after playing 16...♗g7. I have not yet decided which world champion I should blame for that. 17 ♖ab1 ♕c7 18 e4 h5 19 f4 ♖b4 20 ♕d3 ♘b7 21 ♘c2 ♖xb1 22 ♖xb1 h4?! (22...exf4!?) 23 fxe5 dxe5 24 ♘f3! and White's centre pawns will be strong. 24...hxg3 25 ♗xe5 gxh2+ 26 ♗xh2 ♕c8 27 ♘e3 ♘g4 28 ♘xg4 ♗xg4 29 ♘e5 ♘a5 30 ♖f1 ♗h5 31 d6 ♗xe5 32 ♗xe5 ♕e6 33 ♗f6 ♘c6 34 ♕e3 ♔h7 35 ♕xc5 ♘b8 36 ♗e7 ♖e8 37 ♕d5 1-0 Zaid-Kasparov, Leningrad 1977.

17 ♗xb4 cxb4 18 ♘ab1

White's rooks have no open files, therefore the sacrifice comes into consideration. However, Black doesn't even have a pawn for it.

18...♕c7

Petrosian's opponent followed up the exchange sacrifice with 18...♕b6. Then came 19 ♘b3 ♘b7 20 ♘1d2 ♖c8 21 a3 a5 22 axb4 a4 (22...♖xb4!?) 23 ♘a5 ♘xa5 24 bxa5 ♕xa5 25 e3 ♗g7 26 ♖a2 ♘e8 27 ♖fa1 ♖a8 28 e4 ♕c5 29 ♕c3 ♖c8 30 ♗f3 ♗h6 31 ♖b1 ♗xd2 32 ♕xd2 ♕xc4 33 ♖b4 ♕c1+ 34 ♕xc1 ♖xc1+ 35 ♔g2 ♔g7 36 ♗e2 ♘f6 37 f3 g5 38 g4 h5 39 h3 hxg4 40 hxg4 ♘g8

41 ♖b6 1-0 Petrosian-Toran, Bamberg 1968.

19 e3

Two years later Kurajica tried an interesting idea, he gave up the c-pawn with 19 c5 in order to open the file. 19...♕xc5 20 ♕b2 ♘g4 (20...♕b5!?) 21 ♘e4 ♕b6 22 ♗f3 ♗g7 23 ♘bd2 ♘h6 24 ♖ab1 f5 25 ♕xb4 White is ready to give up a piece to open files for his rooks. 25...♕xb4 26 ♖xb4 fxe4 27 ♘xe4 ♘f5 28 ♖c1 ♘d4 29 ♔g2 ♗b5 30 ♖c7 ♗f6 31 ♘xf6+ ♖xf6 32 a4 ♗xe2 33 ♗xe2 ♘xe2 34 ♖b6 ♘d4 35 ♖xa6 ♘ab3 36 a5 ♖f7 37 ♖a8+ ♔g7 38 ♖aa7 1-0 Kurajica-Filipovic, Banja Luka 1983.

19...♗f5

I wanted to retain the knight for use against the bishop. The alternative 19...♖c8 has not disappeared from grandmaster practice and here is a recent example of it. 20 a3 b3 21 ♘xb3 ♗a4 22 ♘1d2 ♘xb3 23 ♘xb3 ♖b8 24 ♖ab1 ♕b6 25 ♖b2 ♘g4 26 ♕e2 ♘xe3 27 fxe3 ♗xb3 28 ♖fb1 ♗xe3+ 29 ♔h1 ♗d4 30 c5 ♗xc5 31 ♕d3 ♗c4 32 ♖xb6 ♖xb6 33 ♕d1 ♖xb1 34 ♕xb1 ♗xa3 35 ♕b8+ ♔g7 36 ♕b7 ♗c5 37 g4 ♗d3 38 g5 a5 39 h4 a4 40 ♗h3 ♔f8 41 ♕a8+ ♔g7 42 ♕xa4 h6 43 ♗e6 hxg5 44 hxg5 1-0 Psakhis-Avrukh, Israel 2001.

Maybe gaining space in the centre by 19...♘g4!? is after all a reasonable option. 20 ♖e1 f5 21 h3 (21 ♘b3?! is Timman's recommendation but Black has an aggressive and good reply in 21...f4!) 21...♘f6 22 a3 (22 c5 e4)

22...b3 23 ♘xb3 ♗a4 It looks like White can live with this pin. 24 ♘1d2 ♖b8 25 ♖ab1 ♘xb3 26 ♘xb3 ♕b6 27 c5 ♗xb3 (27...dxc5 28 ♕xc5 ♗xb3 29 ♕xb6 ♖xb6 30 ♖ec1 and White soon invades on the queenside.) 28 ♕xf5 gxf5 29 cxb6 ♖xb6 30 ♖ec1 and White is better.

20 ♘e4 ♗xe4 21 ♗xe4 ♘b7

In a closed position one usually has time to manoeuvre, however Black now lacks just one move to obtain a favourable setup. After 21...♘xe4 22 ♕xe4 f5 23 ♕c2 ♕xc4 24 ♕a4 ♕c5 25 ♘d2 f4 26 exf4 exf4 27 ♖ad1 White has the better prospects. And if 21...♕xc4 22 ♕xc4 ♘xc4 23 ♗d3 White retains an edge.

22 ♘d2 ♘c5

23 ♗g2!

Interestingly this move fights for the c5-square. Chess can be stunning, indeed. The bishop will cut Black's kingside knight off from the queenside. If 23 a3? b3.

23...♖b8 24 ♖fb1 a5 25 a3!

Weakening b4 and opening the a-file for the rook.

25...e4 26 axb4 axb4 27 ♗h3!

A subtle move which cuts off the f6-knight.

27...♗g7 28 ♖a2 h5 29 ♘b3 ♘d3 30 ♖d1 ♘e5

31 c5!

Black loses an important component of his compensation for the exchange. He relinquishes the c5 post for his knight.

31...♘d3 32 cxd6 ♕xd6 33 ♗f1 ♘e5 34 ♖a6 ♕d7 35 ♖xf6

35 d6!? was also attractive.

35...♗xf6 36 ♕xe4 ♖c8?

Black gives up the pawn for free. 36...♕a4 would still enable him to continue resistance but in the end White's extra pawn should prevail.

37 ♕xb4

White is just winning with his two extra pawns.

37...h4 38 ♕f4 ♔g7 39 gxh4 ♕d6 40 ♘d2 1-0

A.Yusupov – G.Kasparov
World Cup, Barcelona 1989

1 ♘f3 ♘f6 2 c4 g6 3 ♘c3 ♗g7 4 e4 d6 5 d4 0-0 6 ♗e2 e5 7 d5 a5 8 ♗g5 h6 9 ♗h4 ♘a6 10 ♘d2 ♕e8 11 0-0 ♘h7 12 a3 ♗d7 13 b3 f5 14 exf5

See diagram on page 94.

14...gxf5 15 ♗h5 ♕c8 16 ♗e7 ♖e8

I sacrificed the exchange, just like Petrosian. But after some mutual mistakes I went down to Artur.

17 ♗xe8 ♕xe8 18 ♗h4 e4 19 ♕c2 ♕h5 20 ♗g3 ♖f8 21 ♗f4 ♕g4 22 g3 ♘g5 23 ♔h1 ♘f3 24 ♖ac1 ♘c5 25 ♘xf3 ♕xf3+ 26 ♔g1 ♘d3 27 ♕d2 ♗d4

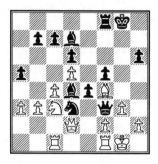

28 ♖c2 ♔h7 29 h3 ♖g8 30 ♔h2 ♕h5 31 ♘d1 ♘e5 32 f3 ♘d3 33 ♘e3 ♘xf4 34 gxf4 ♗b6 35 ♕f2 ♕g6 36 ♖e2 ♗c5 37 fxe4 fxe4 38 f5 ♕h5 39 ♖d2 ♖g5

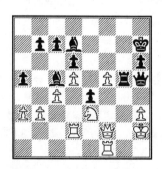

40 ♕f4 ♕e8 41 ♘g4 1-0

J. Van der Wiel – G.Kasparov
World Under 16 Championship,
Wattignies 1976

1 e4 c5 2 ♘f3 d6 3 d4 cxd4 4 ♘xd4 ♘f6 5 ♘c3 a6 6 f4 ♕c7 7 a4 g6 8 ♗d3 ♗g7 9 ♘f3 ♗g4

It's more common to develop the bishop on b7.

10 ♗e3 ♘c6 11 0-0 0-0 12 ♕e1 ♗xf3 13 ♖xf3 e6 14 ♕h4 ♕d8

The queen retreats to defend the king.

15 ♖h3 h5 16 ♗e2

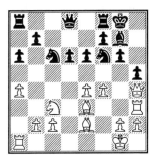

16...d5

This is thematic. As White is attacking on the flank, Black switches to the centre. Black could ease the attack by getting rid of the strong queen on h4 with 16...♘g4. Then 17 ♗xg4 (17 ♕xd8 ♖fxd8 18 ♗xg4 hxg4 19 ♖g3 f5 and Black has a nice game.) 17...♕xh4 18 ♖xh4 ♗f6! 19 ♖h3 hxg4 20 ♖g3 ♘b4 and Black has a good endgame. And after 16...♘b4 17 ♖c1 ♘d7 18 ♕e1 ♕c7 Black is doing well.

17 e5 ♘d7

The queen can still be swapped by means of 17...d4. Then after 18 ♖d1 ♘g4 19 ♗xg4 ♕xh4 20 ♖xh4 dxe3 21 ♗f3 f6 Black has nothing to worry about.

18 ♕f2 ♕e7 19 g4 hxg4

Black can also stir up things with 19...♕b4!?. Then 20 gxh5 d4 21 ♗c1 dxc3 22 bxc3 ♕b6 23 h6 ♕xf2+ 24 ♔xf2 ♗h8 25 h7+ ♔g7 26 f5 ♘dxe5 27 ♗h6+ ♔f6 28 ♗xf8 ♖xf8 29 fxg6 and Black has compensation for the exchange.

20 ♗xg4 ♖ad8

After 20...g5 21 ♔h1 gxf4 22 ♗xf4 ♘dxe5 23 ♖g1 the position is unclear.

21 ♖d1 f5

Black wants to carry out g5 under better conditions than in the previous line.

22 ♗f3!

Van der Wiel is alert. He stops g5.

22...♖f7

If 22...g5 23 ♘xd5.

23 ♔h1!

He wastes no time and goes after the weakness on g6.

23...g5

If 23...♘f8? 24 ♗c5.

24 ♗h5!?

See diagram on page 95.

24...g4?

Black gets some play for the exchange, and White's rooks have no open files – however that factor can be rectified. After 24...♖ff8 25 fxg5 ♘dxe5 (After 25...♗xe5 26 ♗g6 ♕b4 27 ♗h7+ ♔g7 28 g6 Black's king is in danger.) 26 ♗c5 (26 ♗b6 ♖c8 27 g6 ♘d7) 26...♕xg5 27 ♗xf8 ♖xf8 28 ♖g1 ♘g4 29 ♕e2 ♘ce5 30 ♘d1 and Black has to work hard to keep his position together.

25 ♗xf7+ ♕xf7 26 ♖g3 ♕h5 27 ♔g2 ♘f8 28 ♘e2 ♘g6

29 h3!

Interestingly, a similar formation occurred in my game against another Dutchman, Timman, where I sacrificed the exchange. In that game I had a b-pawn (which has the same qualities as the g-pawn). He undermined it with a single move of an edge-pawn. With the same result – he beat me too. Had Black stopped all that he would have had a decent position.

29...♘h4+ 30 ♔f1 ♔f7 31 ♘g1

White is not in a hurry to take on g4, which would free the f5-square.

31...d4 32 ♗c1 gxh3?

This mistake completely relaxes the pressure. White's king is no longer in danger and the rooks start to work. Black should protect g4 with 32...♖g8. Then 33 ♖dd3 (33 ♕e2 ♗f8) 33...♗f8 34 c3 ♗e7 35 cxd4 ♘b4 36 ♖b3 b6 and though Black's position is troublesome it has not fallen apart.

33 ♕e2! ♕xe2+ 34 ♘xe2

Black is just the exchange down.

34...♘g6 35 ♖xh3 ♗f8 36 ♖b3 ♖d7 37 ♖bd3 ♗c5 38 c3

Now John wins a pawn in addition to the extra exchange. It's all over now.

38...♗a7 39 ♗e3 ♖d5 40 cxd4 ♘b4 41 ♖b3 a5 42 ♗d2 1-0

Petrosian also had one remarkable game where he allowed himself to be saddled with a doubled f-pawn and it has remained in my memory.

But when I took on the responsibility of doubled f-pawns, I lost, as you will see in the following two examples...

B.Gurgenidze – T.Petrosian

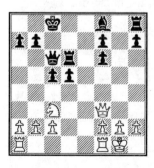

V.Cheskovsky – G.Kasparov

A.Beliavsky – G.Kasparov

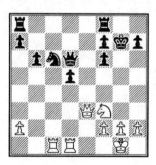

B.Gurgenidze – T.Petrosian
USSR Championship 1967

1 e4 c5 2 ♘f3 d6 3 ♗b5+ ♗d7
4 ♗xd7+ ♕xd7 5 0-0 ♘f6 6 e5 dxe5
7 ♘xe5 ♕c8 8 d4 e6 9 ♘c3 ♘c6
10 ♘xc6 ♕xc6 11 ♗g5 0-0-0

Petrosian puts pressure on d4 at once.
12 ♗xf6
White sacrifices a pawn in order to
create a doubled pawn in Black's camp.
12...gxf6 13 d5 exd5 14 ♕f3 ♖d6

See diagram on page 104.

It looks like Petrosian is defending
the f6-pawn with the rook.
15 ♖fe1 d4
The rook can recapture on c6, which
was the point of 14...♖d6.
16 ♕f5+ ♔b8 17 ♘e4
The knight's aim is to get to f5.
17...♖e6
Petrosian organises his pieces while
White's knight heads for f5.
18 ♘g3 ♗e7 19 ♕h5 ♕e8 20 ♘f5

20...♗d8! 21 ♖xe6
After 21 ♔f1 ♕b5+; or 21 ♕d1 ♕b5
22 b3 ♗a5 and Black wins.
21...fxe6 22 ♕xe8 ♖xe8 23 ♖e1
Black dissolves the doubled pawns,
but the knight has a chance to force
matters and improve his situation.
23...♔c7!
Just in time, the king lends a hand
thanks to the fact that the e1-rook is
unprotected.
**24 ♘g7 ♖e7 25 ♘h5 f5 26 h3 ♔d6
27 g4 fxg4 28 hxg4 e5 29 ♘g3**

29...♔d5
Black's active king prevents an
effective blockade by the knight.
30 f3
If 30 ♘c4 ♖g7 31 f3 h5 wins.
30...♖f7 31 ♖f1
The natural king move 31 ♔g2
allows an exchange of bishop for
knight by 31...♗h4.
31...♗g5 32 ♔g2 b5
White has blocked the kingside but
Black has a winning pawn majority on
the queenside.
**33 ♘e4 ♗e3 34 ♖h1 h6 35 b3 ♖f8
36 ♖b1 ♖f4 37 a4 b4 38 ♖h1**

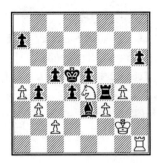

38...Ξxe4

The exchange sacrifice wins because Black has too many pawns for White to cope with.

39 fxe4+ ☗xe4 40 Ξd1 a5 41 ☗g3 ☗d5 42 Ξf1 ☗f4+ 43 ☗f3 c4 44 ☗e2

After 44 bxc4+ ☗xc4 45 ☗e4 ☗c3 46 Ξf2 d3 47 cxd3 b3 48 d4 b2 wins.

44...cxb3 45 cxb3 ☗e4! 46 Ξf3 ☗g5 47 Ξf7

If 47 Ξd3 ☗d5.

47...d3+ 48 ☗d1 ☗d4 0-1

V.Cheskovsky – G.Kasparov
USSR Championship, Tbilisi 1978

1 e4 c6 2 d4 d5 3 ☗d2 dxe4 4 ☗xe4 ☗f5 5 ☗g3 ☗g6 6 h4 h6 7 h5 ☗h7 8 ☗f3 ☗d7 9 ☗d3 ☗xd3 10 ☗xd3 ☗c7 11 ☗d2 ☗gf6 12 0-0-0 e6 13 ☗e4 0-0-0 14 g3 c5 15 ☗f4 c4

This was my novelty. It is an ambitious move which aims to place a knight on d5.

16 ☗e2 ☗c6 17 ☗xf6 gxf6

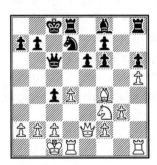

18 d5!

See diagram on page 104.

18...exd5

With a pawn sacrifice, White blocks the d5 square. I was not worried that Petrosian had won with the doubled pawns – and without having any knight.

19 ☗d4 ☗a6 20 ☗b1 ☗d6 21 ☗f3 ☗xf4 22 ☗xf4 ☗e5 23 ☗f5+ ☗b8

24 f4

Unlike Gurgenidze, Cheskovsky manages to win back the pawn.

24...☗d7?!

After 24...☗c6 25 ☗xf6 ☗xd4 26 ☗xd4 White has a small edge.

25 ☗xd5 ☗e5 26 ☗e4 ☗g4?

He should try to enter a slightly inferior rook ending by 26...☗c6 27 ☗xc6+ ☗xc6 28 ☗xc6 bxc6.

27 ☗e2

White has obtained a better position.

27...☗b6

If 27...Ξhg8 28 Ξhe1.

28 c3 f5 29 Ξhe1 ☗c5 30 ☗e7 ☗xe7 31 Ξxe7 Ξhe8

Black could try to hang on the material by playing 31...Ξhf8. After 32 Ξde1 Ξd5 33 ☗c2 Black is rather passive.

32 Ξde1 Ξxe7 33 Ξxe7

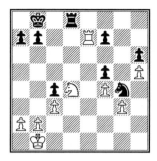

33...♘f6

Reducing the number of pawns on the board does not lead to salvation. After 33...f6 34 ♔c1 (34 a4!? ♖d5 35 ♔a2) 34...♖d5 35 ♔d2 a6 36 ♔e2 Black is struggling.

34 ♖xf7 ♘xh5 35 ♘xf5 ♖d3 36 ♖f8+ ♔c7 37 ♖g8 ♔d7 38 ♖g6 b5 39 a3 ♖d1+ 40 ♔a2 ♖g1 41 ♖d6+ ♔c7 42 ♖xh6 ♘xg3 43 ♘d4

Black loses a second pawn after which his position is hopeless.

43...♘e4 44 ♘xb5+ ♔d7 45 ♖h7+ ♔e6 46 ♖xa7

It's all over now.

46...♘c5 47 ♘d4+ ♔d6 48 ♘f5+ ♔d5 49 ♘e3+ ♔e4 50 ♖c7 ♘d3 51 ♖e7+ 1-0

A.Beliavsky – G.Kasparov
Game 4, Candidates match, quarterfinal, Moscow 1983

1 d4 ♘f6 2 c4 e6 3 ♘c3 ♗b4 4 e3 0-0 5 ♗d3 c5 6 ♘f3 d5 7 0-0 dxc4 8 ♗xc4 cxd4 9 exd4 b6

This system of development is Karpov's favourite variation.

10 ♕e2 ♗b7 11 ♖d1 ♗xc3 12 bxc3 ♕c7 13 ♗d3

13...♕xc3?!

This position with 13...♘bd7 14 c4 has been played many times. 13...♘d5 has not been tested. Black is treading a very narrow path but objectively the move might be playable. 14 ♗d2 ♘xc3 15 ♗xc3 (15 ♗xh7+ ♔xh7 16 ♘g5+ ♔g8! 17 ♕h5 ♘e2+! 18 ♔h1 [18 ♕xe2 ♘d7] 18...♕c2 and Black is in the game.) 15...♕xc3 16 ♖dc1 ♕a5 17 ♖c7 ♕d5 (17...♗d5 18 ♘g5!) 18 ♖ac1 and White has compensation for the pawn.

14 ♗b2

If 14 ♗g5 ♘bd7.

14...♕c7

After 14...♕b4 15 d5 ♗xd5 (15...♘xd5? 16 ♘g5 h6 17 ♕e5 ♘f6 18 ♗h7+ ♔h8 19 ♕xf6 wins.) 16 ♗xf6 gxf6 17 ♘d4 f5 (17...♘c6? 18 ♕g4+ ♔h8 19 ♕h4 f5 20 ♗xf5 and White mates.) 18 ♗xf5 (18 ♕e3 ♘d7 [18...♘c6 19 ♗xf5±] 19 ♗xf5 ♔h8) 18...exf5 19 ♘xf5 ♕e4 20 ♘e7+ ♔h8 21 ♕b2+ f6 22 ♘xd5 and White stands much better. If 14...♕c6 15 d5 exd5 16 ♘d4 ♕e8 17 ♕d2 ♘e4 18 ♗xe4 ♕xe4 19 ♖e1 ♕g4 20 ♖e7 ♗a6 21 ♕c3 and White has tremendous compensation for the two pawns.

15 d5 ♗xd5 16 ♗xf6 gxf6

Just like Petrosian, I did not mind having the doubled f-pawns.

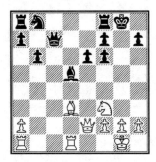

17 ♕e3! ♔g7

Not 17...♕b7 18 ♘g5!

18 ♖ac1 ♘c6

After 18...♕b7 19 ♘e5 ♘d7 20 ♕h3 f5 21 ♗a6 ♕xa6 22 ♘xd7 Black's king remains vulnerable.

19 ♗e4?

After 19 ♘d4 ♕d6! (19...♖fd8 surprisingly loses. 20 ♗b5 ♕b7 21 ♕g3+ ♔f8 22 ♗xc6 ♗xc6 23 ♕f4! ♖d7 [Other moves also lose. 23...♗xg2 24 ♘xe6+; 23...♖ac8 24 ♘xe6+; 23...f5 24 ♖e1; 23...♗d5 24 ♖c7 ♕b8 25 ♘b5] 24 ♕xf6 ♔g8 25 h4!! [25 ♖d3 ♗e4] 25...♗xg2 26 f3 and White wins.) 20 ♘xc6 (20 ♕h3 ♖h8 21 ♘xc6 ♗xc6) 20...♗xc6 and Black probably survives.

After 19 ♗b5! ♖fd8 20 ♖d3!? (20 ♘d4 also wins as it transposes to the line with 19 ♘d4) 20...♖ac8 21 ♘d4 ♕e5 22 ♘xc6 ♕xe3 23 fxe3 ♖d6 24 ♗a4 a6 25 ♖c2 and White wins.

19...♕d6! 20 ♗xd5

If 20 ♖xc6? ♕xc6 21 ♖xd5 exd5 22 ♘d4 ♕a4! 23 ♗c2 ♕e8 and Black wins as Beliavsky pointed out.

20...exd5

See diagram on page 104.

I was happy with the doubled f-pawn.

21 ♖c4 ♕d7?

I gave back one of the pawns but this was an unnecessary concession. After 21...♘e7 22 ♖h4 ♘f5 23 ♖g4+ ♔h8 24 ♕d3 ♘e7 25 ♖h4 ♘g6 26 ♖h5 Black is safe.

22 ♖h4 ♕f5

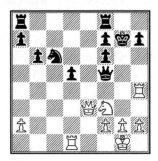

23 ♖xd5 ♘e5

After 23...♕b1+ 24 ♘e1 ♔h8 25 ♖dh5 ♖fe8 26 ♖xh7+ ♕xh7 27 ♖xh7+ ♔xh7 28 ♕h3+ ♔g8 29 ♕g4+ ♔f8 30 ♘c2 is dangerous according to Beliavsky. The knight aims to get to f5 after creating a flight square for his king with h4.

24 h3 ♖fe8

Not 24...♘xf3+? 25 gxf3 and White's heavy pieces catch the king.

25 ♘d4 ♕g6

Not 25...♕g5? 26 ♖g4 winning.

26 ♕f4

Not 26 f4? ♕b1+ 27 ♔h2 ♘g6 28 ♕g3 ♖e1.

26...♖ad8 27 ♘f5+ ♔h8 28 ♖xd8 ♖xd8 29 ♕e4 ♖c8?

If 29...♖g8 30 g4. Alternatively 29...♕g8! to free the g6-square for his knight. 30 ♘e7 (30 ♖h6 ♘g6; 30 f4 ♘g6 31 ♕c6 ♖d1+ 32 ♔h2 ♕d8 33 ♘h6 ♔g7 34 ♘f5+ is a repetition.) 30...♕g7 31 ♖h5! and White has compensation for the pawn. (31 ♘f5 ♕f8 32 ♘e7 ♕g7=; 31 ♔h2 ♖e8 32 ♘d5 ♖e6 and Black may be able to hold on.) 31...a6 (31...♘g6 32 ♔h2; 31...♖e8 32 ♘d5 ♖e6 33 ♘xf6. This is the point of putting the rook on h5; White retains a small edge.) 32 ♔h2 and Black must be careful.

30 ♔h2

Not 30 f4? ♘f3+.

30...♖c4?!

This looks active but it just drops a pawn. After 30...♖d8?! 31 g4 (31 f4 ♘f3+!) 31...♕g8 32 ♖h6 ♕f8!

a) 32...♖d2? 33 ♘e7 ♕g7 34 ♕a8+ wins;

b) 32...♕g5?

b1) 33 f4 ♘xg4+ 34 hxg4 ♕xg4 35 ♘e3! ♕g7 (35...♖d2+ 36 ♔h1 ♕g7 37 ♘g4) 36 ♘g4 wins.

b2) 33 ♖xf6 ♕c5 34 ♘h6 ♔g7 35 ♖f5 ♕d6 36 ♔g2 ♔xh6 37 ♖xe5 ♔g7 and though Black's king is exposed, it is not easy to exploit the situation.

31 ♕a8+ ♕g8 32 ♕xa7 ♖xh4 33 ♘xh4 ♕g5 34 ♕a8+ ♔g7 35 ♕e4

35...h5??

This is a bad blunder as Black drops the knight. Better was 35...♘g6 36 ♘f5+ ♔g8 37 g3 ♕d2 when Black doubtless has problems but he is still in the game.

36 ♘f5+ ♔g6 37 ♘e7+ ♔h6 38 f4

1-0

Similarities in a rook versus bishop endgame – with rook's pawns too.

T.Petrosian – L.Aronin

G.Kasparov – A.Yusupov

T.Petrosian – L.Aronin
USSR Team Championship, Riga 1954

1 e4 c5 2 ♘f3 d6 3 d4 cxd4 4 ♘xd4
♘f6 5 ♘c3 a6 6 ♗g5 e6 7 ♕f3 ♘bd7
8 0-0-0 ♕c7 9 ♕g3 h6 10 ♗xf6 gxf6

This is a risky option.

11 ♔b1 ♘b6 12 f4 ♗d7

13 ♕h4! ♗e7 14 ♕h5

Black has serious problems with his special Rauzer pawn formation.

14...♖h7 15 f5 e5?

Alternatively 15...0-0-0 16 fxe6 fxe6 17 ♕h3 ♔b8 18 ♗e2 and White's advantage is smaller than in the game.

16 ♘e6 ♕c6 17 ♕g4 ♗f8 18 ♕g8 fxe6 19 ♕xh7

White has won the exchange, and in return Black has very little.

19...0-0-0 20 fxe6 ♗xe6 21 ♗e2 d5 22 exd5 ♘xd5 23 ♘xd5 ♗xd5 24 ♖hf1?

Best was 24 ♗g4+! ♔b8 25 ♗f3 winning.

24...♔b8 25 ♕f5 ♗e7 26 ♗f3 e4 27 ♗e2 ♖c8 28 ♕xd5 ♕xc2+ 29 ♔a1 ♕xe2 30 ♖fe1 ♕xg2 31 ♕xe4 ♕xe4 32 ♖xe4

Black can resist.

32...♗d6 33 ♖e2 ♗e5 34 ♔b1 ♖c4 35 ♖d3 h5 36 b3 ♖h4 37 h3 ♖f4 38 ♔c2 ♔c7 39 ♖g2 ♔c6 40 ♔d1 ♖f1+ 41 ♔e2

41...♖f4

The rook is actively placed on the fourth and causes much inconvenience.

42 ♖g8 a5 43 ♖h8 ♖h4 44 ♖a8 ♔b6 45 a4 ♖e4+ 46 ♔f3 ♖f4+ 47 ♔e2 ♖e4+ 48 ♖e3 ♖h4 49 ♖c8 ♖d4 50 ♖d3 ♖e4+ 51 ♔f3 ♖f4+ 52 ♔e2 ♖e4+ 53 ♖e3 ♖d4 54 ♖c2 ♖h4 55 ♖d3 ♖e4+ 56 ♔f3 ♖f4+ 57 ♔g2 ♖e4 58 ♔f3 ♖f4+ 59 ♔e2 ♖e4+ 60 ♖e3 ♖f4

61 ♖c4

Finally he removes Black's rook.

61...♖xc4 62 bxc4 ♔c5 63 ♖b3 ♔xc4 64 ♖xb7 h4 65 ♖b5 ♗g3 66 ♖xa5

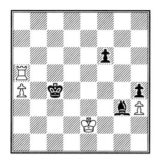

66...♔b4

Black is likely to take the a-pawn and with the h4-pawn he has chances to draw even with the exchange deficit.

67 ♖a7 f5 68 ♔f3 f4 69 ♖a8 ♔a3 70 ♔g2 ♔b4 71 ♖a6 ♔a3 72 ♖a7 ♔b4 73 ♔f3 ♔a3 74 ♔e4

74...♔b4

After 74...♔b3 75 a5 ♔b4 76 a6 ♔b5 77 ♖a8 ♔b6 78 ♔d5 ♗f2 (78...f3 79 a7 f2 80 ♖f8 ♔xa7 81 ♔c6 wins. 81...f1=♕ 82 ♖xf1 ♔b8 [82...♗h2 83 ♖b1] 83 ♔d7 White cuts off the king from b1 and his king goes to g5 and takes the h4-pawn.) 79 a7 ♔b7 (79...♗g3 80 ♖g8 ♔xa7 81 ♔c6 transposes to the game.) 80 ♖f8 ♔xa7 81 ♖xf4 ♗g3 82 ♖b4 wins.

75 ♖a8 ♔b3 76 a5 ♔b4 77 a6 ♔b5 78 ♔d5 ♔b6 79 a7! ♔b7 80 ♖g8! ♔xa7 81 ♔c6

See diagram on page 109.

Petrosian won even though his opponent had an additional f-pawn. I had every reason to be optimistic.

81...♗f2

The forthright 81...f3 82 ♖e8 f2 83 ♖f8 sets up a zugzwang.

82 ♖g2 ♗g3

83 ♖b2!

I recalled that Tigran Vartanovich had won this endgame.

83...♔a8 84 ♖b7 ♗f2

After 84...f3 85 ♖d7 ♔b8 86 ♖h7 f2 87 ♖f7 wins.

Alternatively, 84...♗h2 85 ♔c7 f3+ 86 ♔c8 f2 87 ♖b2 ♔a7 88 ♖xf2 ♗g3 89 ♖b2! White must keep Black's king in the corner. 89 ♖f6 was winning as well.

85 ♔c7!

White not only stalemates the black king but also creates threats of checkmate.

85...♗g3 86 ♔c8 f3 87 ♖e7!

Black is in zugzwang. After 87 ♖b3 ♔a7 88 ♖xf3 ♔b6 Black holds as the king can leave the corner.

87...f2

88 ♖f7

Black has no choice but to drop the pawn because of the zugzwang.

88...♗e5 89 ♖xf2 ♔a7 90 ♖f5! ♗g3

91 ♖b5!

White must make sure Black's king stays in the corner. It is remarkable that Black loses this type of endgame if his king is in any corner, whereas he can draw if his bishop gets on the e1-h4 diagonal and his king reaches the centre. It can be very useful to know these secrets. Incidentally 91 ♖f6 wins as well.

91...♔a6 92 ♖b1 ♔a5 93 ♔d7

White just collects the h-pawn and wins.

93...♔a4 94 ♔e6 ♔a5 95 ♔f5 ♔a4 96 ♔g4 ♔a5 97 ♖b7 1-0

G.Kasparov – A.Yusupov
Linares 1993

1 d4 d5 2 c4 e6 3 ♘c3 ♗e7 4 cxd5 exd5 5 ♗f4 ♘f6 6 e3 ♗f5 7 ♘ge2 0-0 8 ♘g3 ♗e6 9 ♗d3 c5 10 dxc5 ♗xc5 11 0-0 ♘c6 12 ♖c1

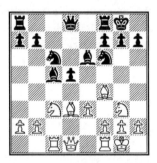

12...♗d6

Artur is ready to defend the isolated pawn middlegame. It looks like Black gets away with exchanging all the central pawns if he were to play 12...d4!? 13 ♘ce4 (after 13 ♘b5 ♗b6 14 e4 ♘g4 Black has a nice position, as in Lautier-Marciano, France 1999) 13...♗e7 14 ♘f5 ♗xf5 15 ♘xf6+ ♗xf6 16 ♗xf5 ♕a5 (16...dxe3 17 ♗xe3 ♕xd1 18 ♖fxd1 ♖fd8 19 ♗d7 ♘e5 20 ♗b5 ♖xd1+ 21 ♖xd1 a6 22 ♗e2 ♖d8 23 ♖c1 ♘c6 and Black is able to live with White's two bishops as in Karolyi-Zahilas, Hungary-Greece, E-mail Olympiad 2000) 17 ♗b1 ♖ad8 18 ♕b3 ♖d7 19 exd4 ♖fd8! and Black is not worse, Gulko-Shabalov, Seattle 2000.

13 ♘h5 ♗e7 14 ♘b5 ♘xh5 15 ♕xh5 g6 16 ♕f3 ♖c8 17 ♖fd1 ♕d7

**18 h3 ℤfd8 19 ♕g3 ♘b4 20 ♘c3
♘xd3 21 ℤxd3 ♗f5 22 ℤd2 ♕e6
23 ℤcd1 h5 24 h4?!**

Taking the pawn with 24 ♘xd5 was better thanks to a little tactic. 24...ℤxd5 25 ℤxd5 h4 26 ♕f3 ♗e4 27 ℤe5!

24...ℤc5 25 f3 ♕c6 26 e4

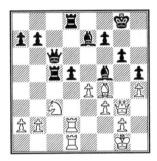

26...ℤxc3!

The exchange sacrifice offers real chances of survival.

**27 bxc3 ♕b6+ 28 ♔h2 dxe4
29 ℤxd8+ ♗xd8 30 ♗e3**

30 fxe4!? offers White a more promising way to enter an endgame. 30...♗xe4 31 ♕e3 ♗c6 32 ♕e5!? (32 ♕xb6 ♗xb6 33 ♗e5) 32...♔h7 33 ℤd2 ♕a5 34 ♕xa5 ♗xa5 35 ♗e5.

**30...♕a5 31 ♕b8 ♕c7+ 32 ♕xc7
♗xc7+ 33 ♔g1 exf3 34 gxf3 b6
35 ♔f2 ♔f8 36 ℤd4**

36...♔e7?!

This allows the exchange of bishops.

37 ♗f4

Reducing the amount of material. On the other hand White will now have more freedom of movement for his king. Another idea is 37 ℤa4 a5 38 ℤc4!?

**37...♗xf4 38 ℤxf4 ♔d6 39 ♔e3 ♔c5
40 ℤd4 ♗e6 41 a3 a5 42 ♔e4 b5**

After 42...f6 43 f4 White can breach the fortress by defending the queenside with the king on c1 and invading with the rook on d8.

**43 ♔e5 a4 44 f4 ♔c6 45 ♔f6 ♔c5
46 ℤb4 ♗c4 47 ♔e7 ♗e6 48 ℤe4 ♔d5
49 ℤd4+ ♔c6 50 ♔d8**

White cannot penetrate yet.

**50...♗f5 51 ♔e8 ♗e6 52 ♔f8 ♔c5
53 ♔g7 ♔c6 54 ♔g8 ♔c5 55 ♔f8 ♔c6
56 ♔g7 ♔c5 57 ♔h8 ♔c6 58 ♔h7 ♔c5
59 ♔h6 ♗f5 60 ♔g5 ♗e6 61 ♔f6 ♔c6**

62 f5!

Reducing the number of pawns while simultaneously freeing the f4-square for the rook.

**62...♗xf5 63 ♔xf7 ♔c5 64 ♔f6 ♗c2
65 ♔e7 ♗f5 66 ♔d8 ♔c6 67 ℤf4!**

It was 62 f5 that enabled him to play this move.

**67...♔d6 68 ℤb4 ♔c5 69 ♔c7 ♗d3
70 ℤd4 ♗e2 71 ♔b7 ♗f1 72 ♔a7 ♗e2
73 ℤe4 ♗d3**

But not 73...♗c4? 74 ♔a6 b4+

75 ♖xc4+! and having the king on c4 enables the g-pawn to promote. If 75...♔xc4 76 cxb4 g5 77 hxg5 wins.

74 ♖b4 ♗c4 75 ♔a6 ♔d5 76 ♔a5 ♔e5

Black can't stay on the queenside with 76...♔c5, because of zugzwang. 77 ♖b1 ♗d3 78 ♖b2. Then 78...♗c4 79 ♖d2 ♗f1 80 ♖d4! ♗e2 (80...♗g2 81 ♖d8 ♗f1 82 ♖c8+ ♔d5 83 ♔b4) 81 ♖e4 ♗f1 82 ♖e5+ wins.

77 ♖b1

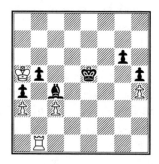

77...g5?

Black reduces the number of pawns but the final endgame is unfortunate for him. Keeping the pawns on with 77...♔f4 was just enough to survive: 78 ♖g1 ♗d3 79 ♔b4 ♔f3 80 c4!? (80 ♔c5 ♔f2 81 ♖g5 ♔f3) 80...♗xc4! (80...bxc4? 81 ♖xa4 ♔e3 82 ♔b4 ♔d2 83 ♖g2+ ♗e2 84 a4! c3 85 ♖xe2+ ♔xe2 86 ♔xc3 g5 87 hxg5 h4 88 g6 h3 89 g7 h2 90 g8=♕ h1=♕ 91 ♕g4+! [or 91 ♕e6+!] 91...♔f2 92 ♕f4+ White can swap queens and win.) 81 ♖xg6 ♔f4 82 ♖g5 ♗e2 83 ♔c5 ♗g4 84 ♔d4 ♔g3 85 ♔e3 ♔xh4 86 ♔f4 Black's king is choked, and it's scary, but Black can hold. 86...♗d7! 87 ♖c5 ♗e8!

88 ♖c3! ♗f7 89 ♖c2 ♔h3 90 ♖c5 ♗c4! (90...h4? 91 ♖xb5 ♔g2 92 ♖b2+ ♔g1 [92...♔f1 93 ♖h2 ♔e1 94 ♔e3 wins] 93 ♔g4 ♔f1 94 ♔xh4

Black's king is in a poor position and now he loses. If his king were instead on f6, that would be enough for him to obtain a draw. If Black's bishop were dark-squared and situated on f8, the position would also be a draw even though White could defend the a-pawn with his rook along the third rank. 94...♔e1 95 ♔g4 ♔d1 96 ♔f4 ♗b3 97 ♔e3 ♔c1 98 ♖h2 ♗c2 99 ♔d4 ♗b2 100 ♔c5 wins. [but not 100 ♔c4?? ♔xa3].) 91 ♖xh5+ ♔g2 92 ♔e3 ♗f1 93 ♖g5 ♗e2 94 ♔d2 ♗c4 95 ♖f5+ ♔g1! 96 ♔e3 ♔g2 and White can make no progress as I pointed out in my *Informant* analysis.

78 hxg5 ♔f5 79 ♖g1 ♔g6 80 ♔b4 h4 81 ♔c5 h3 82 ♔d4

Not 82 ♖h1? ♗e6 83 ♔xb5 ♔xg5 84 ♔xa4 ♔g4 85 ♔b5 ♗d5! and White has to give up the rook for the pawn, while the bishop contains the a- and c- pawns.

82...♗e6 83 ♔e5 ♗d7 84 ♔f4 ♗c6 85 ♔g3 ♔xg5

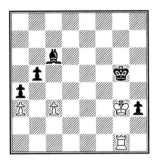

86 ♖d1!!

White exchanges the weak c3 pawn. After 86 ♔xh3+ ♔f4 87 ♖g3 ♔e4 88 ♔g4 ♔d5 89 ♔f4 ♔c4 Black's king is active.

86...h2 87 ♔xh2 ♔f4

If 87...♔f5 88 ♖d4! and White cuts off the king. (On the other hand 88 c4 allows Black to escape into a favourable version of the game. On 88...bxc4 89 ♖d4 c3 90 ♖c4 ♗d5

the bishop would reach b3, and that would save him as his king is in the centre and can't be forced into any corner.) 88...♔e5 89 ♔g3 and White's king has time to return to the centre and push Black back.

88 c4

Now cutting off the king by 88 ♖d4+ is ineffective, as it is only temporary. 88...♔e3 89 ♔g3 (if 89 ♖d6 ♗e4) 89...♗e4! (Black has to approach c3

otherwise White's king invades, e.g. 89...♗e8 90 ♔g4) 90 ♔g4 ♗d3.

88...bxc4 89 ♖d4+ ♔e5 90 ♖xc4

Since the computer programs have reached new levels of analysis we can understand this type of endgame much better. Now the bishop can't reach b3.

90...♗d5 91 ♖b4 ♔c5 92 ♔g3

Not 92 ♖b2? ♗d5!

92...♗b5 93 ♔f4 ♔b6

If 93...♗c6 94 ♔e3 ♗b5 95 ♔e4 ♗c6+ 96 ♔d3 ♗b5+ 97 ♔c3 ♗e8 98 ♖f4 wins.

94 ♔e3 ♔a5 95 ♔d4 ♗e2 96 ♖b1 ♗h5 97 ♖e1 ♗f7

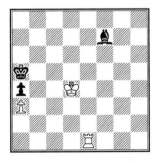

Now the bishop reaches b3 and yet Black is lost because his king is in the corner. If Black's bishop were dark-squared and stood on f8 it would be a draw.

98 ♔c5 ♗b3 99 ♖e8 ♔a6 100 ♔c6 ♔a7 101 ♔b5 ♔b7

102 ⬛e7+??

Petrosian won because his opponent's king was too far away, I hoped that I could chase the king to where Tigran's opponent's king was. Better was 102 ⬛d8! as the king has to be kept in the corner, White wins even if the bishop is on b3. This is the case if Black's pawn were on a5, his bishop on b4 and White's pawn on a4. 102...⬔c7 103 ⬛d3 ⬔c8 Postponing the inevitable. If 103...⬔b7 104 ⬛c3 ⬔d1 105 ⬛c1 ⬔b3 106 ⬔a5 ⬔a7 107 ⬛c7+ ⬔b8 108 ⬔b6 ⬔a2 [if 108...⬔g8 109 ⬛e7] 109 ⬛a7 ⬔b3 110 ⬛d7 ⬔c8 111 ⬛d4

The key position. Black is in a lethal zugzwang.) 104 ⬔c6 ⬔a2 105 ⬛d4 ⬔f7 106 ⬛f4 ⬔e8+ The bishop has to leave the diagonal. 107 ⬔c5 ⬔c7 108 ⬛e4 ⬔d7 109 ⬛e7 ⬔c8 110 ⬔d6 ⬔b5 111 ⬛f7 ⬔e2 (111...⬔d3

112 ⬛c7+ ⬔b8 [112...⬔d8 113 ⬛a7 wins.] 113 ⬔c6 ⬔c2 114 ⬔b6 ⬔b3 115 ⬛d7 ⬔c8 116 ⬛d4 is the same zugzwang.) 112 ⬔c6 ⬔d8 113 ⬛d7+ ⬔c8 (113...⬔e8 114 ⬛d4 wins.) 114 ⬛h7 ⬔f3+ 115 ⬔b6 ⬔d1 116 ⬛h4 ⬔b3 117 ⬛d4! wins. 102 ⬛e4! ⬔c7 103 ⬛d4 ⬔b7 104 ⬛d7+ ⬔c8 105 ⬔c6 ⬔c2 106 ⬔d6 ⬔d1 107 ⬛f7 ⬔b3 108 ⬛h7 ⬔d1 109 ⬔c6 ⬔f3+ 110 ⬔b6 ⬔d1 111 ⬛h4 ⬔b3 112 ⬛d4 also wins.

102...⬔c8 103 ⬔c6 ⬔d8

104 ⬛d7+ ⬔e8!

Black escapes from the corner and that saves him.

105 ⬔c7 ⬔c2 106 ⬛d2 ⬔b3! 107 ⬛e2+ ⬔f7 108 ⬔d6 ⬔c4 109 ⬛e7+ ⬔f8 110 ⬛e4 ⬔b3

111 ⬔d7

If White had one more move, then a rook check would help – just as in the Petrosian game – and he could then rush his king to the b-file and win. He can't allow the black king to reach g5 earlier.

111...♔f7 112 ♖f4+ ♔g6!

Not 112...♔g7? which loses after 113 ♔c6 ♔g6 114 ♔b5 and the king can't get to c8.

113 ♔d6 ♔g5! 114 ♔e5 ♔g6 115 ♖f3 ♔g7 116 ♖f6 ♗c4 117 ♔f5 ♗b3 118 ♔g5 ♗c2 ½-½

When I went home I quickly checked the Petrosian game and noticed that he was in fact Black and actually lost this game.

I had the most annoying experience of all with Petrosian, as he beat me with a particular central pawn structure seen in the diagram below. I learned from that and wanted to use my new found knowledge against Karpov when exactly the same structure arose.

G.Kasparov – T.Petrosian

A.Karpov – G.Kasparov

First here is the game against Petrosian.

G.Kasparov – T.Petrosian
Moscow, 1981

1 d4

This is perhaps my most unfortunate game. I picked up the idea from Petrosian when he beat me. Then I used it at a most critical moment against Karpov in a World Championship match. I lost that game as well when I needed a draw to retain the title. While analysing it for my Predecessors book I realised some of my earlier comments were not quite correct.

1...♘f6 2 c4 e6 3 ♘f3 b6 4 a3

How could I try the Petrosian variation against its inventor? Could that in itself have been a mental blackout?

4...♗b7 5 ♘c3 d5 6 cxd5 ♘xd5 7 e3 ♗e7 8 ♗b5+ c6 9 ♗d3 ♘xc3 10 bxc3 c5 11 0-0 0-0

12 ♕c2 g6 13 e4 ♘c6 14 ♗h6 ♖e8

This time there is no exchange sacrifice.

15 ♖fd1 ♕c7 16 ♕e2 ♖ed8 17 ♕e3 e5 18 d5 ♘a5 19 c4

After 19 a4 c4 20 ♗c2 ♗c8 the position is equal.

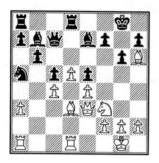

19...♘b3

Petrosian centralises the knight. I lost quite a number of games by leaving a knight on a5 or h5. Nikolaevsky, Zaid, Magerramov, Beliavsky and Gulko beat me in those games.

20 ♖a2 f6 21 h4 ♗c8

Dvoretsky and Yusupov pointed out that Black should have exchanged the bishop with 21...♗f8!.

22 ♖b1 ♘d4 23 ♘xd4 cxd4

I thought the d4-pawn was not bad, but hoped to get a good game in the end.

24 ♕g3

See diagram on page 117.

24...♗f8

25 ♗d2!

Now I can save it.

25...♗d6 26 ♖f1 ♕g7 27 a4?!

Dvoretsky and Yusupov found the right move which was 27 ♗b4, stopping ♗d7. 27...♕e7 28 f4 leaves White a bit better.

27...a5 28 ♖b2 ♗c5 29 f4 ♗d7

Petrosian suggested 29...h6!.

30 h5 ♗xa4?

If 30...gxh5 31 ♕h4 ♗g4. This move was not mentioned in my 1981 analysis. The position is unclear.

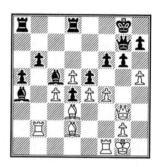

31 h6

As we have already seen, Karpov pushed his pawns as far as this.

31...♕c7 32 f5?!

In 1981 I did not spot that 32 fxe5! would give me an advantage. Then 32...fxe5 33 ♗g5 ♖f8 34 ♗f6. I shall not repeat the analysis from *My Great Predecessors*. Suffice it to say White retains the advantage against all Black defences.

32...g5 33 ♗xg5! fxg5?

Better was 33...♔f7. Petrosian often used his king with great style. For example when he beat Fischer in the 1959 Candidates tournament. After 34 ♗c1 ♖g8 35 ♕h3 White has a slight edge.

34 ♕xg5+ ♔f8

35 ♕f6+?

In time trouble I lose my way. Best was 35 f6! ♕f7 36 ♕xe5 ♖e8 (if 36...♕g6 37 ♖xb6! ♕xh6 38 ♕e7+! wins) 37 ♕g5 ♕g6 38 ♖f5 and the white pawns are too dangerous and he will win. I lost to Kramnik in a 1994 Intel rapid game in a similar fashion. I consolidated a piece on d4, he took it, then he sacrificed a piece, and later the exchange. He went on to defeat me. You can see that game on page 166 in the Smyslov chapter. So even my own analysis helped my rival, making this really the most unfortunate game of all!

35...♔e8! 36 ♖a1

36...♕e7!!

This is a great defensive move. I understand now why Botvinnik did not always anticipate Petrosian's moves.

37 ♕e6?

I should have swapped queens and defended in the endgame.

37...♖d6! 38 ♕g8+ ♕f8 39 ♕g3 ♕xh6

40 ♖xa4?

When I wrote the chapter on Petrosian I discovered that White could still stay in the game or at least resist with 40 ♕g8+. Then 40...♕f8 41 ♕xf8+ ♔xf8 42 ♖xa4 and Black is somewhat better. However it is hard to tell whether he can win.

40...♕c1+ 41 ♔f2 ♕xb2+ 42 ♔f3 ♔f7 0-1

My fourth World Championship match with Karpov stood at 11-11 and I needed to score one more point to retain the title. This was the dramatic end of the match.

A.Karpov – G.Kasparov
Game 23, World Championship,
Seville 1987

1 c4 c5 2 ♘f3 ♘f6 3 ♘c3 d5 4 cxd5 ♘xd5 5 d4 ♘xc3 6 bxc3 g6 7 e3 ♗g7 8 ♗d3 0-0 9 0-0 ♕c7 10 ♖b1 b6

The pawn structure is becoming very similar to my game against Petrosian.

11 ♕e2 ♖d8 12 ♗e4

119

12...♗a6!

To weaken the d4-square.

13 c4 ♘c6 14 d5 f5 15 ♗d3 e5! 16 e4 ♘d4

I got very excited and realised I did not even have to expend tempi like Tigran Vartanovich.

17 ♘xd4 cxd4

See diagram on page 117.

I felt things were really going my way.

It is the same pawn structure and I would be able to use the knowledge I had gained from my loss against Petrosian.

18 ♗g5

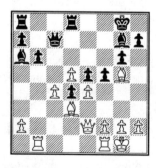

18...♖f8

In addition I have more space on the queenside.

19 ♖fc1 ♖ac8 20 ♗d2 ♖f7 21 a4 fxe4 22 ♕xe4 ♖cf8

I even control the f-file.

23 f3

23...♗c8

I had yet to become acquainted with the analysis of Yusupov and Dvoretsky who pointed out that ...♗c8 was not the best move for Petrosian. I just copied his play.

24 a5

Karpov did not let me fix the a5-pawn. Okay, you can't have everything.

24...♗f5 25 ♕e2 ♖e8 26 ♗e4 ♗f8 27 ♕d3

27...♗c5

Now my bishop has arrived at the same square as Petrosian's. Life can be sweet, I thought.

28 ♖a1 ♕d7 29 ♖e1 ♕c8 30 ♔h1 ♖c7 31 ♖ab1 ♔g7 32 ♖ec1 ♗xe4

33 fxe4

The central pawns are configured in the same way.

33...♖f7 34 ♕g3 bxa5 35 ♗xa5 ♖f4 36 ♖e1 ♕a6 37 ♗d2 ♖f7 38 ♕d3 ♖ef8 39 h3

Karpov doesn't push the h-pawn two squares like I did.

39...♖f2 40 ♖a1 ♕f6 41 ♖g1 h5!? 42 ♖a5

Or 42 ♗e1!? ♖f1 43 ♗g3 ♖xg1+ 44 ♔xg1.

42...♕e7 43 ♖b1

43...h4

Showing my optimism, I don't need to worry about putting pawns onto the colour of Karpov's bishop as there will be no bishop ending here.

44 ♖a6 ♖8f7 45 ♖c6

If 45 ♖e6 ♕f8.

45...♕f8 46 ♖g1 ♗e7 47 ♖e6 ♔h7! 48 ♗e1

If 48 ♖xe5 ♗d6 49 ♖h5+. I was hoping that sacrificing material would not bring any luck, as had happened 16 years earlier. After 49...gxh5 50 e5+ ♔g8 51 exd6 ♕xd6 52 ♕xd4 ♕f6 Karpov and Zaitsev evaluated the position as equal.

48...♖f1 49 ♗d2 ♗c5 50 ♖c6

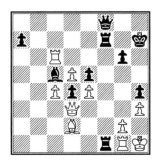

50...♖7f3??

A horrible blunder. I thought everything was going my way and it was time to reap the fruit of my lexical knowledge. I felt it was time for a knockout punch. In a way I was successful as the battle does indeed end fairly quickly. But after the game I was not satisfied. A much better alternative was 50...♗b4!?

51 gxf3 ♖xf3 52 ♖c7+ ♔h8

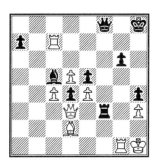

53 ♗h6!

What a shock it was to be on the receiving end of this intermediate move. Suddenly Black is completely lost.

53...♖xd3 54 ♗xf8 ♖xh3+ 55 ♔g2 ♖g3+ 56 ♔h2 ♖xg1 57 ♗xc5 d3 1-0

In the end I won the last game and thus kept my title but, my word, it was a close run thing. Had I lost the match, Petrosian would have had something to do with it.

Mikhail Tal the 8th

Tal decisively defeated Botvinnik in 1960 to become world champion, but he lost a return match in a similarly convincing fashion one year later. The magician from Riga was the last champion to gain the title before I was born and is famous for his very aggressive attacking style. I played some training and blitz games with him and certainly picked up many ideas from these experiences. His calculating ability was one of his strong points. I believe this features in my chess as well.

I do have very nice memories associated with Tal, but also some painful ones. Let's have a look at a few examples.

> With symmetrical pawn islands of four kingside pawns and a- and c-pawns, whoever exerts greater pressure on the opponent's pawn structure should gain the upper hand.

N.Rashkovsky – M.Tal

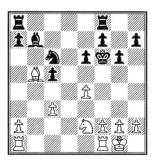

A.Karpov – G.Kasparov

N.Rashkovsky – M.Tal
Chigorin Memorial, Sochi 1973

1 d4 g6 2 c4 ♘f6 3 ♘c3 d5

Interestingly, Tal rarely employed the Grünfeld – according to the databases only four times. It is a bit of surprise as this opening often provides very dynamic positions, ones which Misha would have handled so well.

4 cxd5 ♘xd5 5 e4 ♘xc3 6 bxc3 ♗g7 7 ♗c4 0-0 8 ♘e2 ♘c6

He previously beat Gulko with the main move 8...c5. Tal was extremely good in positions where one player had a rook versus bishop and knight and I lost a slightly similar game to Romanishin in Moscow 1981. Tal played extremely powerfully when there was unbalanced material on the board and my most bitter memory in such circumstances was my loss to Anand in Tilburg 1991.

9 0-0 b6 10 ♗e3 ♗b7 11 ♕d2 ♘a5

12 ♗d3 e6

Let me stress the effect this game had on me. In my game against Korchnoi in the World Cup in Reykjavik 1988 I also played a similar e6 in a main line Grünfeld.

13 ♗h6 c5 14 ♗xg7 ♔xg7 15 ♕f4
Korchnoi put his queen on the queenside – that game ended in a draw.

15...♘c6 16 ♗b5 ♕f6 17 ♕xf6+ ♔xf6 18 dxc5

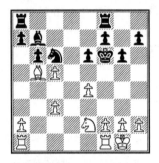

18...bxc5

We have reached a key position. Alternatively, 18...♖fc8 would also have been interesting. Korchnoi beat me only once in our many encounters, the only time I suffered was during our Candidates match in London 1983. He used the pawn sacrifice motif under rather similar conditions after 1 d4 ♘f6 2 c4 e6 3 ♘f3 b6 4 ♘c3 ♗b7 5 a3 d5 6 cxd5 ♘xd5 7 e3 g6 8 ♗b5+c6 9 ♗d3 ♗g7 10 e4 ♘xc3 11 bxc3 c5 12 ♗g5 ♕d6 13 e5 ♕d7 14 dxc5

14...0-0! 15 cxb6 axb6 However the pawn structure doesn't always give Black a good game. For example, Smyslov beat Ribli with White the same year in a Candidates match. 16 0-0 ♕c7 17 ♗b5 ♗xe5 18 ♗h6 ♗g7 19 ♗xg7 ♔xg7 20 ♕d4+ ♔g8 21 ♘g5 h6 22 ♘e4 ♗xe4 23 ♕xe4 ♘a6 24 ♕e3 ♕c5 25 ♕xc5 ♘xc5 26 ♖fb1 ♖fd8 27 ♖b4 ♖d6 28 ♗f1 ♔f8 29 a4 ♖a5 30 g3 ♔e7 31 ♔g2 f5 32 ♗b5 ♖d2 33 ♖d4 ♖xd4 34 cxd4 ♘xa4 35 ♖xa4 ♖xb5 36 ♖a7+ ♔d6 37 ♖h7 h5 38 ♖g7 ♖d5 39 ♖xg6 b5 40 ♔f3 b4 41 ♔e3 b3 42 ♔d2 ♖xd4+ 43 ♔c3 b2 44 ♔xb2 ♖d2+ 45 ♔c3 ♖xf2 46 h4 f4 47 ♖g5 ♖f3+ 48 ♔d4 ♖xg3 49 ♖xh5 ♖e3 50 ♖h6 ♔e7 51 h5 e5+ 52 ♔d5 f3 0-1 Kasparov-Korchnoi, London 1983.

19 ♘c1

Whoever starts exerting pressure on the opponent's pawn structure will be the one who gets the upper hand.

19...♘a5! 20 ♖e1 ♖ab8 21 e5+ ♔g7 22 ♘b3

22 ♗f1!? keeps the pawn structure as it is.

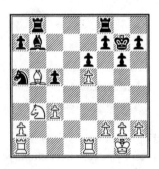

22....♗xg2!

Tal weakens Rashkovsky's pawns on the kingside.

23 c4 ♘xb3 24 axb3 ♗b7 25 ♖xa7 ♖fd8! 26 ♔f1 ♗f3 27 ♗d7 ♖xb3

27...♖b7 also gives reasonable winning chances as after 28 ♖xb7

♗xb7 29 ♗a4 g5 White is rather passive and his pawns are loose.

28 ♗xe6 ♖b7 29 ♖a3 fxe6 30 ♖xf3 ♖d4 31 ♖f6 ♖e7 32 ♖a1

32 ♖c1 ♖e4 33 f4 ♖f7 34 ♖xe6 ♖fxf4+ 35 ♔g1 h5 is tough for Black, but not hopeless.

32...♖e4 33 f4 ♖xc4 34 ♔e2 ♖c2+ 35 ♔d3 ♖xh2 36 ♖c1 ♖h3+ 37 ♔e4??

The king is frequently well-placed in the centre, but not always. These exceptions make chess such a wonderful game. White finds himself in a difficult endgame after 37 ♔c4!, although he has chances of holding on.

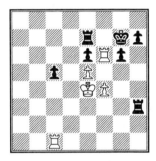

37...♖d7!

Tal grabs the chance to net Rashkovsky's king.

38 ♖c4 ♖dd3! 0-1

Out of the blue White's king is getting checkmated.

Now we look at the game which was inspired by Tal.

A.Karpov – G.Kasparov
Game 27, World Championship, Moscow 1984

1 ♘f3 d5 2 d4 ♘f6 3 c4 e6 4 ♘c3 ♗e7 5 ♗g5 h6 6 ♗xf6 ♗xf6 7 e3 0-0 8 ♕c2 c5 9 dxc5 dxc4 10 ♗xc4 ♕a5 11 0-0 ♗xc3 12 ♕xc3 ♕xc3 13 bxc3 ♘d7 14 c6 bxc6

This is the very same queenside pawn formation that Tal had against Rashkovsky.

See diagram on page 123.

Black's king is less active than in Misha's game, therefore I thought White had better drawing chances. Nevertheless I had no inkling of what was about to happen.

Another famous game by a champion suggested to me that I have a good position because of the pawn structure. Here it is:

L.Portisch – R.Fischer
Piatigorsky Cup, Santa Monica 1966

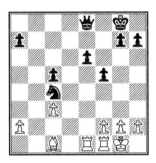

21 ♗f4 h6 22 ♖e2 g5 23 ♗e5 ♕d8 24 ♖fe1 ♔f7 25 h3 f4 26 ♔h2 a6 27 ♖e4 ♕d5 28 h4 ♘e3 29 ♖1xe3 fxe3 30 ♖xe3 ♕xa2 31 ♖f3+ ♔e8 32 ♗g7 ♕c4 33 hxg5 hxg5 34 ♖f8+ ♔d7 35 ♖a8 ♔c6 0-1

15 ♖ab1 ♘b6 16 ♗e2 c5

17 ♖fc1

Karpov places the rook behind his own pawn instead of occupying an open file. I felt good as he was defending the c-pawn before advancing it and generally it is reassuring when your opponent feels obliged to defend. Karpov doesn't go for Rashkovsky's pawn formation with 17 ♘e5 when after 17...♗b7 18 ♘d7 ♖fc8 19 ♘xb6 axb6 the position is equal.

17...♗b7?!

Since this game other players have developed the bishop on d7, following up with ♖fd8 and ♔f8. But I felt I was ready to start applying pressure.

18 ♔f1 ♗d5?!

Out of 17 games played since this game, nobody has lost this position with Black. Perhaps they didn't know Tal's game – and perhaps I was overconfident. Tal also developed his bishop on this square.

19 ♖b5 ♘d7

Not 19...♗xa2? when 20 c4 wins. Better was 19...♖fc8!

20 ♖a5

When Karpov made this move I started to feel even better about life. He had already used his other rook to defend a pawn, thereby giving up the open file. He must have been feeling troubled.

20...♖fb8 21 c4 ♗c6

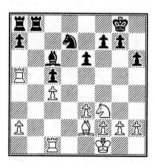

22 ♘e1

Such a superb endgame player as Karpov is now retreating. This made me feel that I was on the right track.

22...♖b4

Exerting pressure on the c-pawn.

After 22...♖b2? 23 f3! White can follow up with ♘d3 (but not 23 ♘d3 ♗xg2+).

22...♗e4 is also met by 23 f3 and after 23...♗g6 24 e4. Later I will show how I was misled in my judgment of such a bishop. Alekhine and Euwe are guilty for creating that impression. Then 24...♖b7 25 ♘d3 ♖c8 enables Black to survive without losing material.

23 ♗d1

Karpov keeps going backward. I was pulling his strings just as if he were a puppet.

23...♖b7

Here I got a bit confused – suddenly I had to retreat as well.

24 f3 ♖d8 25 ♘d3 g5

26 ♗b3

Karpov seems to be in trouble. Indeed he defends c4 with one more piece, when it is not even attacked. However the picture is not so rosy for Black.

Taking the pawn with 26 ♘xc5? led to equality. After 26...♘xc5 27 ♖xc5 ♖b2 28 ♖xc6 ♖dd2 Black's rooks are good enough to draw.

26...♔f8 27 ♘xc5

Now the sobering reality of the game made me forget about Tal's win. I wish I had not known about that game at all.

27...♘xc5

White is just a pawn up for nothing. Very annoying indeed. Misha, Misha what did your magician's spell do to me?

28 ♖xc5 ♖d6 29 ♔e2 ♔e7 30 ♖d1 ♖xd1 31 ♔xd1 ♔d6 32 ♖a5 f5 33 ♔e2 h5 34 e4!? fxe4 35 fxe4

35...♗xe4

Tal was able to take the g2 pawn. I remembered that – and hoped to do it as well. But it never happens.

36 ♖xg5 ♗f5 37 ♔e3 h4 38 ♔d4 e5+ 39 ♔c3

Karpov sends a message that he is going to play on the queenside again.

39...♗b1 40 a3 ♖e7 41 ♖g4

In his analysis Tal preferred 41 h3 to the game continuation but he did not mention his Rashkovsky game – maybe he did not dare to!

41...h3

I made the h-pawn push one of my trademarks. The legacy of Karpov.

42 g3 ♖e8 43 ♖g7!

Classical principles. The rook stands well on the seventh.

43...♖f8 44 ♖xa7 ♖f2 45 ♔b4

45...♖xh2

Fischer also misled me with the power of the edge-pawn due to his game against Taimanov. Tal is not the only one who can be blamed for my loss in this game. However he played the biggest role in it. Simplifying with 45...♖b2 did not help either as then comes 46 c5+ ♔c6 47 ♔c4 ♗a2 48 ♗xa2 ♖xa2 49 ♖a6+ ♔b7 50 ♖b6+ ♔c7 51 ♖h6 ♖xh2 52 ♔d5 ♖h1 53 ♖h7+ ♔b8 (53...♔c8 54 ♔d6!) 54 ♔e4! – a very strong switch.

46 c5+ ♔c6 47 ♗a4+ ♔d5 48 ♖d7+!

In an adjournment it was easy for Karpov. He had so many seconds to analyse for him.

48...♔e4 49 c6 ♖b2+ 50 ♔a5 ♖b8

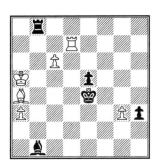

51 c7

That same c-pawn that I pressurised with ♖b4 finally decides the outcome of the game. It was hard to take.

51...♖c8 52 ♔b6 ♔e3 53 ♗c6 h2 54 g4 ♖h8

Here 54...e4 55 ♖h7 wins.

55 ♖d1 ♗a2 56 ♖e1+

Now even the e-pawn falls.

56...♔f4 57 ♖e4+ ♔g3 58 ♖xe5 ♔xg4 59 ♖e2 1-0

Tal refused to work for either of us in our world championship matches. In this game however he helped Karpov.

Let's have a closer look at Tal's win as Black with a particular queenside pawn formation where Black has a potentially powerful passed d4-pawn. Tal's game against Rashkovsky was played in 1973 when I was 10. Of course that age is a very formative period for a young and ambitious player and I was keen to pick up all available knowledge from the former champion's games.

V.Saigin – M.Tal

A.Kochyev – M.Tal

N.Andrianov – G.Kasparov

In the first two diagram positions Tal was Black, whereas in the third I played Black.

I guess you already know the results of these games.

V.Saigin – M.Tal
Game 8, match, Riga 1954

1 d4 ♘f6 2 c4 c5 3 ♘f3 e6 4 g3 cxd4 5 ♘xd4 d5 6 ♗g2 e5 7 ♘f3 d4

8 0-0 ♘c6 9 e3 ♗e7 10 exd4 exd4

See diagram above.

It's a fine line between a pawn being a strong point on d4 or a target.

11 ♘bd2

Smyslov also won this position with Black against Golombek in 1956. Smyslov is covered in the next chapter.

11...♗e6 12 ♖e1 0-0 13 b3 ♕d7 14 ♗b2 ♖ad8 15 a3 a5

16 ♘e5

If White can block the d-pawn and exchange many pieces, it can become a nice target. However it is not easy to achieve both objectives.

16...♘xe5 17 ♖xe5 b6 18 ♘f3 ♗c5 19 ♕d2 ♘g4 20 ♖ee1 d3 21 ♖f1 ♕d6 22 ♕c3?

This is too optimistic. After 22 h3 comes 22...♘xf2 (22...♘f6 23 ♘e5) 23 ♖xf2 ♕xg3. Tal was so good at playing positions with two pieces versus a rook. He won many games like that with both colours.

22...f6 23 ♖ad1 ♖fe8 24 ♖d2 ♗f5 25 ♘g5

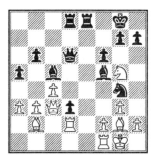

25...♘e3!

Tal, of course, finds a sweet tactical shot like this. He sweeps the white pieces away from the d-pawn, which in turn decides the outcome of the game. An alternative sacrifice, 25...♘xf2, was also promising. 26 ♗d5+ (26 ♖dxf2 ♗xf2+ 27 ♖xf2 d2 wins.) 26...♕xd5 27 cxd5 ♘e4+ 28 ♕xc5 bxc5 and Black should win with the extra pawn.

26 fxe3 ♗xe3+ 27 ♔h1 ♗xd2 28 ♕xd2 ♖e2 29 ♕c3 ♖xg2

29...♕e7 wins as well.

30 ♔xg2

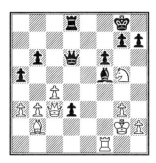

30...d2

Tal's game plan works so well; his d-pawn is irresistible.

31 ♖d1 ♗g4 32 ♘f3 ♕d3 0-1

A.Kochyev – M.Tal
Moscow 4-teams, 1981

1 d4 ♘f6 2 c4 e6 3 g3 c5 4 ♘f3 cxd4 5 ♘xd4 d5 6 ♗g2 e5 7 ♘b3

Retreating the knight is the most popular choice here.

7...d4 8 e3 a5! 9 exd4 a4 10 ♘3d2 exd4

See diagram on page 128.

Again Tal pins his hopes on the d-pawn.

11 0-0 ♗e7 12 ♘a3 ♘c6 13 ♘f3 ♗e6 14 ♗f4 0-0

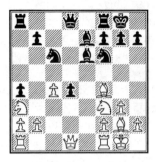

15 ♘g5

The grandmaster from Leningrad doesn't go for exchanges at all.

15...♗g4! 16 ♗f3 ♗f5 17 ♖e1 ♘d7 18 h4 h6 19 ♘e4 ♘de5 20 ♗g2 ♗b4 21 ♖f1

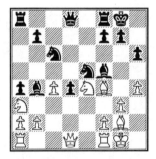

21...d3

Somehow Tal's d-pawn has become a powerhouse again.

22 ♖c1 ♘g6 23 ♗d2 ♖e8 24 ♗xb4 ♘xb4 25 ♖e1

25...d2!

White wins the d-pawn but overall he loses material.

26 ♕xd2 ♘d3

Black wins the exchange and his position is winning.

27 ♖e3 ♘xc1 28 ♕xc1 ♘e5 29 ♘b5 ♘g4 30 ♖e2 ♗xe4

Tal exchanges some pieces in order to invade.

31 ♗xe4 ♘f6 32 ♖d2 ♕e7 33 ♗f3 ♖ad8 34 ♔g2 b6 35 ♖xd8 ♖xd8 36 ♘c3 ♖d4 37 b3 axb3 38 axb3 ♕e5 39 ♕c2 ♕e1 40 ♘b1 ♘d7 41 ♕b2 ♖d3 0-1

N.Andrianov – G.Kasparov
Azerbaijan Team Championship,
Baku 1978

1 d4 ♘f6 2 c4 c5 3 ♘f3 cxd4 4 ♘xd4 e6 5 g3 d5 6 ♗g2 e5 7 ♘f3 d4

When I played this move I hoped the pawn would perform heroically like the d-pawn in Tal's games.

8 0-0 ♘c6 9 e3 ♗c5 10 exd4 exd4

See diagram on page 128.

11 ♗f4 0-0 12 ♘e5

My opponent went for exchanges.

12...♘xe5 13 ♗xe5 ♖e8

14 ♗xf6

And he sticks to his plan. Tal drove his opponents crazy with his knight moves. Although I was left with no knight, I did not feel there were any drawbacks.

14...♕xf6 15 ♘d2 ♕b6 16 ♘b3 ♗e6 17 ♗xb7

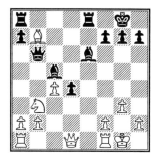

17...♖ad8

I was still optimistic, Black can win back the pawn and simplify to a drawish endgame. I felt the d-pawn has the same latent power as in Tal's game, while White's extra queenside pawn won't start working at all. Tal probably would have won even if he had been missing the b-pawn in those positions. After 17...♕xb7 18 ♘xc5 ♕xb2.

18 ♘xc5 ♕xc5 19 b3

19...d3

My d-pawn gets to the third rank as well.

20 ♖e1 ♕b4 21 ♗c6 ♖f8

Trying to retain as many pieces as possible, but it gives White time to organise his defence. After 21...d2 22 ♖e3 ♗d7 23 ♗xd7 ♖xe3 24 fxe3 ♖xd7 and the strong d-pawn secures a draw, but no more. If 21...♖e7 22 ♗d5 ♗xd5 23 ♖xe7 ♕xe7 24 cxd5 ♖xd5 25 ♕d2 White is a bit worse but with so few pieces he may get away with blocking the d-pawn.

22 ♖e3

22...d2

This looks just as strong as it did in Tal's game.

23 ♕e2 ♖d6 24 ♗e4 ♖fd8 25 ♖d1

But the difference is that it is well blockaded this time.

25...g6 26 h4

White makes room for his king in case of mating threats and will perhaps push his h-pawn all the way to h6 in an attempt to create his own threats.

26...h5?

I just wanted to stop the further advance of the h-pawn.

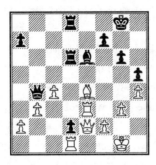

27 ♗xg6

My last move was a blunder, which gave away a pawn.

27...♗xc4 28 ♖e8+ ♖xe8 29 ♕xe8+ ♔g7 30 ♕e5+ ♔xg6 31 ♕g5+

I did not lose just one pawn but several – moreover Black's king becomes exposed.

31...♔h7 32 ♕xh5+ ♔g7 33 ♕g4+ ♔f8 34 ♕c8+ ♔e7 35 ♕xc4 ♕a5 36 b4 ♕e5 37 ♔f1 ♔d8 38 ♕c5 ♖d5 39 ♕f8+ ♔c7 40 ♕xf7+ ♔b6 41 ♕f3 ♕d6 42 ♕e3+ ♔b5 43 a3 ♔a4 44 ♕xa7+

44...♔b3

Other champions have won so many games with long king marches. However I did not have as much luck as they did.

45 ♕e3+ ♖d3

After 45...♔c2 46 ♕e4+! ♖d3 47 ♔e2 White also wins.

46 ♖xd2 1-0

Now even the d-pawn falls.

Let me just add that I finally had something to cheer about when I defeated a tough opponent – the knockout world champion Khalifman. This victory was sweet indeed and I went on to win the tournament as well.

G.Kasparov – A.Khalifman
FIDE Grand Prix, Moscow 2002

15...♘c6 16 b5 axb5 17 cxb5 ♘b4 18 ♘c4 ♕f5 19 ♖e5 ♕c2 20 ♗f4 ♕xd1+ 21 ♖xd1 ♔a8 22 a3 f6 23 axb4 1-0

In the next game Tal's opponent seems to have a dominating king in the centre, but it can also become a target as we will see...

In both these diagrams White's king is better centralised than Black's and surrounded by the opponent's pawns. First we will look at how Tal snares Augustin's king – similar to the way he trapped Rashkovsky on page 125!

I was hoping that I might catch my opponent's king in the centre as Tal did. In any event, no way could I lose with an extra pawn...

<table>
<tr><td>**J.Augustin – M.Tal**</td><td>**S.Rublevsky – G.Kasparov**</td></tr>
</table>

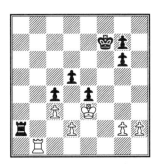

J.Augustin – M.Tal
European Team Championship,
Moscow 1977

1 c4 e5 2 ♘c3 ♘f6 3 ♘f3 ♘c6 4 d3 d6 5 g3 g6 6 ♗g2 ♗g7 7 0-0 0-0 8 ♖b1 a5 9 a3 ♘d4 10 b4 axb4 11 axb4 c6 12 b5 ♗g4 13 ♘xd4 exd4 14 ♘e4 ♘xe4 15 ♗xe4 ♖e8

16 ♖b2?!

If 16 bxc6 bxc6 17 ♖b2 and unlike the game White doesn't have to defend his b-pawn.

16...d5 17 cxd5 cxd5 18 ♗g2 ♖a1

19 h3 ♗e6 20 ♕b3 ♕d7 21 ♔h2 ♖ea8 22 ♗f4 ♖1a3 23 ♕c2 ♖c3 24 ♕d2 b6 25 ♗h6 ♗e5 26 ♗f4 ♗h8 27 ♖a2 ♖ac8 28 ♖b1 ♗f6 29 ♗g5 ♕e7 30 ♗xf6 ♕xf6 31 ♕f4 ♕xf4 32 gxf4 ♖c2 33 ♖bb2 ♖xb2 34 ♖xb2 ♖c5 35 ♔g3 ♔f8 36 ♖b4 ♔e7 37 ♖xd4 ♖xb5

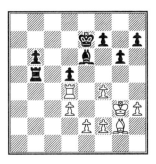

38 f5

With this imaginative pawn sacrifice the Czech player opens a route for his king to the centre. It seems to improve his rook.

38...gxf5 39 ♖a4 ♔d6 40 d4 ♖b2

41 ♗f1 ♖b1 42 ♗g2 b5 43 ♖a6+ ♔c7 44 ♔f4

See diagram on page 133.

White's king can become menacing in the centre.

44...♖b4 45 ♔e5

The king looks like a powerhouse on the e5-square.

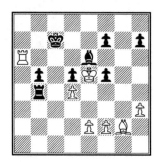

45...♖a4!

Out of the blue, Tal virtually traps White's rook and also exploits his unfortunate king.

46 ♖d6 b4 47 ♗xd5

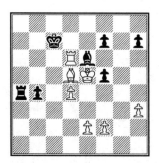

47...♖a5!

A lethal pin shows just how precarious White's king is on e5.

48 ♖c6+ ♔d7 0-1

Tal's b-pawn will win the game.

I wanted to plagiarise the idea! And my punishment came not in court but over the board...

S.Rublevsky – G.Kasparov
EU Cup, Izmir 2004

1 e4 c5 2 ♘f3 ♘c6 3 ♗b5

Rublevsky is quite an expert in the Rossolimo variation, but I also have pleasant memories with White. For instance I beat Salov with it.

3...e6 4 0-0 ♘ge7 5 c3 a6 6 ♗a4

6...c4

This is an ambitious move. The pawn can be a target too.

7 ♕e2 b5 8 ♗c2 ♘g6 9 b3 ♕c7 10 bxc4 ♘f4 11 ♕e3 bxc4 12 ♗a3 ♗e7 13 ♗xe7 ♘xe7 14 ♘a3

This softens up the c4-pawn.

14...0-0 15 ♖ab1

This is Rublevsky's novelty.

15...f5 16 ♕b6 ♕xb6 17 ♖xb6 fxe4 18 ♗xe4

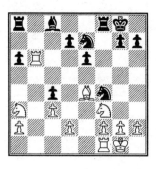

18...d5

Black can hold on tight to the c4-pawn, but his central pawn chain becomes somewhat rigid.

19 ♗c2 ♘eg6 20 ♗xg6 ♘xg6 21 ♘c2 e5 22 ♘e3 ♗f5 23 ♘xf5!

Sergei gets closer to the pawns by exchanging the pieces around it. After 23 ♖e1 ♗d3! 24 ♘xd5 e4 25 ♘d4 ♖fb8 Black has some compensation according to Rublevsky. Alternatively 23 ♘xd5 ♗e4 24 ♘e3 ♗xf3 25 gxf3 ♖f4 26 ♖c6 ♘h4 and Black has nice play.

23...♖xf5

24 ♖fb1! ♖af8

Getting to the second rank attracted me. Not 24...♘f4? 25 g4! ♖ff8 26 ♘xe5 ♖ae8 27 ♘d7 ♘h3+ (27...♖f7 28 ♖b8) 28 ♔g2 ♘f4+ 29 ♔f3 ♖f7 30 ♖b8 and White is clearly better as the winner pointed out. Better was 24...♖f6! although White still has the upper hand after 25 ♖xf6 26 ♖b7.

25 ♖xa6 e4 26 ♘d4 ♖xf2

All so classical – getting to the seventh with the rooks.

27 ♘e6!

Forcing more exchanges.

27...♖2f6

After 27...♖8f5 28 ♖b8+ ♘f8 (28...♔f7 29 ♘g5+) 29 ♖xf8+ ♖xf8 30 ♘xf8 ♖xf8 31 a4! White has decent winning chances.

28 ♘xf8 ♖xa6 29 ♘xg6 hxg6

After 29...♖xg6 30 ♔f2! (30 ♖b5 ♖d6) 30...♖a6 31 ♖b5 d4 32 cxd4 ♖xa2 33 ♔e3 Black is struggling.

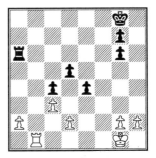

30 ♔f2!!

Bringing the king into the centre. I hoped I was going to catch White's king the same way that Tal did. And in case there were no efficient tactics against the king, I thought the extra pawn would still guarantee a draw.

30...♖xa2

After 30...d4 31 cxd4 ♖a3 32 ♖c1 ♖d3 33 ♔e2 ♖xd4 34 ♖c3 ♔f7 35 a4! wins according to Rublevsky.

31 ♔e3

The king is lured into a cage in the centre of the board.

31...♔f7 32 ♖b7+!

Unlike Tal's opponent, White doesn't step further into the danger zone.

32...♔f6 33 ♖b6+ ♔f7

135

See diagram on page 133.

If 33...♚f5 34 ♖d6 ♚e5 35 ♖xg6 ♖a7 36 ♖g5+ ♚e6 37 h4 Black has a very tough ending.

34 ♖d6 ♖a5

Here I realised White's king could not be caught, but still didn't appreciate the full scale of Black's problem.

35 h4

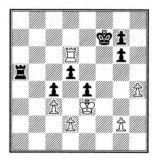

35...g5?

Aware of the trouble, I resorted to desperate measures. However, with 35...♖b5 Black could wait and see – and he has a hidden resource that provides tough resistance if White further improves his king. Then 36 g3!? (White could also play 36 g4 at once, which might create more obstacles for Black.) 36...♖a5 37 ♚f4 ♖b5 38 ♚e5

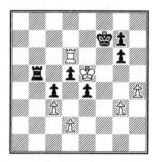

38...♖b3!! This move prompts enough exchanges to create drawing

chances. Interestingly, Black should now look for exchanges.

White could go back with 39 ♚d4!? and push his g-pawn before doing anything else. (After 39 ♖d7+ ♚e8 40 ♖xg7 [40 ♖xd5 e3! 41 dxe3 ♖xc3 Black should be able to hold] 40...e3! 41 dxe3 ♖xc3 42 ♖xg6 ♖xe3+ 43 ♚xd5 c3 and Black saves himself.) Then 39...♖b2 40 ♚e3 ♖b5 41 g4 ♖a5 42 g5 ♖b5 43 ♚f4 Rublevsky gets to this position by a different move order. He stops analysing here, evaluating the position as a clear win. However Black seems to be able to live with passive defence. 43...♖a5 44 ♚e5 ♖a3 45 ♖d7+ ♚e8 46 ♖xg7 e3 47 dxe3 ♖xc3 48 ♚f4 (48 ♚xd5 ♖xe3 49 ♖xg6 ♖h3 and Black survives.) 48...♖c1 49 ♖xg6 c3 50 ♚e5 c2 51 ♖c6 d4 and Black is safe.

36 hxg5 ♚e7 37 ♖c6 ♖a1

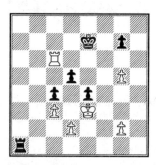

38 ♚d4

The king is in the cage, but there is no way to hurt it. Furthermore, I can't prevent it from carrying out its threat. All so tragic.

38...♖d1

38...♖a3? 39 ♚xd5 e3 40 ♖e6+ wins.

39 ♚xd5 e3

Forcing simplification but not to the desired extent. If 39...♖xd2+ 40 ♚xe4 ♖xg2 41 ♚f5.

40 ℤe6+ ♔d7 41 ℤxe3 ℤxd2+ 42 ♔xc4 ℤxg2 43 ℤe5 ♔d6

If Black could exchange his last pawn the game would be a draw.

44 ℤa5 ℤg4+ 45 ♔b3 ℤg1?!

According to my opponent I should have played 45...♔e6 and then 46 c4 g6 47 ♔b4.

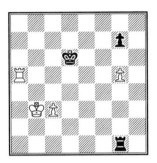

46 ♔b4 ℤb1+ 47 ♔c4 ♔e6 48 ℤa6+ ♔f5 49 g6 ℤg1 50 ♔b5 ♔e5

After 50...ℤb1+ 51 ♔c5 ℤg1 52 c4 ℤc1 53 ℤc6 ♔e5 54 ♔b6 White's king penetrates.

51 c4 ℤb1+

If 51...ℤg2 52 c5 ℤg1 53 ℤd6 (on 53 ♔b6 ℤxg6+ Black would not lose) 53...ℤg2 54 ♔b6 ℤg1 55 ♔c7! White's king walks over to collect the

g7-pawn. On the other hand, giving up the g6 pawn to advance the passed pawn would let Black off the hook, e.g. 55 ♔b7? ℤg2 56 ℤd1 ℤxg6 57 c6 ℤg2 and White is not far enough ahead in the race.

52 ♔c6 ℤg1

After 52...♔f5 53 ♔d7 ℤc1 54 ℤc6 ℤa1 55 c5.

53 ♔d7!

White simply collects the g7-pawn and wins. According to my plan I was supposed to hurt this king in the centre, just like Tal did – but instead it invaded my territory with fatal results.

53...ℤd1+ 54 ♔e7 ℤb1 55 ℤa5+ ♔d4 56 ♔f8 ℤb7 57 ℤf5 1-0

G.Kasparov – Y.Anikaev

From Tal I picked up a way to crack the Rauzer formation when Black castles kingside.

This time I show my position first followed on the next page by two misleading ones from the Magician from Riga.

M.Tal – I.Platonov

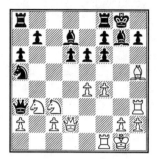

M.Tal – Y.Sakharov

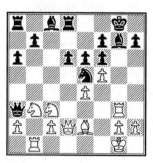

We still start by looking at Tal's games.

M.Tal – I.Platonov
Dubna 1973

1 e4 c5 2 ♘f3 d6 3 d4 cxd4 4 ♘xd4 ♘f6 5 ♘c3 a6 6 ♗g5 e6 7 f4 ♕b6 8 ♕d2 ♕xb2 9 ♘b3

Nowadays the popularity of this line is increasing.

9...♕a3 10 ♗xf6 gxf6 11 ♗e2 ♘c6

12 0-0 ♗d7 13 ♗h5 ♗g7 14 ♖f3
Bringing the rook into play.
14...0-0
Portisch later put his king on the queenside and defeated Tal in a well-known game in 1976.

15 ♖af1 ♘a5 16 ♖h3

See diagram above.

16...♘xb3 17 axb3 ♖ac8 18 ♔h1 f5 19 exf5 ♕b4 20 f6 ♗xf6 21 f5 ♖xc3?

Black misses a win here by 21...exf5! Then 22 ♕h6 (22 ♖ff3 f4) 22...♗g7 23 ♖g3 ♕xc3! decides.

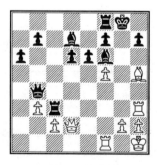

22 ♖g3+ ♔h8??
This loses to a wonderful finesse. With 22...♗g7 Black has a beautiful defence thanks to the weak back rank. 23 f6 (23 ♖xg7+ ♔xg7 24 ♕g5+ ♔h8 25 ♖f4 ♖f3!! forces White to accept a perpetual check.)

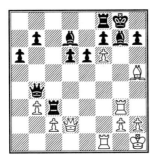

23...♖f3!! 24 ♖xg7+ ♔h8 25 ♕c1 ♖xf1+ 26 ♕xf1 ♕c3 and the position is equal.

23 ♕h6 ♖xg3

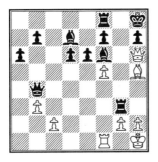

24 ♗g6!! 1-0

White sets up an unstoppable checkmate threat.

Here is his second game cracking the Rauzer formation.

M.Tal – Y.Sakharov
USSR Championship, Kiev 1964

1 e4 c5 2 ♘f3 d6 3 d4 cxd4 4 ♘xd4 ♘f6 5 ♘c3 a6 6 ♗g5 e6 7 f4 ♕b6 8 ♕d2 ♕xb2 9 ♖b1 ♕a3 10 ♗xf6 gxf6 11 ♗e2 ♗g7 12 0-0 0-0 13 ♖f3 ♘c6

14 ♘b3

In this earlier game White wasted a tempo by putting his rook on b1 – and his attack still broke through. This increased my confidence.

14...♖d8 15 f5 ♘e5 16 ♖g3

See diagram on page 138.

16...♔h8 17 ♖f1 ♕b4 18 ♔h1 d5 19 exd5 exd5 20 ♘d4 ♕f8 21 ♖h3 b5

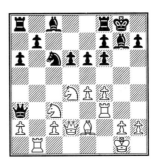

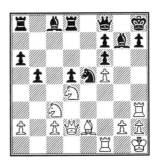

22 ♖f4

Tal brings another piece into the attack.

22...♗b7 23 ♖fh4 ♕g8 24 ♕f4 ♖ac8 25 ♘d1

If 25 ♖h5 ♘d7.

25...♖e8 26 ♘e3

First it was the rooks and the queen, now it is the distant knight that joins the attack.

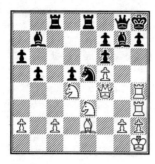

26...♖c3

Black has not obtained enough play on the queenside. He'll make Tal pay attention to that.

27 ♖h5 ♘d7 28 ♗d3 ♖e5 29 ♕h4 ♘f8 30 ♘g4 ♖e8

Giving up the exchange with 30...♖e4 removes some of the attacking pieces and gives him more practical chances after 31 ♗xe4 ♖xh3 32 ♕xh3 dxe4.

31 ♔g1

A careful move.

31...♖c4

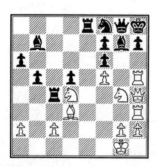

32 ♘xf6

Tal has reached his optimum position so starts the decisive operation which leads to a win of the exchange with no compensation for Black.

32...♗xf6 33 ♕xf6+ ♕g7 34 ♕xg7+ ♔xg7 35 ♖g3+ ♔h8 36 ♗xc4 dxc4 37 ♖h6 ♖d8 38 c3 ♗e4 39 a3 ♖a8 40 ♖d6 a5 41 ♖b6 b4 1-0

Now here is my game:

G.Kasparov – Y.Anikaev
USSR championship, Minsk 1979

1 e4 c5 2 ♘f3 d6 3 d4 cxd4 4 ♘xd4 ♘f6 5 ♘c3 ♘c6 6 ♗g5 a6 7 ♕d2 ♕b6 8 ♘b3 e6 9 ♗e2 ♕c7 10 a4 b6 11 ♗xf6 gxf6

I was happy to have the typical Rauzer pawn formation. One year earlier, back in my home town, I lost a game to Sideif Zade with reversed colours. Here it is: 1 ♘f3 ♘f6 2 c4 g6 3 ♘c3 d5 4 cxd5 ♘xd5 5 ♕a4+ ♗d7 6 ♕h4 e6 7 ♘xd5 exd5 8 ♕d4 f6 9 ♕xd5 ♘c6 10 ♕b3 ♕e7 11 d3 0-0-0 12 ♗d2 ♗g4 13 0-0-0 ♗xf3

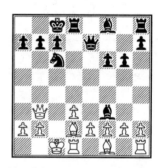

14 gxf3 ♘d4 15 ♕a4 ♘xe2+ 16 ♔b1 ♘d4 17 ♕xa7 ♕c5 18 ♕a8+ ♔d7 19 ♗h3+ f5 20 ♕xb7 ♕c2+ 21 ♔a1 ♗d6 22 ♕d5 ♖a8 23 ♗a5 ♕a4 24 b4

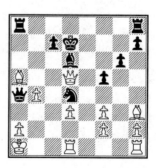

24...♖xa5 25 bxa5 ♘c2+ 26 ♔b2
♖b8+ 27 ♔c1 ♘d4 28 ♔d2 ♕b4+ 0-1
Kasparov – Sideif Zade, Azerbaijan
Team Championship, Baku 1978. So I
thought if he castles long I was ready,
as I knew Tal's game. By the way the
Rauzer formation with Black caused
me another painful memory. I held a
record of winning or tieing for first in
all tournaments for a period of 9 years
and 9 months. I did not make it a clean
10 years because I came 2-3rd in
Linares 1991 where Ivanchuk was the
winner. He beat me in the very first
round.

V.Ivanchuk – G.Kasparov
Linares 1991

1 e4 c5 2 ♘f3 d6 3 ♗b5+ ♘d7 4 d4
♘gf6 5 0-0 cxd4 6 ♕xd4 a6 7 ♗xd7+
♗xd7 8 ♗g5 h6 9 ♗xf6 gxf6

10 c4 e6 11 ♘c3 ♖c8 12 ♔h1 h5
13 a4 h4 14 h3 ♗e7 15 b4 a5 16 b5
♕c7 17 ♘d2 ♕c5 18 ♕d3 ♖g8
19 ♖ae1 ♕g5 20 ♖g1 ♕f4 21 ♖ef1 b6
22 ♘e2 ♕h6 23 c5 ♖xc5 24 ♘c4 ♔f8
25 ♘xb6 ♗e8 26 f4 f5 27 exf5 ♖xf5
28 ♖c1 ♔g7 29 g4 ♖c5 30 ♖xc5 dxc5
31 ♘c8 ♗f8 32 ♕d8 ♔g6 33 f5 ♕h6
34 g5 ♕h5 35 ♖g4 exf5 36 ♘f4 ♕h8
37 ♕f6+ ♔h7 38 ♖xh4+ 1-0

12 f4 ♗h6

This gains a tempo.

**13 0-0 ♗b7 14 ♖f3 ♖d8 15 ♖h3 ♗g7
16 f5 0-0**

Black's king could still walk over to
the queenside, but I decided to look for
safety on the kingside. And I did not
even have to sacrifice for an attack that
looked very promising.

See diagram on page 137.

**17 ♕f4 ♘e5 18 ♖d1 ♕e7 19 ♕h4 h6
20 ♕f2**

I decided to improve the bishop as
well.

**20...♕c7 21 ♘d4 ♗c8 22 ♕f1 ♕b7
23 ♗c4 d5 24 exd5**

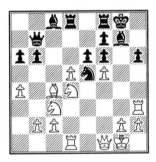

24...exd5

At first it all looked similar to Tal's
game against Platonov, but by now the
pawn structure is the same as in the
Sakharov game. I knew that game as
well so I was still optimistic.

25 ♗b3 ♖fe8 26 ♖g3 ♔h7 27 ♕f2

Bringing the queen closer to the king
by 27 ♕f4, as Tal did, was preferable.

**27...♘c4 28 ♘de2 b5 29 axb5 axb5
30 ♘f4**

Tal transferred the other knight to g4,
but I was happy with my choice.

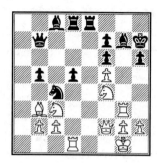

**30...♖e5 31 ♘h5 ♗h8 32 ♖f3 ♘xb2
33 ♖d4 ♘c4 34 ♗xc4 bxc4 35 g4**

This is something Tal did not play, yet I liked it. Sadly my position gradually deteriorates as Anikaev steadily improves his pieces.

**35...♕e7 36 ♕d2 ♗b7 37 ♔f2 ♖e8
38 ♘f4 ♗g7 39 ♖h3 ♔g8 40 ♘ce2
♗f8 41 ♘c3 ♕c5 42 ♘h5 ♕b6 43 ♖f3
♔h7 44 ♔g3 ♖d8**

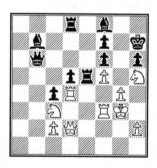

45 ♔h4

Steinitz liked to walk with his king...

45...♗b4 46 ♕f4

After 46 ♖f1 ♖e2! 47 ♕xe2 ♕xd4 White is in trouble.

**46...♕d6 47 ♖g3 ♕e7 48 ♔h3 ♗c5
49 ♕d2 ♖d6 50 ♘f4 ♗xd4**

Black takes the exchange.

51 ♕xd4 ♕d8 52 ♘h5 ♖e8

52...♖a6 followed by ♕b6 was winning.

53 g5 hxg5 54 ♖xg5 ♖g8 55 ♖xg8

After 55 ♕h4 fxg5 56 ♘f6+ ♔g7 57 ♕xg5+ ♔f8 58 ♘h7+ ♔e8 59 ♕xg8+ ♔d7 60 ♕xf7+ ♔c8 61 ♔g4 White has some practical chances.

55...♔xg8 56 ♘b5 ♖c6

56...♖a6! gains a winning tempo.

57 ♕g4+

Unfortunately the queen stands on the same diagonal as the bishop. Best was 57 ♕g1+! ♔f8 58 ♘d4 ♖a6 59 ♘e6+ ♖xe6 60 fxe6 ♔e7 61 exf7 and the position is equal according to Anikaev.

57...♔f8 58 ♘d4 ♖a6

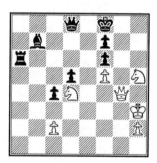

**59 ♘e6+ ♖xe6 60 fxe6 ♔e7 61 ♕g7
♔xe6 62 ♘f4+**

Sometimes Tal caught the king in the centre in endgames even though he had no queen. This time White has no chance even with the queens.

**62...♔e5 63 ♔g3 ♕a5 64 ♔f2 ♕b6+
65 ♔f3 d4+ 66 ♔g4 d3 67 ♕xf7 ♕g1+
68 ♔h4 ♕g5+ 0-1**

Vassily Smyslov the 7th

Smyslov won the world title in 1957 by beating Botvinnik 12½-9½. They had already played a match three years earlier, when they drew 12-12. In 1958 Botvinnik won the rematch but Smyslov kept on playing successfully for four decades. Incredibly he made it to the Candidates matches final, where I met him. The age difference between us is 42 years. He had the longest career, playing the most games of all the champions and with that many games he had a stronger effect on me. I had the most games against the other champions, but only played matches with Karpov and Smyslov. Against the rest I just played a few games. Let me give you a few examples of Smyslov's influence on me.

Firstly, here are a couple of positions from Smyslov's games that caused me particular damage.

White's queenside pawn majority, spearheaded by the pawn on c5, often occurs in the Alekhine defence and Panov attack versus the Caro-Kann.

V.Smyslov – W.Schmidt

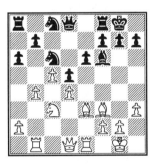

G.Kasparov – A.Yermolinsky

V.Smyslov – H.Azizi

G.Kasparov – A.Dreev

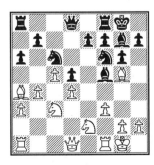

143

Any loss is very painful, two losses are even worse, but to lose two games with White is really pathetic. Making it almost impossible to bear is the fact that one of the games was a regular one. Even now, decades later, I need time to calm down when I think about it. It still upsets me that much!

V.Smyslov – W.Schmidt
Warsaw-Moscow, 1980

1 e4 ♘f6 2 e5 ♘d5 3 d4 d6 4 ♘f3 ♗g4 5 ♗e2 e6 6 c4 ♘b6 7 exd6 cxd6 8 h3 ♗h5 9 0-0 ♗e7 10 ♘c3 0-0 11 ♖e1 a6 12 b3 ♘c6 13 ♗e3 d5 14 c5

White often gains space like this in the Alekhine.

14...♗xf3 15 ♗xf3 ♘c8 16 ♖b1 ♗f6 17 b4

See diagram on page 143.

17...♘8e7 18 ♗g4

Smyslov fights to prevent Schmidt's knights from taking up positions in the centre.

18...g6 19 a4 h5 20 b5 axb5 21 axb5 ♘a5

The knight never comes back into play.

22 ♗e2 ♘f5 23 ♗d3 ♘xe3 24 fxe3 e5

25 ♖b4

It is quite an unusual role for the rook to defend the d4-pawn from b4 in the middlegame.

25...♖e8 26 ♖f1 ♖e6?!

26...e4 would lead to an unclear position after 27 ♗b1 ♘c4 28 ♕c1 ♗g5 29 ♖xc4 dxc4 30 ♗a2.

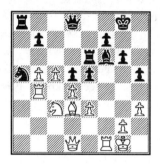

27 e4!

A nice riposte.

27...exd4?

After 27...dxe4 28 ♘xe4 ♗g7 29 ♖a4 f5 (29...exd4 is met by 30 ♘d6) 30 ♗b1 White is better.

28 ♘xd5 ♗e5

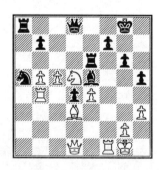

29 ♕f3

With remarkable ease, Smyslov has gained space on the queenside and now wins the game on the other side of the board.

29...f6 30 ♘f4 ♗xf4 31 ♕xf4 ♔g7 32 ♖a4 ♖e5 33 ♕f2 ♖xc5 34 ♖xd4

♕e7 35 ♕xf6+!

The sixth world champion finishes with an elegant petit combination.

35...♕xf6 36 ♖d7+ ♔h6 37 ♖xf6 ♖e5 38 h4 1-0

Smyslov had another win with this pawn structure.

V.Smyslov – H.Azizi
Rilton Cup, Stockholm 1998

1 e4 ♘f6 2 e5 ♘d5 3 d4 d6 4 ♘f3 ♗g4 5 ♗e2 e6 6 c4 ♘b6 7 exd6 cxd6 8 h3 ♗h5 9 0-0 ♗e7 10 ♘c3 0-0 11 b3 ♘8d7 12 ♗b2 ♘f6 13 ♖e1 ♖c8 14 ♘h4

A surprising decision.

14...♗g6?

Better is 14...♗xe2 because you are supposed to exchange when you have a disadvantage in space.

15 ♘xg6?! hxg6 16 ♗d3

The bishop is strong now.

16...a6 17 ♕f3 ♕c7 18 ♖ac1 ♕d7 19 a4 d5 20 c5 ♘a8

To put it mildly, this is not exactly classical chess.

21 b4

See diagram on page 143.

21...♗d8 22 b5 ♘c7 23 b6 ♘ce8 24 a5 ♘h7 25 ♗c2 ♘ef6 26 ♗a4 ♖c6 27 ♘a2 ♗e7 28 ♘b4 ♖fc8

29 ♗xc6 ♖xc6

Even Tigran Vartanovich did not come up with double exchange sacrifices too often.

30 ♘xc6 ♕xc6 31 ♕g3 ♘d7 32 ♕c7 ♘hf8 33 ♖b1 ♗g5 34 ♗c1 ♗xc1 35 ♖exc1 g5 36 ♖f1 g6 37 f4 gxf4 38 ♖xf4 ♔g7 39 ♖bf1 f5 40 ♕xc6 bxc6 41 g4 ♘f6 42 ♔f2 ♘8d7 43 ♔e3 ♘b8 44 ♖4f2 ♘bd7 45 gxf5 exf5 46 ♖g2 ♔f7 47 ♖fg1 ♘f8 48 b7 ♘6d7 49 h4 1-0

Here are some of my own games.

G.Kasparov – A.Yermolinsky
U18 USSR Championship,
Vilnius 1975

1 e4 ♘f6 2 e5 ♘d5 3 d4 d6 4 ♘f3 ♗g4 5 ♗e2 e6 6 0-0 ♗e7 7 h3 ♗h5 8 c4 ♘b6 9 exd6 cxd6 10 ♘bd2 0-0 11 b3 ♘c6 12 ♗b2

To retain the bishop. On e3 it would have been vulnerable to ...♘f5.

12...♗f6 13 a3 d5 14 c5 ♘c8 15 b4

Of course I was satisfied. I thought I would just copy Smyslov's play.

15...a6

See diagram on page 143.

16 ♖c1 ♘8e7 17 ♘b3 ♗xf3 18 ♗xf3 ♘f5

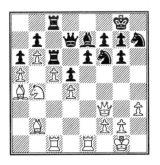

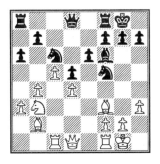

19 ♗g4

My predecessor put this bishop on g4. I reckoned that had to be correct.

19...g6 20 ♕d3 ♗g7 21 ♗c3 ♕f6 22 ♗xf5 ♕xf5 23 ♕xf5 exf5 24 a4 ♘d8

25 b5

All goes according to the Smyslov concept.

25...♘e6 26 ♖a1

I must admit that for just a second I lost my discipline and omitted ...b6, thereby deviating from Smyslov's plan. I felt I could improvise. But a single improvisation and I ended up losing – what a harsh punishment!

26...♖fc8 27 ♖fd1

27...b6! 28 ♖dc1

White should have taken with 28 cxb6, but I was not able to

remember any game with this motive from any champion. 28...♖xc3 29 ♖ac1 ♖c4 30 b7 ♖b8 31 bxa6 ♘c7 32 ♘a5 ♘xa6 33 ♘xc4 dxc4 34 ♖xc4 ♖xb7 35 d5 and White has the upper hand.

28...bxc5 29 b6 cxd4 30 ♗b2 ♖ab8 31 a5

After 31 ♖xc8+ ♖xc8 32 ♖c1 White is still no worse.

31...♖c4 32 ♘d2 ♖xc1+

If 32...♖b4 33 ♗a3 ♖b5 34 ♗d6 ♖d8 35 ♖ab1.

33 ♖xc1 ♔f8 34 ♘b3 ♗e5?!

After 34...♔e7 35 ♗a3+ ♔d7 36 ♘c5+ ♘xc5 37 ♖xc5 ♗e5 Black does better than in the game.

35 ♗a3+ ♔e8?

In principle it is right to bring the king to the centre, however in this particular position it has its tactical drawbacks.

36 ♖e1 f6 37 f4! ♘xf4 38 ♗d6 ♖d8 39 ♗c7 d3?

This is a bad move in a bad position. Black could have played on the exchange down with 39...♘d3, but his position has to be lost. 40 ♖e2 ♔d7 (40...♘b4 41 b7 ♘c6 42 ♘c5) 41 ♗xd8 ♔xd8 42 ♖d2 ♘b4 43 ♘xd4 and the protected b6 passed pawn is too strong to live with.

40 ♔f2?

I not only missed a forced win with this move but actually squandered the full point. I no longer remember exactly but I suspect I was in time trouble. Had Smyslov published annotations to his game I may have been able to memorise it and play faster, thereby avoiding this time trouble blunder. The winning continuation was 40 ♖xe5+! fxe5 41 b7 d2 42 ♘xd2 ♘e2+ 43 ♔f2 ♘d4 44 ♗xd8.

40...d2!

Oh, no. White has to resign.

41 ♖xe5+ fxe5 42 ♘xd2 ♘d3+ 43 ♔e3 ♘c5 44 ♗xe5 ♔d7 45 ♘f3 ♖e8 46 ♔d4 ♘b3+ 47 ♔xd5 ♘xa5 48 ♗f4 ♔c8 0-1

Here is my second game with the same pawn structure.

G.Kasparov – A.Dreev
Moscow PCA-Grand Prix,
Kremlin Stars, Moscow 1996

1 c4 c6 2 e4 d5 3 exd5 cxd5 4 d4 ♘f6 5 ♘c3 ♘c6 6 ♗g5 ♗e6 7 a3 ♗g4 8 f3 ♗e6 9 c5 g6 10 ♗b5 ♗g7 11 ♘ge2 0-0 12 0-0 ♗f5 13 b4

The pawn structure again reminds me of Smyslov's.

13...a6 14 ♗a4

See diagram on page 143.

14...h6 15 ♗e3

Vassily also developed the bishop on e3 in one of his games.

15...♘e8 16 ♕d2 ♔h7 17 ♘g3

I provoked him into pushing his pawns, but maybe it was not in my best interests.

17...e6 18 ♘ge2 g5 19 ♗c2 ♗xc2 20 ♕xc2+ f5 21 ♖ab1 ♘f6 22 a4 ♕e8 23 ♗f2 ♕g6 24 b5

24...♘a5

The knight may become strong on c4.

25 bxa6 ♖xa6 26 ♖b5 ♘d7 27 ♖fb1 ♘b8 28 ♘a2 ♘bc6 29 ♘b4 ♖a7 30 ♘d3 f4 31 ♕d1 ♖f7 32 ♘b2 ♖a8 33 h3 h5 34 ♕d3 ♖a7 35 h4 g4

36 ♕xg6+ ♔xg6 37 ♘d3 ♗h6 38 ♗e1 ♘c4 39 ♖a1 gxf3 40 gxf3 ♔f5

**41 a5 罩g7+ 42 含h1 罩a8 43 奧c3 匂e3
44 罩g1?! 罩xg1+ 45 匂xg1 罩a7 46 匂e2
匂c4 47 含g2 匂4xa5 48 奧xa5 匂xa5
49 匂e5 匂c6 50 匂xc6 bxc6 51 罩b6
罩c7 52 含f2 奧g7 53 含e1 奧f6 54 含d2**

54...奧xh4

Losing a second pawn should be the
end, but it was a rapid game so you
never know.

**55 罩b8 奧f6 56 罩f8 h4 57 匂g1 含g6
58 含d3 罩a7 59 匂h3 罩a3+ 60 含e2
含f5?**

60...罩e3+! simply wins.

**61 匂xf4 含xf4 62 罩xf6+ 含g5
63 罩xe6 h3 64 含f2 罩a2+ 65 含g1 h2+
66 含h1 含f4**

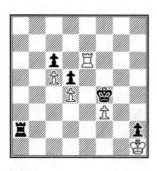

67 罩f6+

67 罩xc6 was another option, but
more fun was 67 罩e2!. This nice
stalemate finesse probably saves the
position. 67...罩a4 68 罩e6 罩xd4
69 含xh2 罩c4 (69...含xf3 70 罩xc6

draws.) 70 罩xc6 d4 71 含g2 (71 罩d6?
含xf3 wins.) 71...罩c2+ 72 含f1 含e3
73 罩e6+ 含d3 74 c6 and White holds.

**67...含g3 68 罩g6+ 含h3 69 罩h6+
含g3 70 罩g6+ 含xf3 71 罩xc6 含g3
72 罩g6+ 含f3 73 c6 罩c2**

After 73...含e4 74 罩g2 罩a1+
(74...罩a7 75 罩c2 罩c7 76 含xh2 含xd4
77 含g2 draws) 75 含xh2 罩c1 76 罩g6
含xd4 77 含g2 White draws.

74 罩h6?

Cutting off the king with 74 罩e6!
was correct.

74...含e4 75 罩h4+ 含d3 76 罩xh2

If 76 罩g4 罩xc6 77 含xh2 罩c4 wins
as well.

76...罩xc6 77 罩h4

77...罩c2?

Here 77...罩c4 78 含g2 罩xd4 79 罩h1
含e2 80 含g3 罩c4 wins, as does
77...罩g6.

78 含g1 罩e2 79 含f1 罩e4

80 ♖h2??

What a dreadful mistake! Even if it was a rapid game this should never have been played. In a way Smyslov is a guilty party for influencing me to conduct the opening the way he did. I must say Levenfish is also partly to blame for this. Together they wrote a classic book on rook endings, which I studied deeply. But they neglected to publish a book on pawn endings.

Simplifying to a pawn ending with 80 ♖xe4! was the solution to the problem. I tried to erase this weakness from my play but even in the very last game of my career I made a losing move against Topalov in a pawn

ending. In the games Karpov-Kasparov Las Palmas 1996, Kramnik-Kasparov, Intel rapid 1995 and in my match in 2003 against Azmaiparashvili, I made serious mistakes, some of which changed or could have changed the result of the game. I did not make these mistakes in pawn endings in a simul against an amateur but against my arch-rivals, Karpov and Kramnik. Yes, Smyslov and Levenfish really should have written a book on pawn endings. 80...♔xe4 (80...dxe4 81 d5 or 81 ♔e1 is also an elementary draw.) 81 ♔e2 ♔xd4 82 ♔d2 resulting in one of the best known drawn positions in chess.

80...♔xd4 81 ♖d2+ ♔c4 0-1

I miss a successful frontal attack by three tempi. My rook should check him from c1 and my king should be on f2. I invested so many hours on his rook ending book and yet here I was not able to gain three tempi.

By the way, this tournament was run on a knockout system – I won the next two games and reached the next round of the competition.

Once Smyslov planted a knight on c4. Here is the position:

I also planted his idea in my mind and reached the following position:

W.Fairhurst – V.Smyslov

Y.Seirawan – G.Kasparov

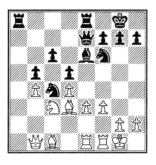

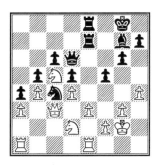

G.Kasparov – V.Kramnik

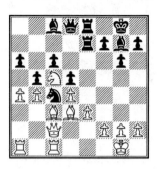

I wanted to encourage my opponent to place a knight on c4. Kramnik was oblivious to the dangers of having such a knight – and beat me!

W.Fairhurst – V.Smyslov
Hastings 1954/55

1 d4 ♘f6 2 c4 e6 3 ♘c3 ♗b4 4 e3 0-0 5 ♘ge2 d5 6 a3 ♗e7 7 ♘g3 b6!?

Smyslov claims he is always searching for harmony but he often goes in for unbalanced fights. Here 7...c5 was better, just to equalise.

8 cxd5 exd5 9 ♗e2 ♗b7 10 ♘f5 ♖e8 11 ♘xe7+ ♕xe7 12 0-0 ♘bd7 13 b4 c6 14 ♗d2 14...a6 15 ♕b3 b5!?

Smyslov's knight is heading for c4.

16 ♖ae1 ♘b6 17 ♗c1 a5 18 f3 axb4 19 axb4 ♗c8 20 ♗d3 ♗e6 21 ♕b1 ♘c4

22 e4?

White pushes forward without proper preparation.

22...♕a7! 23 ♘e2 dxe4 24 fxe4 ♗g4!

Suddenly White's centre falls apart.

25 ♗xc4 bxc4 26 ♘g3 ♕xd4+ 27 ♗e3 ♕d3 28 ♕b2

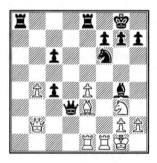

28...♘xe4

The rest is uninteresting.

29 ♘xe4 ♖xe4 30 ♕f2 f6 31 ♗c5 ♗e2 32 ♖a1 ♖ae8 33 ♖fe1 c3 34 ♕f5 c2 35 h4 ♕d5 36 ♕f2 h5 37 ♖ac1 ♗d1 38 ♖xe4 ♖xe4 39 ♖a1 ♕e5 0-1

This Smyslov game was against a relatively unknown player whereas I used his idea against a genuine contender. I should add that it was not only Smyslov who made me think that a knight on c4 would be almost decisive – but also two other champions misled me in one game.

A.Karpov – B.Spassky
Game 11, Candidates Semifinal,
Leningrad 1974

1 d4 ♘f6 2 c4 e6 3 ♘f3 d5 4 ♘c3
♗e7 5 ♗g5 h6 6 ♗h4 0-0 7 e3 b6
8 ♗e2 ♗b7 9 ♗xf6 ♗xf6 10 cxd5 exd5
11 0-0 ♕d6 12 ♖c1 a6 13 a3 ♘d7
14 b4 b5 15 ♘e1 c6 16 ♘d3 ♘b6 17 a4
♗d8 18 ♘c5 ♗c8 19 a5 ♗c7 20 g3
♘c4

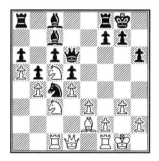

21 e4 ♗h3 22 ♖e1 dxe4 23 ♘3xe4
♕g6 24 ♗h5 ♕h7 25 ♕f3 f5 26 ♘c3
g6 27 ♕xc6 gxh5 28 ♘d5 f4 29 ♖e7
♕f5 30 ♖xc7 ♖ae8 31 ♕xh6 ♖f7
32 ♖xf7 ♔xf7 33 ♕xf4 ♖e2 34 ♕c7+
♔f8 35 ♘f4 1-0

Y.Seirawan – G.Kasparov
Dubai Olympiad 1986

1 d4 ♘f6 2 c4 g6 3 ♘c3 d5 4 ♘f3
♗g7 5 ♗g5 ♘e4 6 cxd5 ♘xg5 7 ♘xg5
e6 8 ♘f3 exd5 9 b4 ♕d6

This move was a novelty then.

10 a3 0-0 11 e3 c6 12 ♗e2 ♗f5
13 0-0 ♘d7 14 ♘a4 a5 15 ♕b3

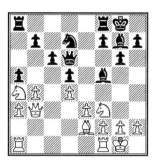

**15...b5 16 ♘c5 a4 17 ♕c3 ♘b6
18 ♘d2 ♖ae8 19 ♖fe1 ♖e7 20 ♗f3
♖fe8**

Now I prefer to transfer the bishop to
g6 after 20...g5!? and start pushing the
f-pawn.

**21 g3 ♗h3 22 ♗g2 ♗xg2 23 ♔xg2
f5 24 h4**

See diagram on page 149.

24...♘c4

I managed to position the knight
just like Smyslov and at this point I was
satisfied and thinking appeciatively of
him.

**25 ♘f3 ♗f6 26 ♖e2 ♖g7 27 ♖h1
♕e7 28 ♖ee1 h6 29 ♕d3 ♖f8 30 ♘d2
♕e8**

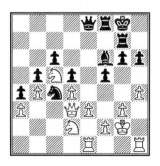

31 ♘xc4

White would have done better not to
have taken the c4-knight.

31...dxc4 32 ♕d1 ♖e7 33 ♖ef1 ♕f7 34 ♕f3 ♕d5 35 ♕xd5+ cxd5 36 ♔f3 ♗g7 37 ♖d1 ♖ff7 38 ♖d2 ♖e8 39 ♖dd1 ♗f8 40 ♖dg1 ♗g7 41 ♖d1 ♔f8 42 ♖d2 ♔e7 43 ♖dd1 ♔d6 44 ♖h2 ♔c6 45 ♖hh1 ♗f8 46 ♖d2 ♗d6 47 ♖dd1

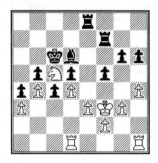

47...♗xc5?!

An impatient move. I should have further improved the positions of my other pieces, for example by 47...♖ee7. Then after 48 ♖d2 (48 ♖h2? ♗xc5! 49 dxc5 ♖e4 wins.) 48...♖h7 49 ♖dd1 g5 Black can exert pressure.

48 dxc5 ♖e4 49 ♖he1 ♖d7 50 ♖d4 g5 51 hxg5 hxg5 52 ♖ed1 ♖xd4 53 ♖xd4 ♖h7 54 ♔e2

54 g4 was interesting.

54...♖h3

If 54...♖h1 55 ♖d1.

55 g4

55...f4?!

Objectively this neither spoils nor improves the position, but puts Black into a situation where he has to find a very subtle plan in order to draw. The practical move 55...fxg4 56 ♖xg4 ♖h5 offered an equal endgame.

56 exf4 ♖xa3 57 fxg5 ♖a2+ 58 ♔f3

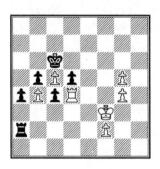

58...c3?

This natural move loses. The c-pawn is closer to promotion than White's g5-pawn, but Black's rook has less effect on it than White's on c3. And that matters at this point. Better was 58...♖a3+! 59 ♔g2 (59 ♔f4 ♖a2)

59...♖a2!!

This pin of the f-pawn is an extremely difficult move to find. It temporarily stops White pushing his passed f and g-pawns as a team. It also gains a tempo to help win the race.

(Not 59...罩a1? 60 g6 罩e1 61 f4! Two connected passed pawns are often advanced together. It is best not to separate them by sending only one out in front. 61...c3

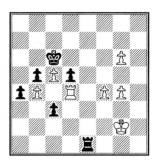

62 罩d1!! I not only investigated the champions' games but also those of other world class players. How hard it was to balance my time between them! Timman also liked to give up his rook on the back rank as in his games against Ivkov at Amsterdam 1971 and Kramnik at Belgrade 1994. The rook can't be taken as White surprisingly checkmates Black's king after queening his g-pawn first, as I first pointed out in my *Informant* analysis. Alternatively:

a) 62...罩e2+ 63 含g3 [63 含f3 罩e8 64 f5 d4] 63...d4 64 g7 罩e8 65 f5 c2 66 罩f1 d3 67 f6 d2 68 f7 d1=豐 69 fxe8=豐+ wins.

b) 62...罩e8 63 f5 d4 64 f6 c2 65 罩f1 d3 66 f7 罩d8 67 g7 d2 68 f8=豐+ d1=豐 69 豐f6+ 含c7 70 g8=豐 罩xg8 71 豐b6+ 含c8 72 豐e6+ 含b7 73 罩f7+ wins. Or 63 g7 c2 64 g8=豐 罩g1+ 65 含h3 罩h1+ 66 含g3 罩g1+ 67 含h4 含c7 [67...c1=豐 68 豐c8 mate] 68 豐f7+ 含c6 69 豐e6+ 含c7 70 豐e7+ 含c6 71 豐d6+ 含b7 72 豐d7+ 含b8 73 c6 White catches Black's king.)

60 g6 (60 含g3 c3 61 g6 罩e2) 60...罩e2 61 罩f4 罩e8 62 罩f6+ 含c7

63 罩f7+ 含c6 64 含f3 a3 65 罩a7 d4 and this unusual position with two connected passed pawns in both camps is probably equal.

59 罩d1 d4

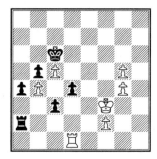

60 g6 d3

Many champions won games by pushing two passed pawns all the way to the sixth rank. The c4 knight that I planted like Smyslov was later transformed into this pawn – but in the end its slow pace is responsible for my defeat.

61 含e3 罩xf2

After 61...d2 comes 62 g7 c2 63 含xd2 cxd1=豐+ 64 含xd1.

62 g7 1-0

I will not analyse in detail my encounter with Kramnik as it is just a blitz game. I happily let my opponent's knight go to c4 and when it arrived there I could not resist a little smile.

G.Kasparov – V.Kramnik
Champions Club, 5 minute game
Kasparovchess.com 2001

1 d4 ❲f6 2 c4 e6 3 ❲f3 b6 4 ❲c3 ♗b7 5 a3 d5 6 cxd5 ❲xd5 7 e3 g6 8 ❲xd5 exd5 9 ♗b5+ c6 10 ♗d3 ♗g7 11 b4 0-0 12 ♗d2 ❲d7 13 罩b1 罩e8 14 0-0 ❲f6 15 豐c2 ❲e4 16 罩fc1 罩c8 17 ♗e1 ❲d6 18 a4 a6 19 ❲d2 罩c7 20 ❲b3

20...b5 21 ♘c5 ♗c8 22 ♖a1 ♖ce7 23 ♗c3 ♘c4 *See diagram on page 150.* **24 ♖a2 ♕d6 25 axb5 axb5 26 ♖a8 ♘b6 27 ♖a2 h5 28 ♖ca1 h4 29 ♕d1 h3 30 g3 ♘c4 31 ♗f1 ♗h6 32 ♖a8 ♗f5 33 ♖xe8+ ♖xe8 34 ♗d2 ♕f6 35 ♗c1 ♗g7 36 ♖a6 ♔h7 37 ♕f3 ♔g8**

38 g4 ♕g5 39 ♗xh3 ♗xd4 40 ♔h1?! ♘e5 41 ♕g3 ♘xg4 42 ♖xc6?

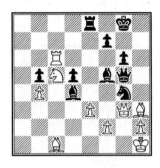

42...♗xc5 43 ♖xc5 ♕h5 44 ♗g2? ♘f6? 45 f3?? ♘e4 46 ♕c7 ♘xc5 47 bxc5 ♗h3 0-1

Smyslov and I both played the Grünfeld quite regularly. Assessing the strength of the d6 passed pawn is not always a simple matter. I knew his win against Euwe, so I also went for a variation in the Grünfeld with a d6-pawn. Very sadly the result was not 0-1 as in Smyslov's game.

Actually the position I reached against Piket was virtually the same.

M.Euwe – V.Smyslov

J.Piket – G.Kasparov

M.Euwe – V.Smyslov
Candidates Tournament, Zurich 1953

1 d4 ♘f6 2 c4 g6 3 g3 ♗g7 4 ♗g2 d5 5 cxd5 ♘xd5 6 e4 ♘b6 7 ♘e2 c5 8 d5 e6 9 0-0 0-0 10 a4

Nowadays players who develop the e2-knight on c3 go there at once with 10 ♘ec3.

10...♘a6 11 ♘a3 exd5 12 exd5 ♗f5 13 ♘c3 ♘b4

Black bases his strategy on the fact

that he has lovely piece play. However White's d-pawn can become dangerous as if he can push and then consolidate it on d6, it could stifle Black.

14 ♗e3 ♖c8

15 d6

I got the impression from this particular game that the d6-passed pawn is not something Black can't handle, especially in the Grünfeld.

15...♗d3 16 ♗xb7 ♖b8 17 ♗g2 ♗xf1 18 ♔xf1

White has reasonable compensation for the exchange.

18...♘d7 19 ♘c4

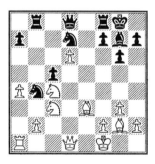

19...♘e5

Smyslov exchanges to get closer to the d6-pawn.

20 ♘xe5 ♗xe5 21 ♗xc5?!

After 21 ♘e4!? ♕a5 22 ♘xc5

21...♕a5 22 ♗e3 ♖fd8 23 ♘e4 ♗xd6

Smyslov makes it so easy to remove the d6-pawn. A fascinating fight starts in the centre.

24 ♘f6+

If 24 ♘xd6 ♕a6+.

24...♔h8 25 ♗d4 ♗e5 26 ♘d7

26...f6?!

Smyslov takes a huge risk. After 26...♗xd4 27 ♕xd4+ ♔g8 28 ♘f6+ ♔f8! (Euwe spotted that the natural continuation 28...♔h8, allowing a battery, gives more than just a perpetual: 29 ♘d5+ ♔g8 30 ♘e7+ ♔f8 31 ♕h8+ ♔xe7 32 ♖e1+ ♔d7 33 ♕d4+ ♘d5 34 ♗xd5 ♖b4 35 ♕e5 ♕a6+ 36 ♔g1 ♕d6 37 ♕c3) 29 ♘xh7+ ♔g8 30 ♘f6+ ♔f8 the players have to settle for a repetition.

27 ♗xe5 fxe5

28 ♕d2?

Going after Black's king with 28 ♕d6 would force Black to return the exchange and settle for a position a pawn down. 28...♖bc8 (28...♖xd7 29 ♕xd7) 29 ♕f6+ ♔g8 30 ♕e7 ♖xd7 31 ♕xd7 and White should win this without too much of a problem.

28...♖bc8 29 ♔g1?

29 ♕d6 was still better than the game. After 29...♕a6+ 30 ♕xa6 ♘xa6 31 ♘xe5 it looks balanced.

29...♕c5!

He makes sure White doesn't get out of the pin.

30 ♗h3 ♕e7 31 ♕e2

If 31 ♖d1 ♖c7.

31...♖xd7

Black wins a piece. Euwe resists but in the long run he has no chance.

32 ♗xd7 ♕xd7 33 ♕xe5+ ♔g8 34 ♕e4 a5 35 h4 ♕d5 36 ♕g4 ♖f8 37 ♖d1 ♕f3 38 ♕c4+ ♕f7 39 ♕c5 ♕f5 40 ♕c4+ ♕f7 41 ♕c5 ♕f5 42 ♕c4+ ♔g7 43 ♕d4+ ♕f6 44 ♕c5 ♖f7 45 ♖d2 ♕e7 46 ♕c3+ ♖f6 47 ♖d4 ♘c6 48 ♖d5 ♕e6 49 ♖c5 h5 50 b3 ♔f7 51 ♖b5 ♕d7 52 ♔g2 ♕e7 53 ♕c4+ ♔g7 54 ♕d3 ♔h6 55 ♖d5 ♖f7 56 ♖d6 ♘e5 57 ♕e3+ ♔h7 58 ♖b6 ♕c7 0-1

I suspected I would face the variation in the next game and was hoping I could prove I was able to neutralise the d6-pawn at least as well as Smyslov.

J.Piket – G.Kasparov

Euwe Memorial, Amsterdam 1995

1 d4 ♘f6 2 c4 g6 3 ♘c3 d5 4 ♘f3 ♗g7 5 ♕b3 dxc4 6 ♕xc4 0-0 7 e4 ♘a6 8 ♗e2 c5 9 d5 e6 10 0-0 exd5

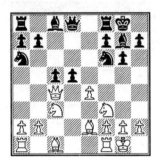

11 exd5 ♖e8

In an earlier game – with 11...♗f5 – the d-pawn did not move yet assumed a great role just by threatening to move. Sadly, I lost that one as well. 12 ♗f4 ♖e8 13 ♖ad1 ♘e4 14 ♘b5 ♕f6 15 ♗d3 ♘b4 16 ♘c7 ♘xd3 17 ♘xe8 ♖xe8 18 ♕xd3 ♕xb2 19 ♖de1 ♕b4 20 ♘d2 ♕a4 21 ♕c4 ♕xc4 22 ♘xc4 ♗c3 23 ♘d2 ♗xd2 24 ♗xd2 ♗d7 25 ♗f4 ♗b5 26 f3 g5 (26...♗xf1 27 ♔xf1 ♘f6 28 ♖xe8+ ♘xe8 29 ♗e5 ♘g7 30 d6 Now the d6-pawn wins.) 27 ♗xg5 ♗xf1 28 ♔xf1 ♘d6 29 ♗e7 ♘c8 30 ♗xc5 ♖d8 31 ♖e5 f6 32 ♖f5 b6 33 ♗d4 ♘e7 34 ♗xf6 ♖xd5 35 ♖g5+ ♖xg5 36 ♗xg5 ♘c6 37 ♔e2 ♔f7 38 ♔d3 ♔e6 39 ♔c4 ♘e5+ 40 ♔d4 ♘c6+ 1-0 Karpov-Kasparov, London/ Leningrad 1986.

12 ♖d1 ♗f5

See diagram on page 154.

13 d6 h6

Piket has his own lines, which he has developed and refined to a high level. I prepared this move to counter his preparation. Gulko defended the position differently with 13...♘e4. Then 14 ♘b5 ♗d7 15 a4! ♘b4? 16 ♕b3! ♕b6?! 17 ♗e3 ♗xb5 18 ♗xb5 ♘c6 19 d7 ♖ed8 20 ♕c4 ♘f6 21 ♗xc5 ♕c7 22 ♗xc6 bxc6 23 ♗d6 ♕xd7 24 ♘e5 1-0 Piket-Gulko, Groningen 1990.

14 ♗f4

I had already played against 14 h3?! when I managed to show that Black's pieces work well and he can even take over the initiative with his piece play. 14...♘b4! 15 ♗f4! ♘d7 16 ♖d2 a6 17 ♕b3 b5 18 ♕d1 c4 19 a4! ♘c5 20 axb5 ♘bd3 21 ♗xd3 ♘xd3 22 ♖xd3? cxd3? (22...♗xd3!) 23 ♘d5! axb5 24 ♘e7+! ½-½ Karpov-Kasparov, Game 15, World Championship, Seville 1987

14...♘d7 15 ♖d2 ♘b4 16 ♕b3 ♗e6

Just like Smyslov I exchanged pieces around the d6-pawn in order to weaken it.

17 ♗c4 ♘b6 18 ♗xe6 ♖xe6

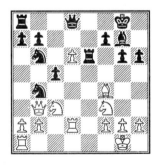

19 ♘a4!?

Tal recommended this and I lost against it. This is one more example where a world champion had a controversial effect on my career. I had faced 19 a3?! in a world title

match: 19...♘d3! 20 ♗g3 c4 21 ♕c2 ♖c8 22 ♖ad1 ♕d7 23 h4 f5 24 ♖xd3 ½-½ Karpov-Kasparov, Game 21, Seville 1987. And I had also come up against 19 ♗g3 in a quite different kind of event: 19...♕d7 20 a3 ♘c6 21 ♕b5 ♖c8 22 ♖ad1 ♗xc3 23 bxc3 ♘e5 24 ♕xd7 and I went on to win in a simultaneous exhibition game, Rao-Kasparov, New York 1988.

19...♖e4?

19...♘xa4 deserves consideration.

20 ♗g3

After 20 ♗e3 ♘c6! 21 ♘xc5 ♖b4 22 ♕d3 ♘c4.

20...♘c4

If 20...♘a6 21 ♘xb6 ♕xb6 22 ♕c2.

21 ♘xc5

21...♘xd2

Everything goes according to plan. Just like Smyslov I win the exchange.

22 ♘xd2 ♖e2

Here 22...♖d4 23 ♘f3 ♖xd6! (23...♖g4 24 ♘e6 wins.) 24 ♘xb7 ♖d3 25 ♕xb4 (25 ♘xd8 ♖xb3 26 axb3 ♖xd8s) 25...♖d1+ 26 ♖xd1 ♕xd1+ 27 ♕e1 and White consolidates his material advantage and has decent chances to win with the two pieces against the rook.

23 ♕xb4 a5 24 ♕xb7 ♖xd2

25 d7

Here some doubt came into my mind as Euwe's d-pawn never got this far, but I still did not worry. In reality Black already has a lost position.

25...♖xb2 26 ♕d5 ♖b5

After 26...♗f8 27 ♘e4! intending ♗e5 is better than 27 ♘d3 ♖d2 28 ♗f4 ♖a7! 29 ♗xd2 ♖xd7 30 ♕xa5 ♖xd3 31 ♕xd8 ♖xd8 32 ♗e3.

27 ♖d1 ♗f8

After 27...♖a7 28 ♕e4! ♗f8 (28...♗f6 29 ♕e8+ ♔g7 30 ♗e5!) 29 ♕e8 ♖a8 30 ♘e4 White wins.

28 ♗d6 ♗xd6

Not 28...♖a7? 29 ♗xf8 ♔xf8 30 ♕e5.

29 ♕xd6

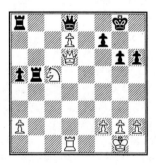

29...♖ab8

Now the d-pawn is almost suffocating me. Black treads a narrow path but it is not enough to stay in the game.

Here 29...♖a7 30 ♘e4 wins.

Alternatively 29...♕f8 30 ♘e4! ♕xd6 (30...♖d8 31 ♘f6+ ♔g7 32 ♕d4 ♖f5 33 ♘e8+ ♔h7 34 g4 ♖b5 35 ♘f6+) 31 ♘xd6 ♖bb8 32 ♖c1 ♖d8 33 ♖c8 ♔g7 34 ♖xa8 wins.

30 h3 ♖b1 31 ♖xb1 ♖xb1+ 32 ♔h2 ♖b6

If 32...♖b8 33 ♕e5 ♔f8 34 ♘e4 ♖b7 35 ♕h8+ ♔e7 36 ♕e8+ wins.

33 ♕e5 ♔f8

And here 33...♖b8 is countered by 34 ♘b7!.

34 ♕h8+ ♔e7 35 ♕e5+ ♔f8 36 f4 h5

After 36...g5 37 f5 ♕b8 38 ♕xb8+ ♖xb8 39 f6 ♖d8 40 ♔g3 wins. And after 36...f6!? 37 ♕d5 ♔e7 38 h4! White keeps Black under pressure.

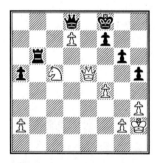

37 ♕d5 h4

Now the pawn ending will not bring victory:

a) 37...♔e7 38 ♕g5+.

b) 37...g5 38 ♘d3.

c) 37...a4 38 ♘b7 ♖xb7 39 ♕xb7 ♔e7 40 ♔g3 and Black can't enter the pawn ending.

38 ♕e5!

After 38 ♘b7 comes 38...♖xb7 39 ♕xb7 ♔e7.

38...g5

This is a desperate attempt, but it can't loosen White's grip. There are three other possibilities.

a) If 38...f6 39 ♕e1!.

b) 38...♖c6 39 ♕h8+ ♔e7 40 ♕xh4+ wins.

c) 38...♖b4 39 ♕h8+ ♔e7 40 ♕xh4+ f6 41 ♕e1+ ♔d6 42 ♕e8 wins.

39 ♕h8+ ♔e7 40 ♕e5+ ♔f8 41 fxg5 1-0

Here I resigned because I saw that I had run out of plausible moves. I never got rid of that damned d6 pawn.

The conclusion of the game mght have been 41...♖g6 (If 41...♖c6 42 g3.) 42 ♔h1 (Black has no move.) 42...♖b6 43 g6 ♖xg6 44 ♕h8+ ♔e7 45 ♕xh4+ ♖f6 46 ♘e4 and wins.

An attacking player like me often obtains positions with unbalanced material. Therefore it quite often happened that my opponent had several connected pawns, while I preferred to have a piece. In this way Smyslov had a very strong influence on me. Two of his games impressed me very much. Here are a couple of critical positions from his games. Then come my games.

V.Smyslov – D.Bronstein

G.Kasparov – B.Spassky

V.Smyslov – J.Timman

G.Kasparov – J.Lautier

This is the third of my losses where there was unbalanced material and a mass of pawns coming in my direction.

No mistake, I lost three games in this way! In fact I may have lost even more, but (luckily for me) I can't remember them.

V.Kramnik – G.Kasparov

V.Smyslov – D.Bronstein
USSR Championship, Moscow 1951

1 e4 c5 2 ♘c3

Smyslov played 56 Closed Sicilians in his career. His first game and first win with it came in 1946, his last was in 1998. His first victim was Kottnauer, his last Arakhamia. 52 years had elapsed between these two games.

2...♘c6 3 g3 g6 4 ♗g2 ♗g7 5 d3 d6 6 ♗e3 ♘h6 7 ♕c1 ♘g4 8 ♗d2 ♘d4 9 h3 ♘e5 10 ♘ce2 ♕b6 11 f4

11...♘xc2+

This is a cute move, but not really a good deal.

12 ♕xc2 ♕xb2 13 ♕xb2 ♘xd3+ 14 ♔f1 ♗xb2 15 ♖b1

See diagram on page 159.

15...♗e6

16 ♗c3

Smyslov prefers to face the three pawns with a piece, rather than have a rook against four pawns. After 16 ♖xb2 comes 16...♘xb2 17 ♗c3 ♘d3 18 ♗xh8 f6 19 ♗g7 h5 20 g4 ♔f7 21 ♗h6 ♗xa2.

16...♗xa2?!

After 16...♗xc3 Bronstein avoids the equation of three pawns against a piece. 17 ♘xc3 ♗c4 18 ♘ge2 (18 ♖xb7 ♘b4+ 19 ♔e1 ♗a6) 18...♖b8 and it is hard to pick a colour. Everyone to their own taste.

17 ♖xb2 ♘xb2 18 ♗xb2

18...罝g8

White has three pieces against a rook and four pawns. This kind of position with unbalanced material is really hard to judge. I have already mentioned one painful experience against Anand in Tilburg 1991; in that game he had a queen, I had three pieces.

19 當f2 盦c4 20 包f3 盦xe2

Black has invested two moves to exchange the bishop for the knight. He could have made two pawn moves instead.

21 當xe2 當d7 22 罝d1 a5 23 包e5+ 當c7 24 包xf7 a4 25 e5 a3 26 盦a1 罝ge8 27 包g5 罝a5 28 包e6+ 當d7

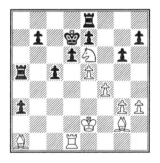

29 盦d5

White simply has too many pieces.

29...a2 30 g4 罝c8 31 包g5 罝f8 32 f5 gxf5 33 gxf5 h6 34 盦e6+ 當c7 35 exd6+ exd6 36 包e4 罝a3

37 包xd6

Smyslov not only takes a pawn, but with his enormous piece power also very quickly catches Bronstein's king.

37...罝xh3 38 盦e5 罝a8

He does not see a checkmate in two, but his position was hopeless anyway.

39 包c4+ 1-0

V.Smyslov – J.Timman
Hoogovens, Wijk aan Zee 1972

1 包f3 g6 2 e4 盦g7 3 d4 d6 4 包c3 盦g4 5 盦e3 包c6 6 盦b5 a6 7 盦xc6+ bxc6

Interestingly, Smyslov himself took on doubled c-pawns with Black against Timman in 1984. Even more interestingly, several decades earlier in 1943, Smyslov also had a similar position against Botvinnik. He lost the first and drew the second game.

8 h3 盦xf3 9 豐xf3 e6 10 e5! 包e7

11 ♘e4

Smyslov plays powerfully.

11...♘d5 12 ♗g5 ♕b8 13 0-0 h6 14 ♗f6 ♗xf6 15 exf6 ♕xb2 16 c4 ♕xd4 17 cxd5 cxd5

See diagram on page 159.

Black has three pawns for the piece. If they start rolling they will be like an avalanche. On the other hand the choking f6-pawn can cause a lot of problems for Black. Interestingly, seven years later Smyslov, in the 9 ♘bd2 variation, introduced a very important novelty which established a new variation. In that line Black also sacrifices a piece for three passed pawns. I beat Shirov in that line (I had the piece of course) in Linares 2001. However the line is still playable for Black nearly three decades after Smyslov first played it.

18 ♘c3 0-0 19 ♖ad1 ♕e5 20 g4 ♖ab8 21 ♖fe1 ♕g5 22 ♖b1

22...c5

Finally the first pawn of the herd moves.

23 ♔g2 ♖b4 24 ♖xb4 cxb4 25 ♘e2 ♖c8 26 ♘d4

Smyslov provokes Black into pushing the pawn.

26...e5 27 ♘e2 ♕d2?!

Timman adopts a risky approach. It is dangerous to release the pressure on the f6-pawn.

28 ♔f1 ♕xa2

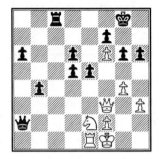

29 ♕e3! ♔h7 30 ♕b6

Of course White's queen is free to invade.

30...♕b3 31 ♔g2 d4 32 ♕xd6 ♕e6 33 ♕xb4 ♕xf6

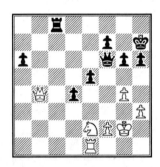

34 ♘g3!

The 'three pawns for the piece' balance is restored, but Black's pawns are no longer in a mass, but separated. The knight will really dominate and sooner or later White will penetrate.

34...♕c6+ 35 ♘e4 ♖c7

After 35...f5 36 gxf5 gxf5 37 ♕e7+ wins.

36 ♕f8 d3

36...g5 would have resisted for longer.

37 ♔h2 d2

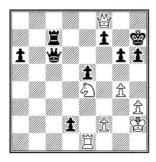

38 ♘xd2

The strongest pawn in Black's position has now disappeared and with it all hope goes too.

38...♛f6 39 ♘e4 ♛f4+ 40 ♔g2 ♜c2 41 ♛d6 a5 42 ♛d5 1-0

Here are my exciting games featuring the topic of a piece against three connected passed pawns.

G.Kasparov – B.Spassky
Niksic 1983

1 d4 ♘f6 2 c4 g6 3 ♘c3 ♗g7

Spassky doesn't often play the King's Indian.

4 e4 d6 5 f3 ♘c6 6 ♗e3 a6 7 ♘ge2 ♜b8 8 ♛d2 0-0 9 h4 b5 10 h5 bxc4 11 g4 ♗xg4!? 12 fxg4 ♘xg4

See diagram on page 159.

Black has three pawns for the piece and no real weaknesses – perhaps only the h-file. I knew how much Smyslov preferred to retain the piece. Black's pawns are a long way from promotion. These two factors made me confident.

13 0-0-0! ♘xe3 14 ♛xe3 e6 15 hxg6 hxg6

If 15...fxg6 16 ♛h3 ♛g5+ 17 ♔b1 ♜xb2+ 18 ♔xb2 ♜b8+ 19 ♔a1 ♘b4 20 ♛xe6+! (In my *Informant* analysis I gave 20 a3 as winning. I can no longer remember why, since it only leads to a draw. 20...♘c2+ 21 ♔a2 ♛a5 22 ♘b1 [22 a4?? ♛b4] 22...♘b4+ 23 ♔a1 and Black has a perpetual.) 20...♔h8 21 a4!! This move wins. 21...♘c2+ (21...♛a5 22 ♜d2) 22 ♔a2 ♘b4+ (22...♛a5 23 ♛xg6) 23 ♔b1! and White wins as there is not enough power in the battery.

16 ♜d2 ♜e8 17 ♘g1! d5 18 ♘f3 a5

19 e5?!

Better was 19 ♜dh2! dxe4 (19...♘e7 20 ♜h8+!! is rather similar to Spassky's ...♜h1 against Larsen. 20...♗xh8 21 ♜xh8+! ♔xh8 22 ♛h6+ ♔g8 23 ♘g5 and White is about to checkmate.) 20 ♘xe4 f5 21 ♘c3 ♘xd4 22 ♘e5 White wins.

19...♘e7 20 ♗h3

20 ♘a4 was not a clear win, though White is better after 20...♘f5 21 ♛f4 ♛e7.

20...c5 21 dxc5

Black has only two pawns, but the path for his d-pawn is open. If 21 ♜dh2 ♘c6.

21...♛c7 22 ♛f4 ♘c6! 23 ♜e1 d4

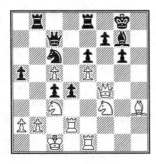

24 ⪼xd4

I knew Smyslov played 24 ⪻e4, but here Black gets nice play after 24...⪻xe5 25 ⪻f6+ ⪻xf6 26 ⪻xe5 c3.

24...⪻xd4

Black recovers the exchange. Although the material no longer favours White, he still has a dangerous attack.

25 ⪻xd4!

After 25 ⪼xd4 ⪼b7 26 ⪼f2 ⪻h6+ 27 ⪸b1 ⪼ed8 28 c6! ⪼xc6 29 ⪻g2 the position is balanced.

25...⪼xc5 26 ⪻f3! ⪼ed8

If 26...⪼b6 27 ⪼e2 ⪼ed8 and I preferred Black's position even a good two decades ago.

27 ⪻g5! ⪼e7?

White has no more than a draw after 27...⪼d7 28 ⪻xe6 fxe6 29 ⪼h2 ⪻h8.

28 ⪼h4 ⪼d3 29 ⪼h7+

Here I started to have problems with my time. The situation has changed, so, just like Smyslov, I might have considered 29 ⪻ce4! Sometimes I copied the champions too much, sometimes not enough. They should have written instructions on their games. If you buy a television you get a manual. 29...⪻xe5! I missed this move in my 1983 *Informant* analysis. (29...c3 30 ⪼f1! ⪼b4 [30...⪼b6

31 ⪼h7+ ⪸f8 32 ⪻xf7! wins.] 31 ⪼h7+ ⪸f8 32 ⪼xf7+ [32 ⪼xg7+ ⪸xg7 33 ⪼xf7+ ⪸h8 34 ⪼h7+ ⪸g8 35 ⪻f6+ ⪸f8 36 ⪻xe6 mate] 32...⪸e8 33 ⪻f6+ ⪸d8 34 ⪻xe6+ ⪸c8 35 ⪼c7 mate) 30 ⪼h7+ ⪸f8 31 ⪼f1 ⪼c3+!! This incredible move saves Black. 32 bxc3 ⪼a3+ 33 ⪸d1 ⪼d8+ 34 ⪻d2 ⪼xd2+ and Black has a perpetual.

29...⪸f8 30 ⪻xe6+ fxe6 31 ⪼f1+ ⪸e8 32 ⪼g8+ ⪻f8

33 ⪼xg6+

I did not see the possibility of 33 ⪻d5!! which forces a draw. Then 33...⪸d7 taking the pawn would lead to the same perpetual. (33...exd5 34 ⪼xf8+ ⪼xf8 35 ⪼e6+ ⪼e7 36 ⪼g8+; 33...⪼xd5 34 ⪼xf8+ ⪼xf8 35 ⪼xe6+) 34 ⪻xe7 ⪻h6+ 35 ⪸c2 ⪼xg8 36 ⪻xg8 ⪼xh3 and the endgame should end in a draw.

33...⪸d8 0-1

Here I lost on time. Maybe I spent too much time trying to work out the similarities between this game and Smyslov's. But the position is lost anyway.

For example: 34 ⪻xe6 ⪼b4! (After 34...⪼b6 35 ⪼g8! ⪼xc3+ 36 ⪸b1! ⪼xb2+! 37 ⪸xb2 ⪼a3+ 38 ⪸b1 ⪼b3+ draws nicely.) 35 ⪻a4 (If 35 ⪻d1 ⪼d2+ 36 ⪸b1 ⪼f3! 37 ⪼g1 [37 ⪼h1

♜f2] 37...♜f2 Black wins.) 35...♛d2+ (Or 35...♝e7! 36 ♗f5 ♛xa4.) 36 ♔b1 ♜f3 37 ♜c1 ♝h6.

Black wins.) 19...♜e8 20 ♛f1 and Black is doing fine here.

17 exf6 ♛xf6 18 ♘b3

See diagram on page 159.

G.Kasparov – J.Lautier
Linares 1994

1 e4 e5 2 ♘f3 ♘c6 3 ♗c4 ♗c5 4 c3 ♘f6 5 d3 d6 6 ♗b3 h6 7 h3 a6 8 ♘bd2 ♗e6 9 ♗c2 ♗a7 10 ♛e2 ♛e7

Black intentionally holds back castling.

11 b4! d5 12 a4 b5! 13 0-0 0-0 14 axb5 axb5

15 d4

Opening up the centre doesn't favour White, and other options offer nothing either. If 15 ♗b2 ♜fd8; 15 exd5 ♘xd5 16 ♗b2 ♘f4 17 ♛e4 ♗d5.

15...exd4

Not 15...dxe4? when 16 ♘xe5 is better for White.

16 e5

Other moves were also harmless for Black.

16...dxc3!?

I saw that Black has time to step aside with 16...♗d7!. Then 17 cxd4 (17 ♜e1 dxc3!) 17...♗xd4! 18 ♜xa8 (18 ♛d3 ♗xe5 wins) 18...♜xa8 19 ♜e1 (19 ♘xd4 ♘xd4 20 ♛d3 ♛xe5 and

Remembering Smyslov's example I retained the piece, but other continuations, like 18 ♛d3 g6, offered nothing but gloom.

18...♘xb4

Four pawns may not be one too many. White has chances to block them as there are holes on Black's queenside.

19 ♗b1

After 19 ♗e3 ♗xe3 20 fxe3 ♘xc2 21 ♛xc2 b4 22 ♘fd4 ♛g5 favours Black; 19 ♗a3 ♘xc2 20 ♛xc2 ♜fd8 and the d-pawn can't be blocked.

19...d4!

Not 19...c5? 20 ♗a3.

20 ♜xa7?!

In such a complicated position it is natural that players cannot always find the best moves. The best choice was 20 ♗a3! This extremely complicated position could take pages of analysis, but for now I'll just show the best defence for White. 20...d3 21 ♗xd3 (21 ♛e4 ♗xb3 22 ♗xb4 ♗xf2+! 23 ♔xf2 ♜xa1 24 ♗xd3 ♛b6+ 25 ♔g3 f5 26 ♛e7 ♛g6+ 27 ♔h2 White is still in the game.) 21...♘xd3 22 ♗xf8 ♘f4! 23 ♕xb5 ♘xh3+! 24 ♔h1 ♘xf2+ 25 ♔g1 and White is still alive.

20...c2

Good is 20...♖xa7! 21 ♘bxd4 (21 ♘fxd4? ♗c4 22 ♕e4 ♕g6! 23 ♘f5 c5!) 21...♖a1! 22 ♕e4 ♕g6! 23 ♕xg6 fxg6 24 ♘xe6 ♖f6 and White is in trouble.

21 ♖xa8 cxb1=♕ 22 ♖xf8+ ♔xf8

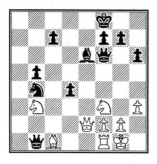

23 ♕xb5??

This is a bad mistake or should we say that it misses the opportunity to play a great move. The position was so exciting that I forgot about Smyslov completely. The surprise is 23 ♗g5!! ♕fg6 (23...♕xf1+ 24 ♕xf1 hxg5 25 ♕xb5 ♘d5 26 ♘bxd4!=) 24 ♕xb5 ♔g8 25 ♕b8+ (25 ♖xb1 ♕xb1+ 26 ♔h2 ♕xb3 27 ♘xd4 White is a pawn behind, but it is not easy to do anything with the extra pawn.) 25...♔h7 26 ♖xb1 ♕xb1+ 27 ♔h2 ♘a6 28 ♕a7 ♕xb3 29 ♘xd4 ♕c4 Despite Black's extra material White can resist.

23...♕xb3

White has only a rook against Black's queen.

24 ♕b8+ ♔e7 25 ♕xc7+ ♔e8 26 ♗d2 ♕d8

Better was 26...♘d3!.

27 ♕e5 ♔f8 28 ♘xd4 ♘d3! 29 ♕e3 ♕c4 0-1

These kinds of positions are harder to play in a rapid game. Maybe that's an excuse for my loss. Because it was a rapid game our analysis was limited.

V.Kramnik – G.Kasparov
PCA Intel-Grand Prix, Moscow 1994

1 ♘f3 ♘f6 2 c4 g6 3 ♘c3 ♗g7 4 e4 d6 5 d4 0-0 6 ♗e2 e5 7 d5 ♘bd7 8 ♗e3 ♘g4 9 ♗g5 f6 10 ♗h4 h5 11 ♘d2 ♘h6 12 f3 ♘f7 13 ♕c2 ♗h6 14 0-0-0 c5 15 dxc6?!

15 ♔b1 came into consideration.

15...bxc6

16 ♔b1 a5

Better was 16...♘c5!.

17 ♘a4 c5 18 ♘c3 ♗e3?

There is no need to think about moving the bishop to d4.

19 ♘d5 ♗d4 20 ♘b3 ♗b7 21 ♘xd4 cxd4 22 f4 ♖b8 23 ♖hf1 ♘h6 24 c5!? ♗xd5 25 exd5 ♘f5

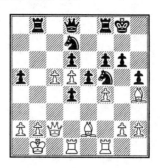

26 fxe5!

Kramnik sacrifices a piece. His pawns are closer to promotion than those of Smyslov's opponents.

26...♘xh4

If 26...♘xe5 27 ♖xf5 gxf5 28 c6.

27 exd6 ♘e5 28 ♖xd4

See diagram on page 160.

28...♘f5

After 28...♖b4 29 ♖xb4 axb4 30 ♕e4 ♘f5 31 ♕xb4 the five queenside pawns might be too much to handle even for Smyslov.

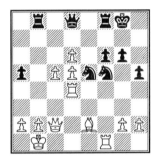

29 ♖xf5! gxf5 30 ♕xf5

Black has a rook for the pawns, but it is hard to make a breach.

30...♔g7

After 30...♖b4 31 ♕e6+ ♔h8 (31...♘f7 32 ♖xb4 axb4 33 d7 [33 ♗xh5 is also sufficient.] White must be winning, e.g. 33...♔g7 34 ♗xf7 ♖xf7 35 c6) 32 ♖xb4 axb4 33 ♕e7! and White's pawns will soon move forward decisively.

31 ♗xh5 ♖h8?

The rook shifts out of play. It was not at all hopeless for Black after 31...♖b4! 32 ♖d2! (32 ♖xb4 axb4 33 ♕e6 ♕a5!) 32...♕c8 33 ♕xc8 ♖xc8 34 c6 ♘c4 and he is still alive and kicking.

32 ♖g4+! ♔f8

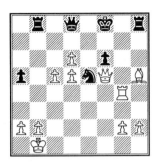

33 ♕e6! ♖b7 34 c6

White's central pawns are just too much to bear.

34...♖xb2+

The rook sacrifice causes some tension, but not much else.

35 ♔xb2 ♕b6+

36 ♔a3!

The king moves up and finds a shelter near the central pawns.

36...♕c5+ 37 ♔a4 ♕c2+ 38 ♔b5 ♕b2+ 39 ♔a6 ♕e2+ 40 ♔b7 ♖h7+ 41 d7 1-0

After all these losses I gave up trusting in the piece against connected passed pawns. The following position occurred in my game against Radjabov at Linares 2003.

G.Kasparov – T.Radjabov
Linares 2003

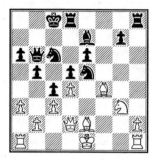

Radjabov has just sacrificed a piece on e5 and in the game I decided not to take it but play 22 ♕e3. However 22 ♗xe5!? ♘xe5 23 dxe5 ♕c7 24 0-0-0 would have given White a clear advantage. I had lost confidence so much in Smyslov's piece against connected passed pawns method, that I did not opt for this possibility which promised a winning position. Black has only two pawns for the piece. Later I even blundered and lost. This painful game prevented me from winning Linares one more time.

Smyslov also influenced me with a lovely checkmate of his opponent's centralised king, just like Tal did.

Here is that sweet finish!

V.Smyslov – L.Oll
Rostov 1993

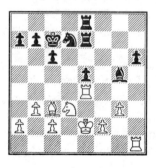

26...♔d6
The young Estonian grandmaster centralises his king.

27 ♖d1 ♔e6 28 f4 ♔f5
Black's king is very active.

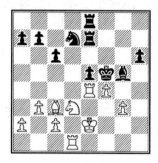

29 g4+!!
People who burn the candle at both ends live shorter lives.

29...♔xe4 30 ♘f2+! ♔xf4

31 ♖g1! 1-0
Smyslov allows Lembit to decide whether he wants to be checkmated by the bishop or the knight, but he has no say as to how many moves it will take to do the deed. Smyslov was 72 when he set up this lovely checkmate.

Vassily is the oldest living world champion. Though I have suffered from his influence, I wish him an even longer and very healthy life.

Mikhail Botvinnik the 6th

Mikhail Botvinnik was the first world champion who did not defeat his immediate predecessor, Alekhine, in a title match. Botvinnik convincingly won the title of world champion in a 5-player match-tournament in 1948, in which he played all his rivals four times. He scored 14 points out of a possible 20, beating each opponent in their individual match. Thereafter, in duels with Bronstein, Smyslov and Tal, he retained his title only by drawing – or winning return matches! But when he lost to Petrosian in 1963, FIDE denied him the right of a re-match and he was finally dethroned.

Botvinnik retired from active play in 1970 but continued working on computer chess programs, something he had started much earlier. He also opened his own school for teaching juniors and I was one of his pupils. He influenced my play not only as a great player but as a trainer as well.

Botvinnik liked to play on the edge of the board, especially the h-file. Though I won games with this method I also lost some. On the right is a position I remember so well. The patriarch attacked on the h-file while his opponent played along the g-file – and in the two positions below I tried to copy Botvinnik's method.

A.Ilyin Zhenevsky – M.Botvinnik

P.Svidler – G.Kasparov

I.Sokolov – G.Kasparov

A.Ilyin Zhenevsky – M.Botvinnik
USSR Championship, Moscow 1927

1 e4 e6 2 ♘c3 d5 3 g3 dxe4

White applies little pressure in the opening.

4 ♗g2 ♗d7 5 ♘h3 ♗c6 6 0-0 ♘d7 7 ♘xe4 ♘gf6 8 d3 ♗e7 9 ♘f4 0-0 10 ♗d2 e5 11 ♘xf6+ ♘xf6

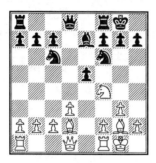

12 ♗xc6

White finally doubles Botvinnik's pawns on the queenside. In exchange Black has a small space advantage.

12...bxc6 13 ♘g2 ♕d7 14 ♘e3 ♘d5 15 ♘c4 f6 16 ♗e3 ♖ae8 17 a3 a6 18 ♔g2 ♗d6 19 f3 f5 20 ♗g1

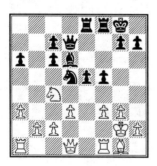

20...♖f6!

Botvinnik slowly but surely builds up an attack on the kingside.

21 ♕e2 h5! 22 ♔h1 h4 23 gxh4

White opens the g-file for himself and the h-file for Botvinnik.

23...♘f4 24 ♕d2 ♖h6 25 ♗e3 ♖xh4

See diagram on page 169.

26 ♗xf4 ♖xf4 27 ♖ae1 ♕f7 28 ♕g2 ♕h5 29 ♖e3 ♖e6 30 ♖g1

30...♕h6

Defending the g7 pawn while assisting his own attack on the h-file.

31 b4 ♖h4

Botvinnik neatly brings up more fire-power to the h-file.

32 ♕e2 ♕f4 33 ♕g2?

White hopes to attack on the g-file, Botvinnik repulses the move nicely.

33...♖g6!

Cute and effective.

34 ♕f2 e4! 35 ♘xd6 ♖xh2+!
36 ♕xh2 ♖h6 37 ♖e2 ♕xf3+ 38 ♖eg2

38...♖xh2+

White survives the attack but has to settle for a lost ending.

39 ♔xh2 ♕h5+ 40 ♔g3 cxd6
41 dxe4 ♕g4+ 42 ♔f2 ♕f4+ 43 ♔e2
♕xe4+ 44 ♔d2 ♕d4+ 45 ♔e2

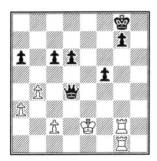

45...♔f7

Black's two connected passed pawns are too much to cope with. Winning the game takes time but is never in doubt.

46 ♖g6 ♕c3 47 ♔d1 d5 48 ♖6g3
♕d4+ 49 ♔e2 ♕e4+ 50 ♔d2 ♕f4+
51 ♔e2 ♕h6 52 ♖1g2 g6 53 a4 f4
54 ♖c3 g5 55 b5 ♕h5+ 56 ♔d2 cxb5
57 axb5 axb5 58 ♖c7+ ♔f6 59 ♖c6+
♔f5 60 ♖c5 ♕f7 61 ♖xb5 g4 62 c4 f3
63 ♖g1 f2 64 ♖f1 g3 65 ♖xd5+ ♔g4
66 ♖d4+ ♔h3 0-1

I also like to attack on the h-file.

P.Svidler – G.Kasparov
Tilburg 1997

1 e4 c5 2 ♘f3 d6 3 c3

This little move is not as harmless for Black as it looks.

3...♘f6 4 ♗e2 ♘bd7 5 d3 b6 6 0-0
♗b7 7 ♘bd2 g6 8 d4!? cxd4 9 cxd4
♘xe4

Black can simply develop, but I could not resist taking the central pawn.

10 ♘xe4 ♗xe4

11 ♘g5 d5

White's attack is very dangerous. The text is probably an 'only move'. Black has no time to retreat the bishop with 11...♗b7? as then comes 12 ♗c4 e6 13 ♗xe6! fxe6 14 ♘xe6 ♕h4 (14...♕c8 15 ♖e1 ♔f7 16 ♕b3 d5 17 ♕f3+ ♘f6 18 ♗g5 ♗e7 19 ♖ac1 ♗c6

20 ♘g7!! ♖f8 21 ♖e6 wins according to Winants.) 15 ♖e1 ♗e7 (15...♔f7

16 ♗g5 ♕h5 17 ♕b3 d5 18 h3!! traps the queen.) 16 ♗g5! ♗xg5 17 g3!! ♕h6 18 ♘xg5+ ♔f8 19 ♕d2! ♔g8 20 ♖e7 ♗c6 21 ♘e6! and White wins according to Peter Svidler's remarkable analysis.

After 11...♗d5 12 ♗f3 ♗xf3 13 ♕xf3 ♘f6 14 ♕c6+ ♘d7 15 ♕d5 e6 16 ♘xe6! (16 ♕f3 ♘f6 17 ♕c6+ ♘d7 18 ♕f3 ♘f6 19 ♕c6+ ♘d7 20 ♕f3 ½-½ Degraeve-Bacrot, France 1996) 16...fxe6 17 ♕xe6+ ♗e7 White stands better. Two of three possible continuations lead nowhere. (17...♕e7 18 ♕d5 ♖b8! 19 ♗g5 ♘f6 20 ♕b3! ♕f7 [20...♕g7 21 ♖fe1+ ♗e7 22 ♖e6±] 21 ♖fe1+ ♗e7 22 ♖e6! 0-0 23 ♖xe7 and White has won a pawn.)

18 ♗g5! ♘f8 (18...♔f8 19 ♗h6+ ♔e8 20 ♖fe1 and White has very nice compensation.) 19 ♕e4 ♖c8 20 ♖fe1 ♖c7 21 ♖ac1 ♖d7! Now all the normal moves do not succeed: 22 ♕f3!! Peter's move is very strong indeed. (22 ♗f6 ♔f7!!) 22...h6 23 ♗xe7 ♖xe7 24 ♖xe7+ ♕xe7 25 ♖c8+ and White wins.

12 ♗b5 ♗g7 13 f3

Here I quote Peter's words from his *Chessbase* analysis: "Then I realized that 13 f3 leads to some very interesting and promising positions and decided

that I should try and have some fun. I know that it doesn't sound the way serious and professional chessplayers are supposed to think during the game, especially if it's a game against the world champion, but that's exactly what I thought. And, after all, it worked."

13...♗f5 14 g4 h6

My plan was based on play along the h-file.

15 gxf5 hxg5 16 fxg6

16...a6!

I was not certain whether my opponent saw this in advance.

17 gxf7+ ♔xf7 18 ♗a4 ♖h5?!

See diagram on page 170.

Trying to force matters on the h-file. 18...♕c7! 19 ♖f2 ♖h4 20 ♗e3 ♖ah8 21 ♖c1 and White can force a draw if he wants (Alternatively 21 ♕d2 b5 22 ♗c2!? ♘b6 23 b3 ♕g3+ also leads to a safe position for Black and in fact after 24 ♖g2 ♖xh2 25 ♖xg3 ♖xd2 26 ♗g6+ ♔xg6 27 ♖xg5+ ♔f7 28 ♖xg7+ ♔xg7 29 ♗xd2 he has a very slight edge.) 21...♖xh2 22 ♖xc7 ♖h1+ 23 ♔g2 ♖8h2+ 24 ♔g3 ♖h3+ 25 ♔g4 ♖h4+ and White must settle for a perpetual as pressing forward would land him in checkmate.

19 ♗e3 ♘f6 20 ♕d2 ♕d6 21 ♖f2

21...♖ah8

I directed all my heavy pieces against the h2 pawn, actually more so than Botvinnik, therefore I was optimistic,

22 ♖g2!

I was not worried about my opponent's play on the g-file, Botvinnik's opponent also had the g-file but got nowhere with it.

22...♖h3?!

I kept attacking when I should have been defending. Botvinnik won so I felt obliged to play for a win as well. 22...♘h7 or 22...♗f6 should have been tried.

23 ♖f1 ♖8h4?

24 ♗c2!

Here I had to realise that my rook on h3 was trapped.

24...♘h5 25 ♗f5 ♘f4 26 ♗xh3 ♘xh3+ 27 ♔h1

Svidler, just like Ilin-Zhenevsky, goes to h1 with his king, so I had reason for hope. In reality, Black simply has insufficient compensation for the pawn.

27...♕f6 28 ♖g3! ♕f5 29 ♗xg5 ♘xg5

After 29...♖xd4 30 ♕g2 ♘xg5 31 ♖xg5 ♕h7 (31...♕f6 32 ♖g1) is given by Winants, then 32 ♖g1 ♗f6 33 ♖h5! wins.

30 ♖xg5

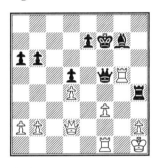

30...♕h3

Black might have hoped for serious counterplay, but not in this case because of the weakness of his own king.

31 ♖g2 ♗f6

If 31...♗xd4 32 ♕d3.

32 ♕d3 ♖xd4 33 ♕g6+ ♔e6 34 ♕e8 ♖c4

After 34...♔d6 comes 35 ♕b8+ ♔c6 36 ♕a8+ ♔b5 37 a4+!

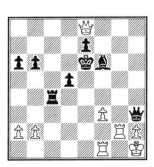

35 ♕d8!

Black's king will stay where it is.

35...♕f5 36 ♖e1+ ♗e5 37 ♕b8

Black loses more material, therefore I resigned.

1-0

This game was not the only time I attacked along the h-file while my opponent was looking for a result along the g-file.

I.Sokolov – G.Kasparov

Hoogovens, Wijk aan Zee 1999

1 d4 ♘f6 2 c4 e6 3 ♘c3 ♗b4

I have never performed really well in the Nimzo – my Psakhis game comes to mind here – but before this game in the tournament I had just won seven games in a row. My opponents were strong grandmasters, but only two of them made it into the top 10. Among these seven Topalov was the strongest.

4 e3

I expected 4 ♕c2 as that is Ivan's main weapon against the Nimzo. I can't be certain why he changed to the 4 e3 line. Maybe he did it because this was Botvinnik's main line.

4...0-0 5 ♗d3 d5 6 ♘f3 c5 7 0-0 ♘c6 8 a3 ♗xc3 9 bxc3 ♕c7 10 ♕c2 dxc4 11 ♗xc4 e5 12 ♗d3 ♖e8 13 e4

This is a sideline.

13...exd4

After 13...c4 14 ♗xc4 exd4 15 cxd4 ♘a5 16 ♗d3 ♕xc2 17 ♗xc2 ♘xe4 18 ♖e1 ♘d6 19 ♗f4 ♘ac4 20 ♗b3 ♗f5 21 ♘e5 ♗e6 22 ♘d3 ♖ad8 23 ♘c5 ♗c8 (23...♗d5?? 24 ♗xd6 wins) 24 ♗xc4 ♘xc4 25 ♗c7 Rogers went on to beat Solomon in Sydney 1999.

14 cxd4 ♗g4 15 e5

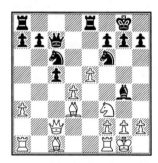

15...♗xf3 16 exf6 ♘xd4 17 ♗xh7+ ♔h8 18 fxg7+ ♔xg7 19 ♗b2 ♖ad8 20 gxf3 ♖h8

See diagram on page 170.

Of course I could select this game under the motif of the doubled f-pawns, but I was hoping to attack on the h-file and I was not worried about the g-file as Botvinnik dealt with this problem well. There was no reason to think that I was not going to handle things equally as well.

21 ♔h1

Just like Ilin-Zhenevsky.

21...♖xh7

Hiding the king with 21...♔f8 and, if necessary, walking over to the queenside, occurred to me. However Botvinnik kept his king on g8, so gave me no hint what to do. He should have told me this in his school.

22 ♖g1+ ♔h8

I decided to step over to the edge. My brain was preoccupied with aggressive ideas along the h-file, not my opponent's play on the g-file.

23 ♖g3 ♕e5

On e5, the queen stops a threat. Not 23...b6? when we see White's threat: 24 ♗xd4+ ♖xd4 25 ♕f5 and wins.

24 ♖ag1

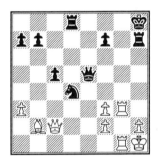

24...♖h4

Ftacnik writes: "The first independent move is very unfortunate, it seems that Black's position instantly becomes hopeless." The Slovak grandmaster did not know that it was not fully independent. I just copied Botvinnik who had put the rook in front and the queen behind. When one attacks a pawn the rook goes in front, however when the king is the target, then often the queen goes in front as an invasion is feasible and it wreaks more

damage. Thus 24...♕h5 25 ♖1g2 f6 (25...♖e8 26 ♕e4 f6 27 ♗c3!) 26 ♕c4 (26 ♕g6 ♕xg6 27 ♖xg6 and White is somewhat better in this endgame.) 26...♕f7 27 ♕xc5! (If 27 ♕d3 ♖h6 28 ♕d2 ♕h7 29 ♕f4 b6?? [29...♖e8 or 29...♖f8 should have been tried.] 30 ♖h3 and White was winning in the game Joshi-Shankar, Mumbai 1999. But Sokolov is thinking of an exchange sacrifice.) 27...♘e2 28 ♕g5 ♖d1+ (28...♘xg3+ 29 fxg3 ♖d6 30 ♖c2 ♖h5 is equally unclear.) 29 ♖g1 ♘xg3+ 30 fxg3 ♖d6 White certainly has compensation for the exchange and Black must be careful. Nevertheless, to be objective, Black may well survive.

25 ♕c1?

Ivan wants to improve his queen, and in the end he does, but he needs some input from me. My opponent missed an almost winning continuation in 25 f4! when White opens the second rank for the queen to get to g2! 25...♕h5 (25...♕d6 26 ♕f5) 26 f3! ♕h6 (26...♖h3 27 ♖g4) 27 ♕g2! ♕f8 28 ♖g7 White overwhelms Black on the g-file. Then 28...♖h6 29 ♕g5 wins.

25...♔h7??

Botvinnik gave no instructions on his game. I lost track of what to do with

175

my king. Anyway I wanted to attack Sokolov's king, not start defending my own. Better was 25...♕h5! 26 ♖1g2 (26 ♖3g2 f6 (26...b6 27 ♕e3 ♕d5 28 ♕e7 wins.) 27 ♕e3 ♖e8 28 ♗xd4 cxd4 29 ♕b3 ♕h7 and though Black is living very dangerously, according to Tsetsarsky, he will get away with it.) 26...♖e8 27 ♕g1 ♕e5 28 ♖g8+ ♖xg8 29 ♖xg8+ ♔h7 30 ♖f8 ♕f4 (30...♕g7 31 ♕b1+! ♔h6 32 ♗c1+ ♔h5 33 ♗e3 and Ftacnik calls it a win at the end of his line.) 31 ♕g8+ ♔h6 32 ♕g2 ♔h7 33 ♕g3 White is better.

26 ♕b1+!

A subtle check forces the king to h8.

26...♔h8

After 26...f5 27 ♗xd4 cxd4 28 ♕xb7+ ♔h8 29 ♕f7! Black gets checkmated.

27 ♕f1

Now Black can't ease the g-file pressure with ...♖g8 as White would take the rook with check. On other moves Black's king will be caught on the g-file.

27...♕e6 28 ♕g2

1-0

Both ♖g8+ and ♖h3!, threatening ♕g7 mate, are menaced. I could have postponed the checkmate for another six moves, but there was no point in doing so. It is remarkable that there are nine Kasparov versus Sokolov games in the database and only one draw, when I was White against Andrei Sokolov in the USSR Championship 1988 – the other 8 times the result was 1-0. In addition I lost to Andrei at the Reykjavik 1988 World Cup where I missed a battery and dropped a piece.

Botvinnik affected my play in many ways. I also picked up his idea in the English Opening of allowing the opponent to push a black pawn to the e3-square and letting him keep it there.

M.Botvinnik – V.Smyslov

G.Kasparov – A.Karpov

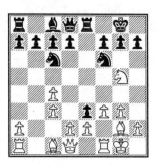

M.Botvinnik – V.Smyslov
USSR Spartakiad, 1964

Until my matches with Karpov these two great players held the record of playing the most games at the very top of world chess. This game was their first since their final match in 1958. In the sixties they played seven games. Botvinnik won two and the rest were drawn. My score after my last match with Karpov produced a somewhat similar picture – relatively few games and one champion who won no more games. I won 5 of the 12 regular games we played together.

1 c4 ♘f6 2 ♘c3 e5 3 g3 ♗b4 4 ♗g2 0-0 5 a3 ♗xc3 6 bxc3 e4

This is quite ambitious.

7 ♘h3 ♖e8 8 0-0 d6 9 ♘f4 b6 10 f3 e3

See diagram on page 176.

Smyslov sacrifices the e-pawn in return for the doubling of White's pawns.

11 d3

Botvinnik doesn't take it – if he had done so, then the game would become unclear. Now the e3-pawn cuts White's camp into two but at the same time it can itself become a target.

11...♗b7 12 ♕e1 ♘bd7

13 g4
Pushing the g-pawn was one of Botvinnik's specialities.

13...h6 14 h4
A pawn move that I also employed regularly.

14...♘f8 15 ♕g3 ♘g6 16 ♘h3 ♘h7 17 h5 ♘h4

It is quite unusual to put a knight on the edge like this, but Smyslov soon makes sure he can rescue it.

18 ♗h1 f5 19 ♗b2 ♕f6

20 f4
White can exploit the fact that the queen is on f6.

20...♗xh1 21 g5 hxg5 22 fxg5 ♕e5 23 ♕xh4 ♗c6 24 ♖f4 g6
Opening the kingside helps White.

25 hxg6 ♘f8

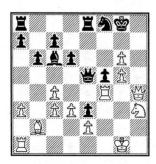

26 ♕h6 ♕g7 27 ♖xf5 ♘xg6 28 ♖af1 ♖f8 29 ♖f6

White has not only exerted pressure against Black's king but has cleared the way to the e3-pawn.

29...♕xh6 30 gxh6 ♖xf6 31 ♖xf6 ♔h7

32 ♗c1

Botvinnik captures the e3-pawn.

32...♖g8 33 ♘g5+ ♔xh6 34 ♗xe3 ♔h5 35 ♖f7

White is now winning easily.

35...♖e8 36 ♖h7+ ♔g4 37 ♔f2 ♘e7 38 ♘e6 ♘f5 39 ♘d4 ♘xd4?!

Smyslov makes sure he loses. After 39...♘xe3 40 ♘xc6 ♘d1+ 41 ♔e1 ♘xc3 42 ♔d2 ♘xe2 43 ♖xc7 Black struggles with his cut-off king.

40 cxd4 ♖c8 41 d5 ♗a4 42 ♗d4 a6

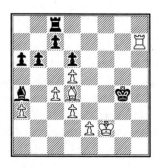

43 e4 c5?

Black is lost anyway.

44 ♗f6 1-0

Black resigned as White will deliver checkmate.

G.Kasparov – A.Karpov
Game 2, World Championship,
Seville 1987

1 c4 e5 2 ♘c3 ♘f6 3 ♘f3 ♘c6 4 g3 ♗b4 5 ♗g2 0-0 6 0-0 e4 7 ♘g5 ♗xc3 8 bxc3 ♖e8 9 f3 e3!?

See diagram on page 176.

A novelty in this particular position. It was Igor Zaitsev's idea.

10 d3!

I could have taken but I knew Botvinnik's game, he had beaten such a great player as Smyslov. Why not just follow him?

10...d5

Karpov plays differently.

11 ♕b3

I changed sides because Karpov was playing on a different flank. I was able to adjust.

11...♘a5 12 ♕a3 c6 13 cxd5 cxd5 14 f4 ♘c6 15 ♖b1 ♕c7 16 ♗b2 ♗g4

178

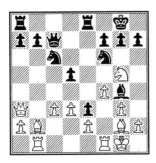

17 c4

After 17 ♘f3 ♕d7 18 ♗a1 ♖e7!?
19 ♖fc1 ♗h3 20 c4 White is a bit better.
17 ♖fe1! and White has an edge
according to Karpov and I. Zaitsev.

17...dxc4 18 ♗xf6

Doubling the f-pawn, as we know, is
a tricky matter.

18...gxf6 19 ♘e4 ♔g7

After 19...♖xe4!? 20 ♗xe4 f5!
21 ♗f3 ♘d4 22 dxc4 ♗xf3 23 exf3 e2
24 ♖fe1 ♕xc4 Black is safe.

20 dxc4

This is an inaccuracy. I thought I was
getting closer to the e3-pawn – just like
Botvinnik.

a) If 20 ♕c3 ♕d8! (not 20...♕e7
21 ♖xb7).

b) 20 h3 ♗xe2 21 ♘xf6 ♗xf1
22 ♕c3 ♖e5! and with this beautiful
move Black takes charge.

c) 20 ♘d6 Karpov and Zaitsev show
a very nice way to a perpetual, and I
should have gone for it. 20...♖e6
21 ♘xc4 ♖d8 22 f5 ♖ee8 23 ♖b2 ♘d4
24 ♖xb7 ♘xe2+ 25 ♔h1

25...♘xg3+! 26 ♔g1! (26 hxg3?
♕xg3 wins) 26...♘e2+ (26...♘xf1
27 ♖xc7 e2 28 ♕xa7 e1=♕ 29 ♖xf7+
♔h6 30 ♖xf6+! ♔g5 31 ♕g7+ ♔f4
32 ♕h6 mate) 27 ♔h1 ♘g3+.

20...♖ad8 21 ♖b3 ♘d4

22 ♖xe3

Finally I took the pawn, but there
are too many pieces left on the
board, many more than in Mikhail
Moiseevich's game.

22...♕xc4

After 22...♘c2 23 ♕c3 ♘xe3
24 ♕xf6+ ♔f8 25 ♕h6+ ♔e7
they miss the precise check 26 ♕g5+!
which covers the c5-square. (26 ♕f6+
♔d7) 26...♔d7 27 ♘c5+ and White is
in the game.

**23 ♔h1 ♘f5 24 ♖d3 ♗xe2 25 ♖xd8
♖xd8 26 ♖e1 ♖e8**

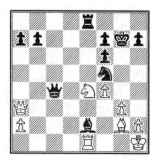

27 ♕a5

After 27 ♘d6 ♘xd6 28 ♕xd6 ♗f3!! and the battery exploits the weakness of the back rank.

27...b5 28 ♘d2 ♕d3 29 ♘b3

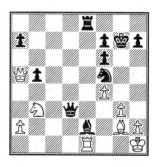

29...♗f3!! 30 ♗xf3 ♕xf3+ 31 ♔g1 ♖xe1+ 32 ♕xe1 ♘e3 0-1

To make things even more annoying, with Black I pushed my e-pawn all the way to e3 in a 1982 game against Romanishin. Do you know what happened? I lost the following position as well!

O.Romanishin – G.Kasparov
USSR 1982

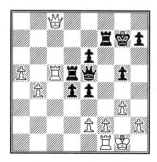

32...e3 33 f4 gxf4 34 ♖xf4 ♖xf4 35 gxf4 ♕f5 36 ♖xd5 ♕xd5 37 ♕c7+ ♔g6 38 ♕c2+ ♔f6 39 a6 ♕a8 40 ♕c4 ♕e4 41 ♕c5 ♕b1+ 42 ♔g2 ♕d1 43 ♕g5+ ♔f7 44 ♕h5+ ♔g7 45 a7 1-0

One of my specialties was to push my g- and especially my h-pawn. I won games with both, but sometimes the idea backfired. First I show you a diagram of the inspirational Botvinnik game and then, on the next page, my games.

M.Botvinnik – A.Pomar

N.Short – G.Kasparov

V. Anand – G.Kasparov

M.Botvinnik – A.Pomar
IBM, Amsterdam 1966

1 c4 c6 2 ♘c3 d5 3 cxd5

Though I played a few Exchange Slavs and French defences, these variations do not suit my style. By the way I beat Dolmatov in an Exchange Slav. I didn't select my loss against him for this book but he did beat me in a Youth tournament in the USSR in 1977. I set up a battery but it very quickly lost. The opening of the Botvinnik game did not catch my imagination but the game did.

3...cxd5 4 d4 ♘f6 5 ♘f3 ♘c6 6 ♗f4 ♗f5 7 e3 e6 8 ♗b5 ♗b4 9 ♘e5 ♕a5 10 ♗xc6+ bxc6 11 0-0 ♗xc3 12 bxc3 ♖c8 13 c4 0-0 14 g4

See diagram on page 180.

Going after the bishop also occurs in this line, sometimes Black can even do this to White, one example being Seirawan-Beliavsky, Brussels 1988.

That game went like this: 1 d4 d5 2 c4 c6 3 ♘c3 ♘f6 4 cxd5 cxd5 5 ♗f4 ♘c6 6 e3 ♗f5 7 ♘f3 e6 8 ♗b5 ♘d7 9 0-0 ♗e7 10 ♗xc6 bxc6 11 ♖c1 ♖c8 12 ♘a4

12...g5! 13 ♗g3 h5 14 h3 g4 15 hxg4 hxg4 16 ♘e5 ♘xe5 17 ♗xe5 f6 18 ♗g3 ♔f7 19 ♖e1 ♖h5 20 ♕d2 ♗e4 21 ♔f1 ♗f3 0-1.

14...♗g6 15 c5 ♘e4 16 f3 ♘d2 17 ♖f2 ♘c4

Black saves the bishop, but it will remain rather passive.

18 ♘xc4 dxc4

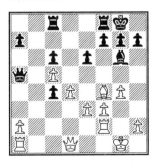

19 ♗d6

The bishop targets nothing but still it is very useful as it keeps both black rooks very passive.

19...♖fe8 20 e4 f5 21 ♕c2 fxe4 22 fxe4 ♕a3 23 ♖e1 ♕h3 24 ♖g2 ♖cd8 25 ♖g3 ♕h6 26 ♕xc4 ♕d2 27 ♕c3 ♕xa2

Black wins back the pawn, but material often doesn't count in opposite coloured bishops middlegames. White's pieces are pretty active.

28 ♖g2 ♕a6

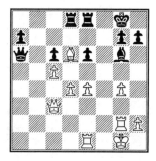

29 h4

Pushing the h-pawn is a nice plan and further restricts the bishop.

29...♖d7 30 h5 ♗f7 31 ♖a1 ♕c8 32 ♕f3 ♕d8 33 g5 g6

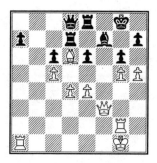

34 h6

Botvinnik's h- and g-pawns are suffocating the Spanish grandmaster.

34...e5 35 ♗xe5 ♖b7 36 ♕f4 a5 37 ♖f2 ♗b3 38 d5 cxd5 39 c6

Botvinnik chooses to win with the c-pawn. He could have triggered an execution on the long diagonal as well.

39...♗a7 40 c7 ♕e7

41 ♗d6 1-0

N.Short – G.Kasparov
Game 16, PCA-World Championship,
London 1993

1 e4 c5 2 ♘f3 d6 3 d4 cxd4 4 ♘xd4 ♘f6 5 ♘c3 a6 6 ♗c4 e6 7 ♗b3 b5 8 0-0 ♗e7

I tried several set-ups against the Sozin, but this was my final choice in the match.

9 ♕f3 ♕c7 10 ♕g3 ♘c6 11 ♘xc6 ♕xc6 12 ♖e1 ♗b7 13 a3

13...♖d8! 14 f3

The standard sacrifice 14 ♘d5? need not worry Black, e.g. 14...exd5 15 exd5 ♘xd5 16 ♕xg7 ♔d7 17 ♕xf7? (17 ♕g4+ ♔c7 18 ♗xd5 ♕xd5 19 ♖xe7+ ♔b8 Black is very active.) 17...♖de8 18 ♗g5 ♖hg8! 19 ♗xe7

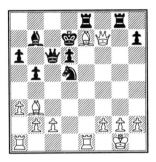

19...♖xg2+!! Black finds an effective way to destroy White's king. 20 ♔xg2 ♘e3+ 21 ♔g3 ♕g2+ 22 ♔f4 ♕e4+ 23 ♔g5 (23 ♔g3 ♕g4 mate) 23...h6+! 24 ♔xh6 (24 ♔h5 ♕g4+ 25 ♔xh6 ♖h8+ 26 ♕h7 ♘f5 mate; 24 ♔f6 ♕e5+ 25 ♔g6 ♗e4+) 24...♖h8+ 25 ♔g7 ♕h7+ 26 ♔f6 ♕h4+ 27 ♔g7 ♕h6 mate.

14...0-0 15 ♗h6 ♘e8 16 ♔h1 ♔h8 17 ♗g5 ♗xg5 18 ♕xg5 ♘f6 19 ♖ad1 ♖d7 20 ♖d3 ♖fd8 21 ♖ed1

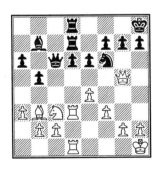

21...♕c5

Black has fully equalised.

22 ♕e3 ♔g8 23 ♔g1 ♔f8 24 ♕f2 ♗a8 25 ♘e2 g6?

I should have exchanged queens and settled for an equal endgame. However I had won the previous game quite convincingly and had not yet lost a single game in the match. All of which made me fall asleep.

26 ♘d4 ♕e5 27 ♖e1 g5

See diagram on page 181.

I advanced my g-pawn further – the same way Botvinnik did so many times.

28 c3 ♔g7

29 ♗c2!

Now Nigel starts softening up my queenside with a strong regrouping of his pieces.

29...♖g8 30 ♘b3 ♔f8 31 ♖d4 ♔e7

My king presented problems on the e7-square not only in this game, but also when I was Black against Kramnik in the Korchnoi-tribute tournament at Zurich 2001.

32 a4! h5 33 axb5 axb5 34 ♖b4 h4 35 ♘d4

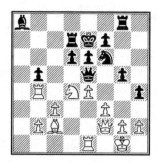

35...g4

It was too late to back down from Botvinnik's pawn onslaught. If 35...♖b8 36 ♗d3.

36 ♖xb5

The unusual queen exchange with 36...♕h2 offered no hope either.

36...d5 37 ♕xh4 ♕h5

After 37...gxf3 38 ♘xf3 ♕h5 39 ♕f2 White wins.

38 ♘f5+! 1-0

V.Anand – G.Kasparov
Frankfurt Giants 1998

1 e4 c5 2 ♘f3 d6 3 d4 cxd4 4 ♘xd4 ♘f6 5 ♘c3 a6 6 ♗e3 ♘g4 7 ♗g5 h6 8 ♗h4 g5

See diagram on page 181.

This is not the Botvinnik-effect as the variation goes like this, but maybe indirectly there is an effect as I was entering a g- and h- pawn pushing line.

9 ♗g3 ♗g7 10 ♗e2

10...h5

Of course I advance my h-pawn.

11 ♗xg4 ♗xg4

I later played the simpler 11...hxg4.

12 f3 ♗d7 13 ♗f2 ♘c6 14 ♕d2 ♘e5

15 b3!

If 15 0-0 then 15...g4! After all, sometimes Mikhail Moiseevich's ideas really work. Two years earlier we had a play-off in the PCA Geneva rapid tournament. In the blitz, improving on our rapid game from the same event, I pushed my g-pawn. I got a fabulous game, yet I spoiled it. 16 f4 ♘c4 17 ♕e2 ♖c8! 18 b3 ♘a3 19 ♘d5 e6 20 ♘b4 ♕a5 21 ♕e1

21...h4! I keep following Botvinnik's play. 22 ♗e3 h3 23 g3 ♘b5 24 ♖d1 ♘c3 25 ♘d3 ♕c7 26 ♖c1 ♘xe4 White has very little for the pawn, yet Black has to play carefully. 27 f5 e5 28 f6 ♘xf6 29 ♘f5 ♗xf5 30 ♖xf5 ♕c6

31 ♕e2 ♕e4 32 ♖f2 ♘d5 33 ♖e1 ♕xe3?? A dreadful mistake. 33...0-0 wins simply. 34 ♕xg4! Suddenly White is winning. 34...0-0 35 ♖xe3 ♘xe3 36 ♕xh3 and though I played on I no longer was in a position to save the game.

15...e6 16 ♘de2! ♖c8 17 ♗d4! b5 18 ♘d1! ♖g8 19 ♘e3! a5

I decided to do what Botvinnik did on the other side of the board as well.

20 0-0-0!

Vishy has handled the opening in great style, but that offers me little consolation. Maybe Botvinnik had mentioned that the opponent could castle on the other side, but he certainly did not emphasise it sufficiently.

20...a4 21 ♔b1 axb3 22 cxb3 ♖a8 23 ♗c3 ♖a6 24 ♘c2 ♗f8 25 ♘b4 ♖a8 26 ♘d4 ♗e7

27 ♖he1

Black's problem is that he can do nothing as any move would expose his own king. But in the long run White will still open up Black's king.

27...♕c8 28 ♗b2 ♕b7 29 ♘dc2 f6 30 ♘d4

30...h4

I have tightened my grip on absolutely nothing! That's because Anand has no pieces on the kingside – and especially not his king.

31 g3 g4

The same push but with a different effect.

32 f4 ♘f3 33 ♘xf3 gxf3 34 f5 hxg3 35 hxg3 ♖xg3 36 ♕h2 ♖g5 37 ♗c1 ♖g7 38 ♕h5+ ♖f7

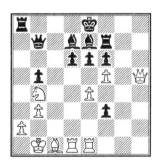

39 ♕xf3 1-0

I resigned as in a moment or two my king will be caught.

Botvinnik's influence came from so many different directions. It is almost impossible to summarise. I'll just show you one more example where, without any fear of losing, I went for a queenless isolated pawn endgame.

G.Veresov – M.Botvinnik

A.Karpov – G.Kasparov

G.Veresov – M.Botvinnik
USSR Championship Semi-Final
Leningrad 1938

1 d4 ♘f6 2 c4 e6 3 ♘c3 ♗b4 4 ♕c2 d5 5 cxd5 exd5 6 ♗g5 ♗e6 7 ♘f3 ♘bd7 8 a3 ♗e7 9 e3 h6 10 ♗h4 0-0 11 ♗e2 c5 12 0-0 ♖c8 13 ♖fc1 a6 14 dxc5

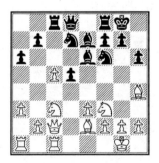

14...♘xc5
Botvinnik had quite a number of nice wins in isolated pawn middlegame positions.
15 b4 ♘ce4 16 ♕d3 ♘xc3

It is an interesting idea to exchange when you have an isolani, but Black's quick play justifies it.
17 ♖xc3 ♖xc3 18 ♕xc3 ♕b6 19 ♕d4 ♕xd4 20 ♘xd4 ♖c8

See diagram above.

Black has solved his problems.
21 f3 ♔f8 22 ♔f1 ♗d7 23 ♗d3

23...g6
I also played this – it covers the f5-square.
24 ♔e2 ♖c3 25 ♔d2 ♖c8 26 ♔e2

♗a4 27 g4 ♘e8 28 ♗xe7+ ♔xe7 29 h4 ♘d6 30 ♔d2

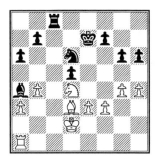

30...♗b5

Karpov also had a similar example, he beat Karasev brilliantly by exchanging pieces to obtain control over the c4-square in a queenless isolated pawn endgame.

31 ♗xb5 axb5 32 ♔d3 ♔d7 33 ♘b3 ♘c4 34 ♘d4 ♖e8 35 ♘c2

After 35 ♘xb5 ♖xe3+ 36 ♔d4 ♖xf3 37 ♔xd5 ♘b6+ 38 ♔e4 ♖h3 39 ♖c1 White is not worse.

35...♘e5+ 36 ♔e2 ♖c8 37 ♘d4

37...♖c3

Botvinnik's rook became annoying.

38 ♖a2?! ♘c4 39 ♘xb5 ♖xe3+ 40 ♔f2 ♖d3 41 ♔e2 ♖b3 42 ♖c2 b6 43 ♖a2 ♖e3+ 44 ♔f2 ♖d3 45 ♔e2 ♖b3 46 ♖a1 ♖e3+ 47 ♔f2 ♖d3 48 h5

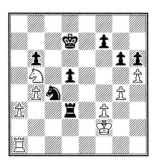

48...d4?!

Botvinnik pushes his pawns, although there were other candidate moves. Possible was 48...g5!? or 48...gxh5 49 ♖h1!? You will see that I have to face a problem like this when my opponent did not automatically recapture after I took his h-pawn. Botvinnik did not mention this possibility in his school.

49 hxg6

Best was 49 g5! Interestingly, Botvinnik missed a similar pawn breakthrough in his book on Karpov. I discovered it and published it first in the Predecessors book. 49...hxg5 (49...♘e5 50 gxh6 ♖xf3+ 51 ♔g2 ♖f5 52 ♖h1 the h- pawn is dangerous.) 50 h6 ♖d2+ 51 ♔g1 ♘e5 52 ♖f1 ♖c2 53 ♘xd4 ♖c8 54 ♔g2 White has an edge.

49...fxg6 50 a4

After 50 ♖e1! ♘xa3 51 ♘xa3 ♖xa3 52 ♖e4.

50...♖d2+ 51 ♔g3 d3

The d-pawn becomes strong. On the other hand I lost to Karpov when I had a d6-pawn with the white pieces. That was the sixth game of our first 1984 match.

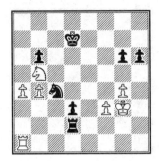

In this game, however, the d-pawn becomes so powerful that it decides the outcome, whereas in the earlier game I just dropped it.

52 a5 bxa5 53 bxa5 ♖b2 54 ♘c3 ♖c2 55 ♘d5??

In my game the same move would have been a mistake by Karpov. After 55 ♘e4! d2 56 ♘xd2 ♖xd2 57 a6 ♘b6 58 a7 ♘a8 59 ♖h1 White holds.

55...d2 56 ♖d1 ♖c1 57 ♘e3 ♔c6 58 ♔f4 ♔b5 59 ♔e4

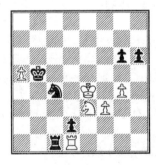

59...h5 60 gxh5 gxh5 61 ♔d3 h4 62 ♔e2 h3 63 ♘g4 ♖xd1 0-1

I trusted Botvinnik so much that I even employed one of his ideas in my very first world title match against Karpov in 1984.

A.Karpov – G.Kasparov
Game 9, World Championship,
Moscow 1984

1 d4 d5 2 c4 e6 3 ♘f3 c5 4 cxd5 exd5

In the Predecessors book I looked at chess culture in general. In this work I do not go into details of the giants other than the champions. Nevertheless do keep in mind that this defence is named after Siegbert Tarrasch.

5 g3 ♘f6 6 ♗g2 ♗e7 7 0-0 0-0 8 ♘c3 ♘c6 9 ♗g5 cxd4 10 ♘xd4 h6 11 ♗e3 ♖e8 12 ♕b3 ♘a5 13 ♕c2 ♗g4 14 ♘f5 ♖c8

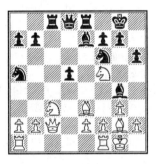

15 ♗d4 ♗c5 16 ♗xc5 ♖xc5 17 ♘e3 ♗e6 18 ♖ad1 ♕c8 19 ♕a4 ♖d8 20 ♖d3 a6 21 ♖fd1 ♘c4 22 ♘xc4 ♖xc4 23 ♕a5 ♖c5 24 ♕b6 ♖d7 25 ♖d4 ♕c7 26 ♕xc7 ♖dxc7

See diagram on page 186.

Just like Karpov I strengthened the c-file, toying with idea of invading on the c-file.

27 h3 h5

Botvinnik paid a lot of attention to gaining space. For this reason, it is a question whether I should put my pawn on the same colour square as Karpov's bishop. If it is a mistake I will have to work out who encouraged me to do this.

28 a3

28...g6

Another pawn goes to the white squares, but Botvinnik played this move as well.

29 e3 ♔g7 30 ♔h2 ♖c4 31 ♗f3 b5 32 ♔g2 ♖7c5 33 ♖xc4

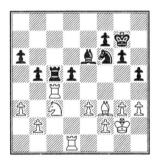

33...♖xc4

I had a chance to recapture with either pawn. 33...dxc4 maintains the balance by dynamic means, which comes to me more naturally, but Botvinnik's game was in my mind and I wanted to follow it. After 33...dxc4 34 ♖d6 a5 35 ♖b6 (35 ♘a2 ♘d5) 35...♘d7 36 ♖xb5 ♖xb5 37 ♘xb5 ♘c5 Black retains a material balance and has a secure position.

34 ♖d4 ♔f8 35 ♗e2 ♖xd4

I should have kept the rooks on, but his rook was a tower of strength on d4. I hoped my d-pawn would work like Botvinnik's.

36 exd4 ♔e7 37 ♘a2 ♗c8

Geller suggested 37...♘e4 which is a Karpov-style move.

38 ♘b4 ♔d6 39 f3 ♘g8 40 h4 ♘h6 41 ♔f2 ♘f5 42 ♘c2 f6 43 ♗d3 g5 44 ♗xf5 ♗xf5

Karpov beat Van der Wiel in Amsterdam 1980 when they had a very similar pawn structure endgame (the pawn islands were the same). Karpov had a bishop versus a knight, but a pair of rooks remained on the board. I thought, okay, I will not win but there was no way I could imagine losing it.

J. van der Wiel – A.Karpov
IBM, Amsterdam 1980

But back to my game...

45 ♘e3 ♗b1 46 b4

Daniel King mentions in his analysis that the position was reminiscent of the game Saidy-Fischer, New York 1964. This was the U.S. Championship where Fischer made 100 percent. Maybe he spent less time investigating the games of the world champions.

46...gxh4?

I missed Karpov's reply, but at least I contributed to the development of endgame theory. Daniel King analyses in depth the position after 46...♗g6. His conclusion is that Black can hold.

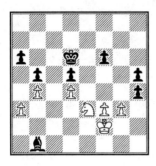

47 ♘g2!

This is against all principles, I did not think that when I have the bishop, and he a knight, that he would open the position. You can see how fair I am, here I could blame my seconds for missing this move. Such a move becomes part of our chess heritage, but why does it happen against me? It would take pages to show you all finesses of this endgame. I'll just show you some interesting points.

47...hxg3+ 48 ♔xg3 ♔e6 49 ♘f4+ ♔f5 50 ♘xh5 ♔e6 51 ♘f4+ ♔d6 52 ♔g4 ♗c2 53 ♔h5 ♗d1 54 ♔g6 ♔e7

55 ♘xd5+?

Taking the pawn is a mistake, as Black's king can cause problems by approaching the queenside. On the other hand 55 ♘h5!! wins. 55...♗xf3 56 ♘xf6. From this point g4-e5-c6-a5-b3-c5 attacks the a6-pawn; then with a king move White will bring the opponent into zugzwang. When Black drops the a6-pawn, then the direct manoeuvre ♘b8-c6-♘a7 forces him to defend the b5-pawn. After any casual king move the knight returns to e3 via c6-e7-f5. If White accomplishes these things, he just has to march to a7 to win the game.

55...♔e6

Better according to Geller was 55...♔d6. He is right.

56 ♘c7+ ♔d7 57 ♘xa6 ♗xf3 58 ♔xf6 ♔d6 59 ♔f5 ♔d5 60 ♔f4 ♗h1 61 ♔e3

61...♔c4

Finally I do something active on the c-file, just like Botvinnik did.

62 ♘c5 ♗c6 63 ♘d3 ♗g2?

Averbakh and Taimanov suggested 63...♗e8! keeping the bishop on this diagonal.

64 ♘e5+ ♔c3 65 ♘g6 ♔c4 66 ♘e7

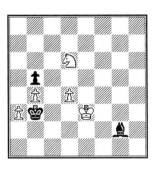

66...♗b7

The amazing move 66...♗h1!! still holds. I thought of this but could not remember any champion playing anything like it before. 67 ♘f5 ♚d5 This is the difference compared with the game: here the ♗h1 stops ♚d3. After 68 ♚f4 ♗e4 69 ♘d6 ♗c2 70 ♘xb5 ♚c4 Black draws.

67 ♘f5 ♗g2?

That damned g2-square in this game! Key moves keep taking place there. 67...♚d5 was the best move, but the legacy of Botvinnik's game is to remain active on the c-file, therefore I did not return with my king.

68 ♘d6+ ♚b3

69 ♘xb5 ♚a4 70 ♘d6 1-0

Botvinnik also set an example that I sadly followed. He trained me and passed on his knowledge. I also gave lectures to young juniors, including Shirov and Kramnik. But Botvinnik undertook coaching only after he had retired, whereas I made the mistake of doing the same thing while I was still an active player. So I helped to improve the play of the champions who dethroned me. What a mistake that was! Had he worked on his own maybe I would have stayed champion for longer. However, when all is said and done, overall I am of course very appreciative of our great first Soviet world champion.

Max Euwe the 5th

Euwe was the last champion still alive when I was born. He and Petrosian were able to form an opinion on my play as they both died in the 1980s when I was already a decent player. Not everyone knows that Euwe won the world title back in 1928. But that was the World Amateur Championship. Later, in 1935, he defeated Alekhine by the narrowest of margins: 15½-14½. Though their rematch began with Euwe dominating, in the sixth game Alekhine commenced a winning streak of three games and convincingly regained his title with a final score of 15½-9½.

In 1946 Euwe still played very well, but the 1948 World Championship final showed that he had lost touch with the very best players of the world. Nevertheless he continued to write many fine articles and books. Though he was an amateur world champion I always considered him to be a true world champion too and began studying his games when I was young – and not only for my Great Predecessors series.

I followed Euwe's play where he cut the position into two with a d5-pawn and paralysed the b7-bishop. Then he gave up the strong d5 pawn.

M.Euwe – A.O'Kelly de Galway

I played the same idea in a very important last round rapid stage of a match against Kramnik. We drew 4 regular games, I won the first rapid and then we drew 4 games.

I show the position of my last rapid game where I should have drawn – and thereby won the match – by adopting Euwe's idea.

This game was extremely important to me because I wanted to prove my superiority over Kramnik after losing the title – and so there was a lot of pride at stake.

G.Kasparov – V.Kramnik

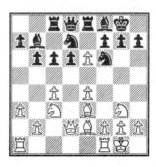

M.Euwe – A.O'Kelly de Galway
Groningen 1946

**1 d4 ♘f6 2 c4 e6 3 ♘c3 ♗b4 4 e3 b6
5 ♘ge2 ♗b7 6 a3 ♗e7**

7 d5

The pawn chokes Black. It is quite hard to undermine it.

7...0-0 8 e4 d6 9 g3 c6 10 dxe6

See diagram on page 192.

White hopes to get play on the e6-square which is why he gives up the strong pawn.

**10...fxe6 11 ♘d4 ♗c8 12 ♗g2 e5
13 ♘f5 ♘a6 14 0-0 ♘c5 15 ♗e3 ♔h8**

16 ♗xc5

Rather a surprise. Euwe voluntarily keeps on taking pieces.

**16...bxc5 17 b4 cxb4 18 axb4 ♗e6
19 ♘e3 a6 20 ♕d3 ♘g4 21 ♘xg4
♗xg4**

22 ♘a4!

In the next few moves the Dutch world champion increases the pressure in a very subtle way.

**22...♕b8 23 ♕c3 ♕a7 24 ♖a2 ♗e6
25 ♖d2 ♖ad8 26 c5 ♕c7 27 cxd6
♗xd6**

28 ♘c5

By now the position has crystallised thanks to very fine positional play by Euwe. Black has two many weak pawns.

**28...♗xc5 29 ♕xc5 ♖xd2 30 ♕xf8+
♗g8 31 ♖a1 ♕b6**

32 ♗f1 ♖b2?

A bad blunder in an inferior position. After 32...♖d4 33 ♖xa6 ♕xb4 34 ♕xb4 ♖xb4 35 f3 Black would suffer with his pawn structure.

33 ♗c4 ♕xf2+ 34 ♕xf2 ♖xf2 35 ♗xg8 1-0

G.Kasparov – V.Kramnik
Botvinnik Memorial 2001

1 d4 ♞f6 2 c4 e6 3 ♞c3 ♗b4 4 e3 b6 5 ♞ge2 ♗b7 6 a3 ♗e7 7 d5

I happily followed the same variation.

7...0-0 8 ♞g3

I too did not allow the g3-square to remain vacant.

8...♖e8 9 ♗e2 ♗f8 10 e4 d6 11 0-0 ♞bd7 12 ♗e3 c6 13 ♕d2 ♖c8 14 dxe6

See diagram on page 192.

Playing 7 d5 was somehow a way of following Euwe, but this is an opening line. On the other hand here it is in black and white that I am behaving like a pupil following his instructions. But I should have been more cautious as, after all, White hereby gives up his centre. But Euwe played this because he appreciated the special circumstances. He did such a tremendous job with his writings, adding significantly to chess culture. How unfortunate he did not publish his analysis here.

14...fxe6

I knew I would not be able to attack e6 like Euwe, but I was able to gain space.

15 f4 ♕e7 16 ♖ad1 ♖cd8 17 ♔h1 ♕f7 18 ♕c2 ♔h8

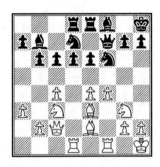

19 b4

Just like Euwe. However, under different circumstances. I wish I knew why Kramnik refrained from placing his knight on c5 earlier. Because of this I was prevented from taking it with the bishop. You know, it's hard to adjust to new situations.

19...e5

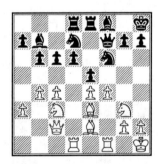

20 ♞f5

Missing the best move because of the desire to obtain a certain type of position against a particular player. It is interesting that before he beat me I called him Vladi. But when he didn't dare to give me a rematch I referred to him as Kramnik. We know language constantly changes, but Russian has not changed that much in the last few years.

My main weapon throughout my career was to stir up complications and because of my special orientation when there was a jungle of variations I outplayed my opponent many times. However after my game with the black pieces against Kramnik at Linares 2000 I realised that I should play for open positions. In our match I did not succeed in getting those positions because of the damned Berlin defence. Later, in the first rapid game of the 2001 Botvinnik Memorial, I managed to beat Kramnik after obtaining an open position, despite the fact that he had an edge early on.

Here, objectively, keeping the position closed with 20 f5! was a better plan. I have never investigated deeply how far the Dutch world champion adapted his way of playing against particular opponents, or whether he played the same way whoever he faced. I see now that I had made a mistake in this game, but why did I receive such harsh punishment?

20...d5 21 exd5 cxd5

22 ♘b5

Maybe White is still okay, but from now on Black is kicking. After 22 fxe5 ♘xe5 23 cxd5 was nice for White and in little danger of losing.

22...♕g6 23 ♗f3 ♖c8 24 ♕b1 e4 25 ♘h4 ♕f7 26 ♗e2 a6 27 ♘c3 dxc4 28 ♕b2

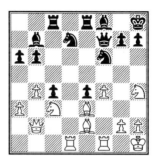

28...b5

I was expecting to create some weaknesses, instead I had to live with a protected passed pawn. Slowly my compensation for the pawn was dissipated.

29 ♘f5 ♘d5 30 ♘xd5 ♕xf5 31 ♘c3 ♘f6 32 h3 ♖cd8 33 ♖xd8 ♖xd8 34 ♖d1

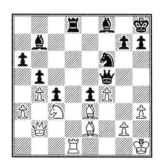

34...♖xd1+

With an extra pawn it is not out of place to exchange. Tigran Vartanovich might have played 34...♖d3.

35 ♗xd1 ♕d7 36 ♗e2 ♗c6 37 ♕c1 g6 38 ♕g1 ♗g7 39 ♗d4 ♔g8 40 ♗e5 ♘d5 41 ♗xg7 ♕xg7

42 ♘xd5 ♗xd5 43 ♕c5 ♕a1+

Putting the queen on the edge of the board is fraught with danger. Better was 43...♕d7.

44 ♔h2 ♗f7 45 ♗g4

If 45 ♕a7 ♕f6 (but not 45...♕xa3?)

45...♔g7

46 ♕c7

I try to pin like Karpov, but for me here it did not work.

46...♕f6 47 ♗d1 h5 48 a4 ♕d4 49 ♗c2 e3 50 f5 e2

51 fxg6 e1=♕ 52 ♕xf7+ ♔h6 0-1

Time and again Euwe was happy giving up the e4-square in the King's Indian. And unfortunately I too didn't mind giving up the e4-square – twice!

G.Fontein – M.Euwe

A.Veingold – G.Kasparov

Kleefstra – M.Euwe

FRITZ X3D – G.Kasparov

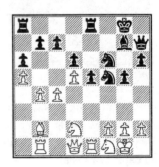

G.Fontein – M.Euwe
Dutch Championship,
Amsterdam 1924

1 d4 ♘f6 2 ♘f3 g6 3 c4 ♗g7 4 ♘c3 0-0 5 e4 d6 6 h3 e5 7 d5 ♘bd7 8 ♗d3 h6 9 ♗e3 ♔h7 10 ♕c2 b6

Players no longer play ...b6 in such positions.

11 0-0 ♘c5 12 ♘e1 ♘h5 13 ♗e2

13...♕h4 14 b4 ♘a6 15 ♘f3 ♕e7 16 ♖ab1 f5 17 exf5

Or 17 ♖fe1 fxe4 18 ♘d2!?.

17...♗xf5 18 ♗d3

See diagram on page 196.

18...♘b8

Playing such a casual move on the other side of the board shows that he is not paying much attention to the e4-square at all.

19 ♘d2 ♘d7 20 ♘ce4

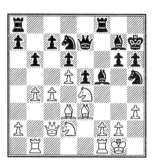

20...♘f4

Black's pieces are alive and the f4-knight has special vitality. Nevertheless White panics by taking the f4-knight, thus opening up the g7 bishop and giving Black the e5-square.

21 ♗xf4 exf4 22 ♘c3 ♗xd3 23 ♕xd3 ♘e5 24 ♕e4 f3! 25 g3

25...♕g5

Euwe plays fluent chess.

26 ♖fd1 ♖ae8 27 ♘b5 ♕d8 28 ♖b3 ♕d7 29 ♔h2 ♖f5 30 g4?

Once more Fontein panics. This time he creates an even bigger problem. 30 ♘d4 ♘xc4 31 ♘e6 ♘xd2 32 ♖xd2 c6 leads to a position in which he is just a pawn down.

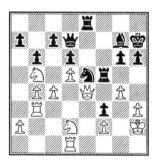

30...♖g5! 31 ♕f4 ♘xg4+ 0-1

This sacrifice wins against any reply by White.

Kleefstra – M.Euwe
Amsterdam Chess Club Championship
1927

1 e4 g6 2 d4 d6 3 ♗e3 ♘f6 4 ♘d2 ♗g7 5 ♗e2 0-0 6 c3 e5 7 d5 ♘bd7 8 ♕c2 b6 9 h3 a5 10 a4 ♘c5

11 ♗xc5?
This is clearly not a testing move.
11...bxc5 12 ♗b5 ♘h5 13 ♘df3 f5 14 ♘e2 fxe4 15 ♕xe4 ♘f4 16 ♘xf4

16...♖xf4
There is no black knight to go to a vacant e5-square. This explains why he captured this way.
17 ♕e2 ♕f6 18 ♘d2

See diagram on page 196.

18...♕f7 19 0-0 ♔h8 20 ♗c4

20...♗b7
Interestingly, Euwe did not mind that both his bishops had very limited prospects on their respective diagonals.
21 ♕d3 ♖f8 22 ♘e4 ♗c8 23 ♘g5 ♕f6 24 ♘e4 ♕f5 25 ♖ae1 ♕h5 26 ♕g3

26...♖h4
Euwe puts his pieces on the edge. I played something similar when I lost to Ivanchuk at Linares in 1991. I did not realise this game might have had an effect in that respect as well. This was the first tournament I did not win for almost a decade. What a pity I was not able to make it a full ten years.

27 ♕g5?
White blunders a piece in a playable position.
27...♕xg5 28 ♘xg5 ♖xc4 0-1

A.Veingold – G.Kasparov
USSR Spartakiad 1979

1 d4 ♘f6 2 ♘f3 g6 3 c4 ♗g7 4 ♘c3 d6 5 e4 0-0 6 ♗e2 e5 7 d5 a5 8 ♗g5 h6 9 ♗h4 ♘a6 10 0-0 ♕e8 11 ♘d2 ♘h7 12 a3 f5

13 exf5

In 1977 I played a game against my trainer Nikitin in which he replied 13 f3. That game ended in a draw.

13...♗xf5

Maybe I should have taken with the g-pawn.

14 g4 ♗d7

See diagram on page 196.

15 ♘de4 a4 16 f3 b6 17 ♗d3 ♗f6 18 ♘xf6+

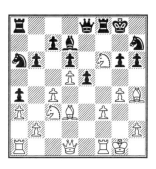

18...♘xf6

My knight never reached h5 as Euwe's had done.

19 ♕d2 ♘c5 20 ♗c2 ♔g7 21 ♖ae1 ♘b3 22 ♕d3

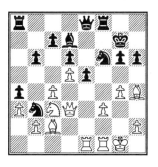

22...g5

There is very little dynamism in Black's position.

23 ♗g3 ♘c5 24 ♕d2 ♕f7 25 h4 ♘h7 26 ♗xh7 gxh4 27 ♗xe5+ dxe5 28 ♗b1

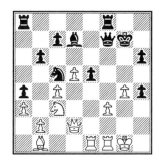

28...♕f4

Defending the king was also an unpleasant choice.

29 ♕xf4 ♖xf4 30 ♖xe5 ♖af8

It looks as though Black has achieved some activity.

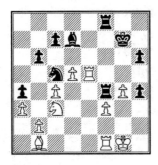

31 ♖e7+

But this check hurts.

31...♖8f7 32 ♖xf7+ ♔xf7 33 ♘e4 ♘b3 34 ♔f2 ♗xg4 35 ♔e3 ♖f5

Stepping into a battery.

36 ♖f2 ♗h5

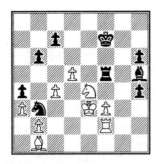

37 ♘d6+ cxd6 38 ♗xf5 ♔f6 39 ♗c2 ♘c5 40 ♖h2 ♔g5 41 ♗d1 1-0

What a miserable defensive game that was!

The Veingold accident happened when I was only 14. Sadly I lost one game like this when those numbers turned around to 41! Everything has advantages and disadvantages – my memory has served me well during my career, but in these games influenced by Euwe it helped only my opponent.

FRITZ X3D – G.Kasparov
Match, New York 2003

1 e4 e5 2 ♘f3 ♘c6 3 ♗b5 ♘f6 4 d3 d6 5 c3 g6

This time the King's Indian pawn structure arises from a Spanish.

6 0-0 ♗g7 7 ♘bd2 0-0 8 ♖e1 ♖e8 9 d4 ♗d7 10 d5 ♘e7

11 ♗xd7

Without the light-squared bishop Black's attack develops more slowly.

11...♘xd7 12 a4 h6 13 a5 a6 14 b4 f5 15 c4 ♘f6 16 ♗b2 ♕d7 17 ♖b1

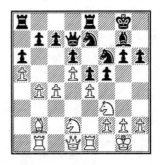

17...g5 18 exf5 ♕xf5 19 ♘f1 ♕h7 20 ♘3d2 ♘f5

See diagram on page 196.

21 ♘e4 ♘xe4 22 ♖xe4 h5 23 ♕d3 ♖f8 24 ♖be1 ♖f7

25 ℤ1e2

This is not very natural, yet it defends f2 satisfactorily.

25...g4 26 ♕b3 ℤaf8 27 c5 ♕g6 28 cxd6 cxd6 29 b5 axb5 30 ♕xb5 ♗h6 31 ♕b6 ♔h7 32 ♕b4 ℤg7?

Euwe also put his rook and queen on the g-file, however in this particular position I drop a pawn.

33 ℤxe5!

Chopping off my pawn! If the electricity had gone off maybe the blackout would have driven the chips of the computer crazy and they might have missed this tactical shot. But no such luck for me.

33...dxe5 34 ♕xf8 ♘d4?!

In a bad position this merely hastens the end.

35 ♗xd4 exd4 36 ℤe8 ℤg8 37 ♕e7+ ℤg7 38 ♕d8 ℤg8

39 ♕d7+ 1-0

Alexander Alekhine the 4th

Alekhine is the last champion to be born in the 19th century. He beat José Raúl Capablanca by 6-3 in 1927. Maybe that match generated the greatest interest of all matches until World War Two. Looking back, that duel still attracts my interest like few other matches in the whole history of chess. Alekhine won the all-Russian Championship in 1909 for the first time. I won it in a tie with Karpov in 1988 and on my own in 2004.

In the late 1920s and early 1930s he enjoyed one of the strongest periods of domination in chess history. Alekhine and Capablanca (probably it is more precise to say Alekhine) avoided each other for nine years and their next game took place only in 1936. In fact they played only three more games against each other. In 1935 he lost his title to Euwe, however two years later he took his revenge and beat him 15½-9½. He died in 1946 in Portugal. As Fischer played a rematch with Spassky, I am the only player who retired as world number 1, while Alekhine is my only predecessor who died as the defending champion.

Maybe there is a similarity between his play and mine. Both of us are very hard to follow. Even so I tried to use some of his ideas.

Alekhine was such an imaginative player, playing some stunning attacks, but, interestingly, the strongest effect he had on me was positionally: freezing the Slav bishop on the kingside, opening the position in the centre and then forcing a win on the queenside where Black misses his Slav bishop.

A.Alekhine – E.Bogolyubov

G.Kasparov – GENIUS

A.Alekhine – E.Bogolyubov
Game 5, World Championship,
Germany/Holland 1929

1 d4 d5 2 c4 c6 3 ♘f3 ♘f6 4 ♘c3 dxc4 5 a4 ♗f5 6 ♘e5 e6 7 ♗g5 ♗e7 8 f3 h6 9 e4 ♗h7 10 ♗e3

See diagram on page 202.

10...♘bd7 11 ♘xc4 0-0 12 ♗e2

12...c5

This is a difficult decision. In a way it helps, as Black exchanges the d4-pawn, plays e5 and f6 and the bishop may come back. Then, with the control over the b4 and b3 squares, the flow of play could go Black's way. On the other hand this may prompt the following plan: by opening the queenside and exchanging a number of pieces he will effectively have an extra piece with which to invade the queenside. Let's have a look to see whose strategy prevails.

13 dxc5 ♗xc5 14 ♗xc5!

The fewer pieces on the queenside, the easier it is to invade.

14...♘xc5 15 b4 ♘a6

16 ♕xd8!

White is happy to keep on exchanging – normally that would just help the opponent develop.

16...♖fxd8 17 ♘a2 ♘b8 18 ♔f2 ♘c6 19 ♖hd1

Intending to exchange even more pieces.

19...♘d4 20 ♖ac1 ♔f8 21 ♗f1 ♘e8 22 ♘c3 f6

Black's last three moves indicate that he clearly wants to bring the bishop into play.

23 ♘a5 ♖ab8

24 ♘b5!

Further exchanging.

24...♘xb5 25 ♖xd8!

Enviable dedication to the task.

25...♖xd8

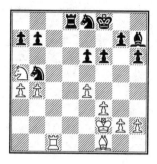

26 ♘xb7!

He is not only playing a great strategic game, but the tactics are on Alekhine's side too.

26...♖b8 27 ♘c5 ♚e7 28 axb5

It was not necessary to accept the doubled pawns. After 28 ♗xb5 ♘d6 29 ♘a6 ♖b7 30 ♗c6 wins.

28...♘d6 29 ♖a1 ♘c8 30 ♗c4 ♗g8 31 f4 ♗f7 32 e5

Alekhine pushes his opponent back.

32...fxe5 33 fxe5 ♖b6 34 ♚e3 ♗e8 35 ♖a5 ♗d7

The bishop finds another diagonal but it is not too active here either.

36 ♚d4 ♗e8 37 h4 ♗d7 38 ♗e2 ♖b8

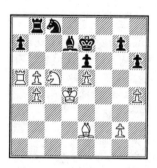

39 ♘xd7!

In order to invade, he keeps on exchanging. Now, when I analyse this game, it occurs to me that maybe Fischer too was copying the other champions! How many congratulations he received for his win over Petrosian, but it may have just been a copy, almost plagiarising Alekhine when he took a bishop with his knight on d7! If there is a reprint of *My Great Predecessors* I may add an extra comment on that.

39...♚xd7 40 ♗f3 ♖b6 41 ♚c5 ♖b8 42 h5 ♚d8 43 ♗c6 ♚e7 44 ♖a3 ♚f7 45 ♗e4 ♚e7

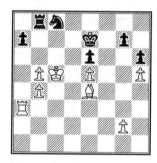

46 ♚c6

Finally the world champion invades nicely with his king.

46...♚d8 47 ♖d3+ ♚e7 48 ♚c7 1-0

G.Kasparov – GENIUS

PCA/Intel-Grand Prix rapid 1994

1 c4 c6 2 d4 d5 3 ♘f3 ♘f6 4 ♕c2 dxc4 5 ♕xc4 ♗f5 6 ♘c3 ♘bd7 7 g3 e6 8 ♗g2 ♗e7 9 0-0 0-0 10 e3 ♘e4 11 ♕e2 ♕b6 12 ♖d1 ♖ad8 13 ♘e1 ♘df6 14 ♘xe4 ♘xe4 15 f3 ♘d6 16 a4 ♕b3

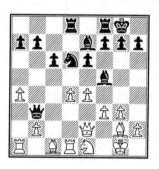

17 e4

I was optimistic about this game as the bishop on g6 is really out of play.

17...♗g6

See diagram on page 202.

18 ♖d3 ♕b4 19 b3 ♘c8 20 ♘c2 ♕b6 21 ♗f4

21...c5

All goes according to the super instructive Alekhine game!

22 ♗e3 cxd4 23 ♘xd4 ♗c5 24 ♖ad1 e5 25 ♘c2 ♖xd3

I am not at all against exchanges.

26 ♕xd3 ♘e7 27 b4 ♗xe3+

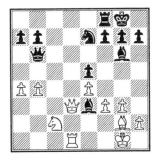

28 ♕xe3

Further swapping just like Alekhine and an invasion will not be long coming as well. I was already thinking how nice it would be to penetrate with my king.

28...♖d8

The computer doesn't know those classical games. It (or should I say he or she) seems to play into my hands.

29 ♖xd8+

The first element was not in my plan, I wanted to exchange queens not the rooks but I thought, okay, it is after all an exchange.

29...♕xd8 30 ♗f1 b6 31 ♕c3

The computer's 24...e5 was strong as it gained space.

31...f6 32 ♗c4+

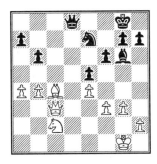

32...♗f7

Black offers another exchange which fits into my plan, but I was no longer happy as the computer's bishop was supposed to be frozen on the kingside.

33 ♘e3 ♕d4

Black keeps exchanging!

34 ♗xf7+ ♔xf7 35 ♕b3+

Maybe entering an equal knight ending would have been more practical against a never tiring opponent.

35...♔f8 36 ♔g2

If 36 ♔f1!? ♕d2 37 ♘c4.

36...♕d2+

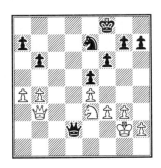

37 ♔h3

Alekhine had activated his king. I wanted to start a march as well, but on the edge the king remains isolated.

37...♕e2 38 ♘g2 h5 39 ♕e3 ♕c4 40 ♕d2 ♕e6+ 41 g4 hxg4+ 42 fxg4

White's pawns have been separated and e4 is now a target.

42...♕c4 43 ♕e1 ♕b3+ 44 ♘e3 ♕d3 45 ♔g3

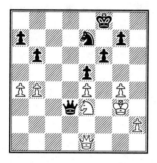

45...♕xe4

Going a pawn down is already a very gloomy prospect.

46 ♕d2 ♕f4+ 47 ♔g2 ♕d4 48 ♕xd4

The knight ending gives little hope of survival.

48...exd4 49 ♘c4 ♘c6 50 b5 ♘e5 51 ♘d6

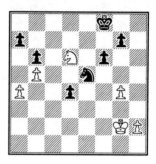

51...d3 52 ♔f2 ♘xg4+ 53 ♔e1 ♘xh2 54 ♔d2 ♘f3+ 55 ♔xd3 ♔e7 56 ♘f5+ ♔f7 57 ♔e4 ♘d2+ 58 ♔d5 g5 59 ♘d6+ ♔g6 60 ♔d4 ♘b3+ 0-1

Alekhine caught some of his opponents on their back rank. I was really impressed by those examples and it is natural that I wanted to do something similar to that...

E.Bogolyubov – A.Alekhine

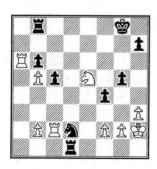

A.Alekhine – E.Colle

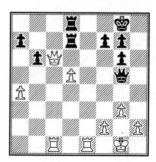

...so here are a couple of my attempts at checkmate on the back rank.

G.Kasparov – N.Short

DEEP BLUE – G.Kasparov

E.Bogolyubov – A.Alekhine
Game 22, World Championship match
Germany/Holland 1929

1 e4 e5 2 ♘f3 ♘c6 3 ♗b5 a6 4 ♗a4
d6 5 c3 ♗d7 6 d4 g6 7 ♗g5 f6 8 ♗e3
♘h6 9 0-0 ♗g7 10 h3 ♘f7 11 ♘bd2
0-0 12 dxe5 dxe5 13 ♗c5 ♖e8 14 ♗b3
b6

15 ♗e3 ♕e7

Alekhine stabilises his position.

16 ♕e2 ♘cd8 17 ♗d5 ♗c6?! 18 c4
♗xd5 19 cxd5 f5 20 ♘c4 ♘b7

21 ♖ac1 ♖ad8 22 d6 ♘bxd6 23 ♘xd6
♖xd6 24 ♕xa6 ♕d7

The position is equal.

25 ♖c2 c5 26 a4 f4 27 ♗d2 g5

28 ♕b5

Bogolyubov panics unnecessarily, as
Black's attack is not yet that dangerous.

28...♕xb5 29 axb5 ♖d3 30 ♖a1 ♘d6
31 ♖a6

The rook leaves the first rank, but it
is not yet a matter of decisive concern.

31...♖b8

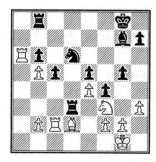

32 &c3?

White opens the way to his back rank. He should exchange the active rook by 32 &c3!

32...&xe4 33 &xe5

In a bad position he goes for a direct loss. Better was 33 &e1.

33...&xe5 34 &xe5 &d1+ 35 &h2 &d2!

See diagram on page 206.

Of course I found this move because of my talent not because of Alekhine's influence! Incidentally I also caught Karpov like this in our 1986 world title match.

G.Kasparov – A.Karpov
World Championship, Leningrad 1986

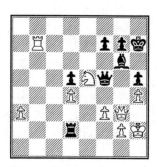

In Game 22 of the match, I had to seal my move at adjournment. My seconds and all the commentators were now expecting 41 &b4, covering the d4-pawn. However only one move had entered my head and as the time control had been passed I was able to spend 17 minutes checking the variations before writing down...

41 &d7!!

Even today, this move still pleases me. It threatens 42 &f8+ &h6 43 &b8! followed by 44 &xg6 and 45 &h8+ mating the boxed in king.

41...&xd4

Karpov takes the pawn in the hope of swapping queens, but...

43 &b4!!

Ruling out his intended 43...&f4, while upon 43...&xb4 I had planned the beautiful idea 44 axb4 d4 45 b5 d3 46 b6 d2 47 b7 d1=& 48 b8=& &c1 49 &xg6 &xg6 50 &h8+ &h7 51 &gxg7 mate.

43...&c4 44 &xc4 dxc4 45 &d6!

Now I have a mate from a different angle. If 45...f6? 46 &d2+.

45... c3 46 &d4

And Karpov resigned as the c3 pawn is lost and with it game, set and match!

But back to Alekhine's game:

36 h4 &e8 37 &f3 &xf3+ 38 gxf3

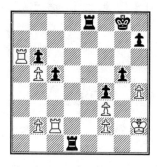

38...&ee1!

Setting up a lovely mating net.

39 &h3 h5 0-1

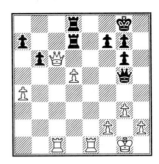

A.Alekhine – E.Colle
Paris 1925

1 d4 d5 2 c4 ♘c6

Smyslov played the Chigorin against me once in our Candidates match final.

3 ♘f3 ♗g4 4 ♕a4 ♗xf3 5 exf3 e6 6 ♘c3 ♗b4 7 a3 ♗xc3+ 8 bxc3 ♘ge7 9 ♖b1 ♖b8 10 cxd5 ♕xd5 11 ♗d3 0-0 12 0-0 ♕d6 13 ♕c2

White has got little from the opening.

13...♘g6?! 14 f4 ♘ce7 15 g3 ♖fd8 16 ♖d1 b6 17 a4 ♘d5 18 ♗d2 c5 19 f5 exf5 20 ♗xf5 cxd4 21 cxd4 ♘de7 22 ♗b4 ♕f6 23 ♗xe7 ♕xe7 24 ♖bc1 ♖d5 25 ♗e4

White only has a small advantage.

25...♖d7 26 d5 ♕f6 27 ♖e1 ♖bd8 28 ♕c6

28...♕g5?

Black must be able to hold with 28...♘e7!

29 ♗xg6!! hxg6

See diagram on page 206.

29...fxg6! would have prolonged the game and delayed resignation. Nevertheless after 30 ♕e6+ ♔f7 31 ♖c8 ♖xc8 32 ♕xc8+ ♖f8 33 ♕e6+ ♖f7 34 d6 White's advantage is overwhelming.

30 ♕xd7!!

A wonderful and unusual way of exploiting the weakness of the first rank.

30...♖xd7 31 ♖e8+ ♔h7 32 ♖cc8

Black can do nothing.

32...♖d8 33 ♖exd8 1-0

G.Kasparov – N.Short
Game 3, exhibition match,
London 1987

1 ♘f3 d5 2 d4 ♗g4

The bishop develops in a similar fashion to the Alekhine game. Naturally I did not anticipate any back rank chances.

3 ♘e5 ♗f5 4 c4 f6 5 ♘f3 c6 6 ♘c3 e6 7 g3 ♗b4 8 ♗g2 ♘e7 9 0-0 0-0 10 ♕b3 a5 11 a3 ♗xc3

209

12 bxc3

White has emerged from the opening with a small advantage, but it will evaporate.

12...♘d7 13 ♘d2 a4 14 ♕a2 ♗g6 15 e4 ♗f7 16 ♖b1 ♖b8 17 ♕c2 b5 18 cxd5 cxd5 19 ♕d3 ♕a5 20 ♖e1 ♖fc8 21 ♖b4 ♘c6 22 ♖b2

22...♘e7

By now Nigel has equalised. There follows a long manoeuvring phase.

23 ♖c2 ♘b6 24 h4 ♖b7 25 ♗h3 ♖c6 26 ♖b2 ♘c4 27 ♖b4 ♕c7 28 ♘xc4 ♖xc4 29 ♗d2 ♕c6 30 e5 f5 31 ♗f1 ♗h5 32 ♕e3 h6 33 ♖eb1 ♔f7 34 ♖1b2 ♔g8 35 f3 ♕a6 36 ♖b1

36...♘c6

Nigel sacrifices the exchange. The position is very closed, so the move is justified.

37 ♗xc4 dxc4 38 ♖4b2 ♘e7 39 d5

It is worth giving up a pawn in order to open the position.

39...♘xd5 40 ♕c5 ♗xf3 41 ♖xb5 ♖c7

42 ♖b8+

Suddenly Alekhine's back rank checkmates came to mind. I should have just taken the a-pawn after 42 ♖a5 and pushed my own a-pawn. 42...♕c8 43 ♕d6.

42...♔h7 43 ♕f8

See diagram on page 207.

I was trying to catch the h7-king just like Alekhine.

43...♕a7+ 44 ♔f1 ♖e7 45 ♖1b2

45...♔g6!

Nigel had a similar win against Timman in an Alekhine defence in Tilburg 1991! In that game he set up a mating net, here Nigel escapes with his king intact.

46 ♗c1 ♔h5 47 ♖a8 ♕c5?

Here 47...♘e3+ wins. 48 ♔e1 (48 ♗xe3 ♕xe3 49 ♕xe7) 48...♗xa8.

48 ♖c8?

White could keep Black busy with defensive duties. 48 ♖e8 should have been played.

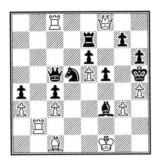

48...♕xa3

Suddenly Black's pieces can attack White's king, leaving him lost.

49 g4+ ♗xg4 50 ♖xc4 ♕a1 0-1

I trusted the back rank attack of Alekhine so much that I even played for it against the calculation monster super computer Deep Blue. Normally knowledge is an asset but, though I knew Alekhine's back rank tactics, after my experience in the next game they left me feeling blue. Even today, a decade later, whenever I think of that computer, it makes me ... deeply blue!

DEEP BLUE – G.Kasparov

Match, Philadelphia 1996

1 e4 c5 2 c3 d5

I beat Sveshnikov with the other main line in the USSR Championship at Minsk 1979. My opponent missed a very interesting blockade of my king in a bishop ending.

3 exd5 ♕xd5 4 d4 ♘f6 5 ♘f3 ♗g4 6 ♗e2 e6 7 h3 ♗h5 8 0-0 ♘c6 9 ♗e3 cxd4 10 cxd4 ♗b4! 11 a3 ♗a5 12 ♘c3 ♕d6 13 ♘b5 ♕e7 14 ♘e5 ♗xe2 15 ♕xe2 0-0

Black has equalised.

16 ♖ac1 ♖ac8 17 ♗g5 ♗b6 18 ♗xf6 gxf6 19 ♘c4 ♖fd8 20 ♘xb6 axb6 21 ♖fd1 f5 22 ♕e3 ♕f6

23 d5!

I was taken completely by surprise. This is the kind of positional sacrifice computers are not supposed to play. Later we found that by sheer brute force Deep Blue had calculated that it could win back the pawn after 23 ♕g3+ ♔f8.

23...♖xd5

Friedel pointed out that White is better after 23...exd5 24 ♕xb6 ♕xb2 25 ♕xb7 ♖b8 26 ♕xc6 ♖xb5 27 ♖c3.

24 ♖xd5 exd5

211

25 b3!

Deep Blue adopts my style! A quiet move after a sacrifice. Maybe I have a way to stay in the game, but it is very hard to find among the many complicated variations.

25...♔h8

I have already shown games in which I tried to force a checkmate on the g-file. I think Botvinnik passed on this idea to me. After 25...♘e7 26 ♕g3+!? (This is Nunn's suggestion. After 26 ♖xc8+ ♘xc8 27 ♕e8+ ♔g7 28 ♕xc8 ♕a1+ 29 ♔h2 ♕e5+ 30 g3 ♕e2 31 ♕xf5 ♕xb5 Black should hold.) 26...♔f8! and Black stands his ground. Alternatively, after 25...♖d8 26 ♕xb6 ♖d7 White has a small edge.

26 ♕xb6 ♖g8 27 ♕c5

Not 27 ♕xb7?? ♕g5.

27...d4

If 27...♕g5 28 g3 ♕d2 29 ♘d6 Black's pawns are all separated.

28 ♘d6 f4

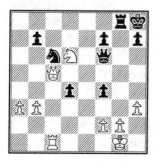

29 ♘xb7

Sadly White has time to grab a pawn.

29...♘e5 30 ♕d5 f3 31 g3 ♘d3

Forcing my way through on the g-file with 31...♕f4 did not work.

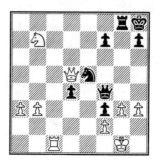

32 ♖c8!! (32 ♔h2? ♖xg3!! and Black mates) 32...♕g5 33 ♘d8! leaves Black in trouble. White can control matters with 33 ♖c5! as well.

But not 33 h4?? when 33...♖xc8!! 34 hxg5 ♖c1+ 35 ♔h2 ♘g4+ 36 ♔h3 ♘xf2+ 37 ♔h4 ♖h1 is mate.

32 ♖c7 ♖e8

After 32...♘f4 33 ♕xf3.

33 ♘d6!

After 33 ♕xf7 the Alekhine-like back rank play 33...♖e1+ 34 ♔h2 ♕xf7 35 ♖xf7 occurred to me and some commentators thought it would win as well. But after 35...♘e5 36 ♖f8+ ♔g7 37 ♖d8 ♘d3 38 g4 ♘xf2! (Playing on the back rank, just like Alekhine.) 39 ♔g3 (On 39 ♖xd4 ♘h1! Black is better. But not 39...♘e4 40 ♖xe4 ♖xe4 41 ♔g3) 39...♘xh3 40 ♔xf3 ♖e3+ the game ends in a draw.

33...♖e1+ 34 ♔h2

34...♘xf2

I set up a mating net just like Alekhine. But there is a small difference between our games – my checkmate can be parried.

35 ♘xf7+ ♔g7

If 35...♕xf7 36 ♕d8+ ♔g7 37 ♖xf7+ ♔xf7 38 ♕d5+ ♔e7 39 ♕xf3 wins.

36 ♘g5+

We have arrived at the next motif I learned from Alekhine and this position is an example of his effect on me. I underestimated the power of the discovered check arising from the battery.

36...♔h6 37 ♖xh7+

1-0

I resigned as I drop the f3-pawn which cages in the king. Without it I am just desperately lost.

After 37...♔g6 38 ♕g8+ ♔f5 comes 39 ♘xf3 and now Black's mating threat has disappeared and I am hopelessly behind on material.

I continue to show Alekhine's effect on me when it came to handling batteries. In the next game he rightly ignored the power of the opponent's battery.

M.Euwe – A.Alekhine

V.Kramnik – G.Kasparov

213

Most chessplayers know that Alekhine and Euwe played two matches for the world title. However they also had a third or should I say a first match in 1926. Later on Euwe also played a match against Capablanca, who beat him 6-4 with no losses. Bogolyubov also beat him 5½-4½ in two different matches.

In the Alekhine-Euwe match of 1926 Alekhine won two games early on but lost the seventh and the eighth, and they drew the ninth. We look at their decisive last game with the match standing at 4½-4½.

M.Euwe – A.Alekhine

Game 10, match, Amsterdam 1926

1 ♘f3 e6 2 c4 f5 3 g3 ♘c6 4 d4 ♗b4+ 5 ♗d2 ♗xd2+ 6 ♕xd2 d6 7 ♘c3 ♘f6 8 ♗g2 0-0 9 ♖d1 ♘e7 10 0-0 ♘g6 11 ♕c2 c6

12 e4
White occupies the centre.
12...♕a5 13 exf5 exf5 14 d5!
Euwe cuts Black's camp into two.

14...cxd5 15 ♘xd5 ♗d7 16 ♘d4 f4

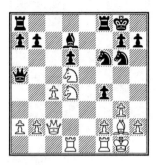

17 ♖de1?
This is a bit too subtle. Winning a pawn for nothing with 17 b4 was the simplest. 17...♕d8 18 ♘xf6+ ♕xf6 19 ♗xb7.
  17...♘xd5 18 ♗xd5+ ♔h8 19 ♘e6 ♖f6 20 ♘g5

20...♖af8
Black's pieces come into the game.
21 ♕b3 fxg3 22 ♕xg3
White has compensation for the pawn after 22 hxg3 ♖xf2 23 ♕e3.
Black's pieces have now become threatening.
23 ♖e7 ♖g6 24 ♖f7??
Even after 24 ♘f7+ ♖xf7 25 ♖xf7 ♘e2+ 26 ♔h1 ♘xg3+ 27 fxg3 h5 28 ♖xd7 White is worse, but it is far from over.

24...♖xf7 25 ♘xf7+ ♔g8

See diagram on page 213.

Alekhine intentionally steps into the discovered check of a battery. I knew this example when I played my last World Championship match.

26 ♘e5+

26...♕xd5!!
Euwe must have missed this.
27 cxd5 ♘e2+
And Euwe resigned.
0-1

You might say Euwe was unlucky. Yes and no. Looking at this match only, yes, but probably he learned from the extremely tense situation. When he played the last game of the 1935 match he was able to handle the pressure and he was successful. He probably became wiser because of this painful experience, whereas I derived no benefit from it because I got no chance of a return match.

V.Kramnik – G.Kasparov
Game 10, World Championship
London 2000

1 d4 ♘f6 2 c4 e6 3 ♘c3 ♗b4

In the match the Grünfeld did not work well. It is a pity Grünfeld did not become a world champion, then I could blame him for losing the second game of this match.

4 e3 0-0 5 ♗d3 d5 6 ♘f3 c5 7 0-0 cxd4 8 exd4 dxc4 9 ♗xc4 b6

I employed Karpov's variation, but Alekhine is also not 100 percent free from guilt for this loss.

10 ♗g5 ♗b7 11 ♖e1 ♘bd7 12 ♖c1 ♖c8 13 ♕b3 ♗e7 14 ♗xf6 ♘xf6 15 ♗xe6

15...fxe6
I've already showed you that I was not worried by the battery, and in fact this time the battery is not dangerous after 15...♖c7!. Then 16 ♘g5 (16 ♗c4 ♗xf3 17 gxf3 ♖d7 and Black is safe.) 16...♕xd4! 17 ♘e2 (17 ♘xf7 ♗c5 18 ♘e5+ ♔h8 is okay; 17 ♖cd1 ♕h4 18 ♘xf7 ♗c5 and Black can move despite the discovered check.) 17...♕d2 18 ♘xf7 ♕xe2 and Black is doing all right. In this game all the motifs are here that I picked up from Alekhine – the back rank included.

16 ♕xe6+ ♔h8 17 ♕xe7 ♗xf3 18 gxf3

After 18 ♕xd8 ♖cxd8 19 gxf3 comes 19...♖xd4.

18...♕xd4 19 ♘b5

19...♕xb2

The excellent Hungarian junior trainer Hazai, playing the White pieces, had a game where he was faced with 19...♕f4. He did not mind taking a walk in the centre. 20 ♖xc8 ♖xc8 21 ♘d6 ♕xf3 22 ♘xc8 ♕g4+ 23 ♔f1 ♕h3+ 24 ♔e2 ♕xc8 25 ♔d2 and went on to win in Hazai-Danielsen, Valby 1994.

20 ♖xc8 ♖xc8 21 ♘d6 ♖b8

21...♖a8 was better as the rook would be less vulnerable if Black's king goes in front of its pawns. 22 ♘f7+ ♔g8 23 ♕e6 h6 24 ♘xh6+ ♔h7 25 ♘f7! (25 ♘g4 ♖f8) 25...♖e8 (25...♕d2 26 ♖e4!?) 26 ♕f5+! and White has good winning chances.

22 ♘f7+ ♔g8 23 ♕e6

See diagram on page 213.

This is the battery I did not mind. Thanks to Alekhine.

23...♖f8

Trying to include the rook in the defence, but in vain. Other moves did not help either. Kramnik showed how White wins with 23...h5. Then

24 ♘g5+ ♔h8 25 ♕f5 ♕xa2 (25...♕c3 26 ♖e6 [26 ♖e7 ♕c5] 26...♕c7 [26...♔g8 27 h4!] 27 ♕g6 ♖f8 28 ♖xf6 gxf6 29 ♕h6+ ♔g8 30 ♕xf8+ a nice check follows.) 26 ♕g6 ♕a3 (26...♖f8 27 ♖e7) 27 ♖e6 ♔g8 28 h4 White wins.

If 23...h6 24 ♘xh6+ ♔h7 25 ♕f5+! ♔h8 (25...♔xh6 26 ♕f4+ ♔h7 27 ♕xb8 This is why putting the rook on a8 creates a bigger obstacle.) 26 ♘f7+ ♔g8 27 ♘g5 ♕xa2 (27...♕c3 28 ♖e7 ♕c5 29 ♖xg7+) 28 ♖e6 ♖c8 (28...♖e8 29 ♖xe8+ ♘xe8 30 ♔g2 wins; or 28...♖d8 29 ♔g2) 29 ♕g6 wins.

24 ♘d8+

The battery looks innocent as the knight wins nothing, however it still blocks the eighth rank.

24...♔h8

I did not have the same luck as Alekhine and was not able to take the piece at the base of the battery.

25 ♕e7 1-0

I resigned, because the d8 knight makes it possible to trap my rook or, if it moves away, there is a back rank checkmate or even worse a nightmare smothered mate. All Alekhine's motifs that I wanted to employ played a role in this game. I knew them all and still lost.

After this game I started to understand that the crown won't stay with me till I die as happened with Alekhine. It was a very important game.

The world champions have had a strongly negative effect on me, something which has probably escaped everybody's attention. I learned from them never to be behind at a decisive final stage of a World Championship match but, unlike Euwe, I was inexperienced when I played this game against Kramnik.

Indirectly, Alekhine affected me as well, since Kramnik learned from him how to avoid a rematch. He never gave me a chance to prove my superiority over him in a match, the same way that Alekhine denied Capablanca. So Alekhine had an especially marked and controversial influence on my career.

José Raúl Capablanca the 3rd

Capablanca beat Emanuel Lasker in 1921 to become the third world champion. Capablanca won 4 games and 10 were drawn, therefore the result was 9-5. The match took place in Cuba, where the weather favoured him, but anyway the great Cuban was destined to become world champion. Actually he may have been the best player earlier or, more precisely, during World War I. At that time there was hardly any chess activity in Europe and Capablanca was performing at his best in America. In a way, among the world champions he is the most dissimilar type of player to myself. He had a very positional style, whereas I prefer complications. He was a laid back easy-going person, whereas I am a hard worker and have conflicts. Of course there are similarities too, He was very talented and had better results in individual tournaments against a very strong player who beat him and never gave him a chance for a rematch. What did I pick up from him? Well, there are a few indications of his style in my play but these are rather superficial. First I'll show you the games that inspired me – and also cost me dearly.

J.Capablanca – L.Molina
Casual game, Buenos Aires 1911

1 d4 d5 2 c4 e6 3 ♘c3 ♘f6 4 ♗g5 ♘bd7 5 e3 c6 6 ♘f3 ♗e7 7 cxd5?! ♘xd5 8 ♗xe7 ♘xe7 9 ♗d3 c5 10 0-0 0-0 11 dxc5 ♘xc5

See diagram below.

12 ♗xh7+!?
Capablanca had a positional style, but also very sharp tactical vision. It is very hard to foresee all the components of this sacrifice.
12...♔xh7 13 ♘g5+ ♔g6

Because Capablanca had won with the bishop takes h-pawn sacrifice, I settled for a draw when I was faced with it – instead of trying for more.

J.Capablanca – L.Molina	**G.Kasparov – DEEP JUNIOR**
	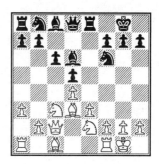

218

13...♔h6?? loses to 14 ♘xf7+; and there is no way back with 13...♔g8 as after 14 ♕h5 ♖e8 15 ♖ad1 ♗d7 16 ♕xf7+ ♔h8 17 ♕h5+ ♔g8 18 b4 wins.

14 ♕g4 f5

This is the only move.

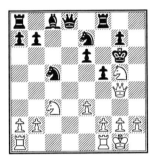

15 ♕g3 ♔h6

After 15...f4 16 exf4 ♘f5 17 ♕g4 ♘h6 18 ♕h4 White has two pawns and play for the piece – enough compensation for the material deficit. And after 18...♖h8 19 ♖fd1 ♕f6 20 ♖ac1 he will play b4 with an edge.

If 15...♔f6 16 ♖ad1 ♕b6 (16...♕a5 leaves White two ways to look for play. 17 ♘h7+ ♔f7 18 ♘xf8 ♔xf8 19 ♖d4 or 17 e4 ♘xe4 18 ♘cxe4+ fxe4 19 ♘xe4+ ♔f7 20 b4) 17 e4 (17 ♘h7+) 17...♘xe4 18 ♘cxe4+ fxe4 19 ♕f4+ ♘f5 20 ♘h7+ ♔f7 21 ♘xf8 ♔xf8 22 ♕xe4 with easier play for White.

16 ♕h4+ ♔g6 17 ♕h7+ ♔f6

Not 17...♔xg5?? 18 ♕xg7+ ♔h5 19 ♘e2! f4 20 exf4 ♘f5 21 ♕h7+ ♘h6 22 ♘g3+ ♔g4 23 ♕xh6 and checkmate follows on the next move.

18 e4! ♘g6

If 18...e5 19 ♖ad1 ♕b6 20 ♕h4 ♗e6 21 ♘xe6+ ♔xe6 22 exf5+ ♔f7 23 ♕c4+ ♔e8 24 b4 ♘a6 25 ♘e4 and White has nice prospects.

19 exf5 exf5 20 ♖ad1 ♘d3 21 ♕h3!

21 ♕h5 could lead to a perpetual. 21...♖h8 22 ♘ce4+ fxe4 23 ♘xe4+ ♔f7 24 ♘g5+ ♔f6 25 ♘e4+ ♔f7.

21...♘df4

There's nothing better. If 21...♖h8 22 ♕e3 ♘gf4 23 g3 and White wins back the piece. Or 21...♘gf4 22 ♕g3 ♖h8 23 h4 ♗e6 24 ♖fe1 ♖e8 25 ♘e2 and Black's position has deteriorated.

22 ♕g3 ♕c7

After 22...♕a5 23 h4.

23 ♖fe1 ♘e2+

After 23...♖d8 24 ♖xd8 ♕xd8 25 h4 Black is in trouble. And if 23...♖h8 24 h4 ♘xh4 25 ♖d6+! ♕xd6 26 ♘ce4+ White wins.

24 ♖xe2 ♕xg3

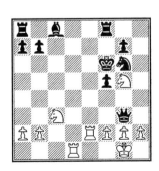

25 ♘h7+

This is an effective intermediate move. It crushes Black's position.

25...♔f7 26 hxg3 ♖h8 27 ♘g5+ ♔f6 28 f4 1-0

G.Kasparov – DEEP JUNIOR
Game 5, Man v Machine,
New York 2003

1 d4 ♘f6 2 c4 e6 3 ♘c3 ♗b4 4 e3 0-0 5 ♗d3 d5 6 cxd5 exd5 7 ♘ge2 ♖e8 8 0-0 ♗d6 9 a3 c6 10 ♕c2

See diagram on page 218.

10...♗xh2+?

Seeing this move on the screen had the effect of a cold shower. It struck me that perhaps it was my turn to lose to an opening trap, the same way that Karpov once lost horribly to Korchnoi. Then, with the Capablanca game rapidly flashing across my mind, my heart nearly missed a byte's worth of beats.

11 ♔xh2 ♘g4+

12 ♔g3

The only move – and just like the Capablanca game.

12...♕g5 13 f4

Things are developing in a very similar way to the Capablanca game.

13...♕h5

This represents a slight difference.

14 ♗d2 ♕h2+ 15 ♔f3

15...♕h4

The pieces are placed in a similar fashion to the Capablanca game.

16 ♗xh7+?

Here I was virtually settling for a draw because of the game of the Cuban champion. I thought it would be dangerous to play on because Capablanca had won with the sacrifice. However I should have continued with 16 g3!! as the centre is not as open as in the Capablanca game.

Then 16...♘h2+

a) 16...♕h2 This is surely the move Capablanca would have chosen. 17 f5 (17 ♖ae1) 17...♘d7 (17...h5 18 e4 or 17...♕h3 18 ♖h1 ♘h2+ 19 ♔f2 wins.) 18 ♔xg4 ♕g2 19 e4 ♘f6+ 20 ♔f4 dxe4 21 ♗xe4 ♘xe4 22 ♘xe4 ♕xe2 23 ♖ae1 ♖xe4+ 24 ♕xe4 ♕xd2+ 25 ♕e3 and Black runs out of play.

b) 16...♕h5 17 ♖h1 ♘xe3+ 18 ♖xh5
♗g4+ 19 ♔f2 ♘xc2 20 ♖ah1 ♗xh5
21 ♖xh5 ♘a1 22 ♗xh7+ wins.

17 ♔f2 ♘g4+

Now White's king can run away with
18 ♔e1!.

Before we continue with this line
let's see the continuation if White's
king stays in the area with 18 ♔g2,
which allows Black to hold. There
follows 18...♕h2+ 19 ♔f3 g6!! (19...f5
20 ♗xf5 ♕h5 21 ♗xg4 wins.)

20 f5 (20 e4 dxe4+ [Black can force
a draw by 20...♕h5 21 ♔g2 – 21 ♖h1
♘e5+ – 21...♕h2+ 22 ♔f3 ♕h5]
21 ♗xe4 ♘f6 22 f5 ♕h5+ 23 ♔f2
♘xe4+ 24 ♘xe4 ♕xf5+ 25 ♔e3 ♕g5+
26 ♔d3 [26 ♔f2 ♕f5+ 27 ♔e3]
26...♗f5 27 ♘2c3 ♕xg3+ 28 ♗e3 ♕h3

Maybe White is somewhat better, but
this is by no means certain and things
can easily go wrong for White.)
20...♘d7 (threatening ♘e5 mate) 21 e4
c5 (Black is not worse in the line
starting 21...dxe4+ which might end in
a particular perpetual check. 22 ♘xe4
[22 ♗xe4 ♘df6] 22...gxf5 23 ♘4c3
♖e3+ 24 ♗xe3 ♘de5+ 25 dxe5 ♘xe5+
26 ♔f4

26...♕h6+ 27 ♔xe5 ♕g7+ leads to a
draw.) 22 ♗g5 (White should settle for
a draw. It is too risky to play for a win
by 22 ♔xg4? cxd4 23 ♗g5 [23 ♖h1??
♘e5+ 24 ♔f4 h6 – 24...g5+ 25 ♔xg5
h6+ 26 ♔f4 ♕f2 mate – 25 ♘xd4 ♕f2+
and checkmate on the next move.]
23...dxe4 24 ♘xe4 ♕h5+ 25 ♔f4 gxf5
26 ♘xd4 ♕g4+ 27 ♔e3 ♕xg5+ 28 ♔f2
fxe4 29 ♗xe4 ♘f6 and Black takes
over.) 22...gxf5 23 ♘xd5 cxd4 24 exf5
♕h5 25 ♔g2 ♕h2+ is another
perpetual.

Meanwhile back to 18 ♔e1! when
play continues 18...♕h3 (18...♕h2!?
19 ♘d1 ♘d7 20 e4 dxe4 21 ♗xe4 ♕h5
22 ♖h1 ♘h2 23 ♘e3 ♘f6 24 ♗g2
♘fg4 25 ♕c5 leaves White an edge.)

19 ♖g1 (Had I not known Capablanca's game I might have tried 19 ♘d1!?. I am not saying this wins but I knew he had won with the rook move and I trusted his idea.) 19...♘d7 20 e4 dxe4 21 ♘xe4 ♕h2 (21...♘df6 22 ♘d6 ♖e6 23 ♘c4 and White keeps his position together.) 22 ♔d1 ♘df6 23 ♘xf6+ ♘xf6 24 ♖e1 ♗g4 25 ♕c4 and White is tied up.

16...♔h8 17 ♘g3 ♘h2+ 18 ♔f2 ♘g4+

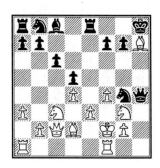

19 ♔f3 ♘h2+ ½-½

And the game ended in a perpetual. But I should have won this game or at least pressed harder. So, planted deep in my mind in my junior years was Capablanca's game – and it returned to me much later when I played Deep Junior.

Capablanca beat Alekhine in an endgame in which he was a pawn up and with a particular pawn structure.

Here is my position – also from a world title match – and with similar characteristics.

J.Capablanca – A.Alekhine

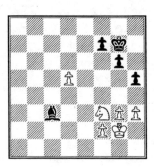

G.Kasparov – A.Karpov

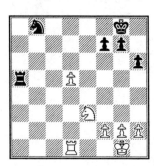

J.Capablanca – A.Alekhine

Game 29, World Championship,
Buenos Aires 1927

1 d4 d5 2 c4 e6 3 ♘c3 ♘f6 4 ♗g5 ♘bd7 5 e3 c6 6 ♘f3 ♕a5 7 ♘d2 ♗b4 8 ♕c2 dxc4 9 ♗xf6 ♘xf6 10 ♘xc4 ♕c7 11 a3

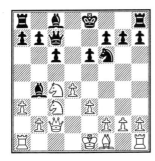

11...♗e7

There are problems assessing this type of middlegame. This bishop may be worth as much as White's extra space. For example, players once considered the Moscow variation to be slightly better for White. By the end of the 1990s masters began to sacrifice the c4-pawn instead. I also beat Dreev with this idea in an extremely important game in the 2004 Russian Championship.

12 g3 0-0 13 ♗g2 ♗d7 14 b4 b6 15 0-0 a5 16 ♘e5 axb4 17 axb4 ♖xa1

If 17...♗xb4 18 ♘b5 ♕c8 19 ♘a7 wins.

18 ♖xa1 ♖c8

If 18...♗xb4 19 ♘b5 ♕c8 20 ♗xc6! Capablanca liked this continuation and he had a point.

19 ♘xd7 ♕xd7 20 ♘a4 ♕d8

21 ♕b3 ♘d5

Here Alekhine missed a chance to reduce his disadvantage with 21...b5. Then 22 ♘c5 ♗xc5 and Black is only a fraction worse.

22 b5 cxb5 23 ♕xb5 ♖a8 24 ♖c1 ♖a5 25 ♕c6

White soon wins the b6-pawn.

25...♗a3 26 ♖b1 ♗f8 27 ♗xd5 ♖xd5

28 ♘xb6

White has excellent chances of converting his advantage.

28...♖d6 29 ♕b7 h5 30 ♘c4 ♖d7 31 ♕e4 ♖c7 32 ♘e5 ♕c8 33 ♔g2 ♗d6 34 ♖a1 ♖b7 35 ♘d3 g6 36 ♖a6 ♗f8 37 ♖c6

It is interesting that Capablanca chooses not to attack with h3 and g4.

37...♖c7 38 ♖xc7 ♕xc7 39 ♘e5 ♗g7 40 ♕a8+ ♔h7 41 ♘f3 ♗f6 42 ♕a6 ♔g7

43 ♕d3

Capablanca starts creating a passed d-pawn.

43...♛b7 44 e4 ♛c6 45 h3 ♛c7 46 d5 exd5 47 exd5

Had the Cuban not exchanged rooks ten moves earlier, and if the game had proceeded in a similar way, by now his advantage would have been greater.

47...♛c3 48 ♕xc3

Another small surprise when it was possible to keep the queens on.

48...♗xc3

See diagram on page 222.

49 ♔f1 ♔f6 50 ♔e2 ♗b4 51 ♘d4 ♗c5 52 ♘c6 ♔f5 53 ♔f3 ♔f6

54 g4 hxg4+ 55 hxg4 ♔g5

An unfortunate move, as it fixes White's king. However, it does provide freedom for the knight. Moving the

bishop along both diagonals was better so perhaps b6 is the best square for the bishop. Then Black has real chances of survival.

56 ♘e5! ♗d4

If 56...f5 57 d6! fxg4+ 58 ♔g2! wins. Alternatively, 56...♗a3 57 d6 ♔f6 58 d7 ♔e7 59 ♘xf7 is decisive.

57 ♘xf7+ ♔f6 58 ♘d8 ♗b6 59 ♘c6 ♗c5

60 ♔f4!

Capablanca can now use his king and returns a pawn for a winning endgame. 60 ♔e2 ♗d6 (60...♔g5 61 ♘e5) 61 ♔d3 ♔g5 62 ♘d8 ♔xg4 63 ♔e4 also wins.

60...♗xf2 61 g5+

As Capablanca played g5, I too opted for the same idea – see the next game!

61...♔f7

If 61...♔g7 62 d6.

62 ♘e5+ ♔e7

After 62...♔g7 63 d6 wins.

63 ♘xg6+

Winning a second pawn. The rest is simple.

63...♔d6 64 ♔e4 ♗g3 65 ♘f4 ♔e7 66 ♔e5 ♗e1 67 d6+ ♔d7 68 g6 ♗b4 69 ♔d5

Not 69 g7?? ♗c3+ draws.

69...♔e8 70 d7+ 1-0

This game looked very convincing to me.

G.Kasparov – A.Karpov
Game 40, World Championship,
Moscow 1985

1 d4 ♘f6 2 c4 e6 3 ♘f3 d5 4 ♘c3 ♗e7 5 ♗g5 h6 6 ♗h4 0-0 7 e3 b6 8 ♗e2 ♗b7 9 ♗xf6 ♗xf6 10 cxd5 exd5 11 b4 c5 12 bxc5 bxc5

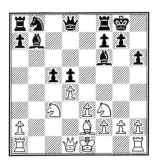

There are 126 games with this particular position in the database. Karpov and I played this position five times in our World Championship matches, all ending in draws. These games do not belong to the most exciting pages of World Championship history but as far as I was concerned they were justified because of my standing at the time in those matches.

13 ♖b1 ♕a5 14 ♕d2 cxd4 15 ♘xd4 ♗xd4 16 exd4 ♗c6 17 ♘b5 ♕d8

18 0-0 a6 19 ♘a3 ♖e8 20 ♘c2 ♖xe2 21 ♕xe2 ♗b5 22 ♖xb5 axb5 23 ♕xb5 ♖xa2 24 ♘e3

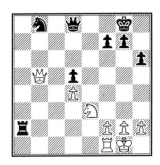

24...♖a5?

Karpov hangs on to the pawn, but soon he has to relinquish it. Geller recommended 24...♘a6!? which loses the pawn but might hold the game. For example, 25 ♖c1 (25 ♘xd5 ♖a5 26 ♘e7+ ♔f8 27 ♘c6 ♖xb5 28 ♘xd8 ♘b8) 25...g6! 26 ♘xd5 (26 ♕b7 ♕f6) 26...♖a5 27 ♘e7+ ♔g7 28 ♘c6 ♖xb5 29 ♘xd8 ♘b4 30 ♖b1 ♖b8 and Black seems to escape.

25 ♕b7 ♕e8 26 ♘xd5 ♖b5 27 ♕a8 ♕d7 28 ♘c3 ♖b4 29 d5 ♕c7 30 ♘d1 ♖b5

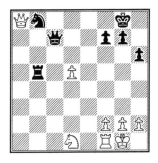

31 ♘e3

White has consolidated his extra pawn. However it is not so simple to convert it.

31...♕a5

I had no choice, but it was not against my wishes as Capablanca had exchanged queens as well.

32 ♕xa5 ♖xa5 33 ♖d1

See diagram on page 222.

There are rooks on the board and Black has a knight. But I thought the rooks could be swapped and the difference between having a knight instead of a bishop is not significant. Capablanca won his game, therefore I was hoping to win my endgame as well.

33...♘d7 34 g4 g6 35 ♔g2 ♖a4 36 h3 ♔g7 37 d6

Capablanca advanced his pawn at a much later stage.

37...♖a6 38 f4 ♖c6 39 h4 ♔f8

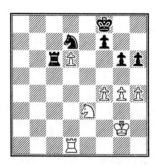

40 g5

The great Cuban pushed the g-pawn later. But he pushed nevertheless and why shouldn't I do the same? That's what I thought. On the other hand Geller preferred 40 h5.

40...hxg5 41 hxg5 f5!

Karpov does not allow my king to penetrate.

42 ♖d4

After 42 gxf6 comes 42...♔f7!

42...♔f7 43 ♘c4 ♔e6 44 ♔f3 ♖c5 45 ♔e3 ♖b5 46 ♔d2 ♖d5 47 ♖xd5 ♔xd5

We too have simplified to one piece against one piece. But I was not so lucky as Capa.

48 ♘e5 ♔xd6

49 ♘xg6

My simplification is different from the previous game. White's king is unable to improve its position and so no progress can be made. Oh, it's all so sad!

49...♘c5 50 ♘h4 ♔e6 51 ♔e3 ♘e4 52 ♘f3 ♔f7 53 ♔d4 ♔e6 54 ♔c4 ♘f2 55 ♔d4 [55 ♘g1!?] 55...♘e4 56 ♘e1 ♔d6 57 ♘c2 ♘c5 58 ♔e3 ♘e6 59 ♘d4 ♘g7 60 ♔d2 ♔c5 61 ♔d3 ♔d5 62 ♘e2 ♘h5 63 ♔e3 ♘g7 64 ♘g3 ♔d6 65 ♔f3 ♔e7 66 ♘e2 ♘e6 67 ♘g3 ♘g7 68 ♘f1 ♔f7 69 ♘e3 ♔g6 70 ♘d5 ♘e6 ½-½

But not all my memories were sour as regards the particular pawn structure with three pawns on the kingside and one extra d-pawn. Here is my game against Shirov:

A.Shirov – G.Kasparov
Astana 2001

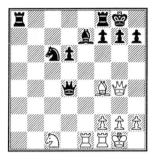

22...♕c4 23 ♖ae1 ♘c6 24 ♘c1 ♕xd4 25 ♘e2 ♕a4 26 ♕g3 ♖fd8 27 ♘c3 ♕b3 28 ♖e3 d5 29 ♗h6 ♗f8 30 ♘e4 ♕b2 31 ♘c5 ♗xc5 32 ♖c3 ♗xf2+ 33 ♖xf2 ♖a1+ 34 ♖f1 ♕b6+ 35 ♖e3 ♖xf1+ 36 ♔xf1 ♕d4 37 ♕c7 ♕c4+ 0-1

I have sacrificed a piece on b5 a few times, of course this occurs most frequently in the Sicilian defence. So my main recourse to employing this idea came from other games and I very clearly remembered one of Capablanca's wins where he sacrificed a bishop on b5. He played it in his first European tournament at San Sebastian 1911 after which he was universally regarded as a world-class player.

Here is the position where Capablanca had just sacrificed on b5:

And here you can see the moment when I unleashed the same move.

J.Capablanca – O.Bernstein

G.Kasparov – J.Lautier

J.Capablanca – O.Bernstein
St. Petersburg 1914

1 d4 d5 2 ♘f3 ♘f6 3 c4 e6 4 ♘c3
♘bd7 5 ♗g5 ♗e7 6 e3 c6 7 ♗d3 dxc4
8 ♗xc4 b5 9 ♗d3 a6 10 e4 e5 11 dxe5

I have had two games in which my opponent had doubled e-pawns in the opening and I lost. One was only a blitz game again Kramnik, but the second one was a regular game against Hübner. Tal, Euwe and Steinitz all won games against such a pawn structure.

11...♘g4 12 ♗f4 ♗c5 13 0-0 ♕c7
14 ♖c1 f6 15 ♗g3 fxe5

Against Hübner I did not mind him taking back the e-pawn, as I based my play on my queenside pawn majority.

16 b4 ♗a7 17 ♗xb5!

See diagram on page 227.

In return for the bishop Capablanca obtains three pawns and prevents Bernstein from castling.

17...axb5 18 ♘xb5 ♕d8 19 ♘d6+
♔f8 20 ♖xc6 ♘b6 21 ♗h4 ♕d7

22 ♘xc8
This is a surprising solution. He gives up his well placed knight for an undeveloped bishop.

22...♕xc6 23 ♕d8+ ♕e8
If 23...♔f7 24 ♘d6+.

24 ♗e7+ ♔f7 25 ♘d6+ ♔g6
26 ♘h4+ ♔h5 27 ♘xe8 ♖xd8

28 ♘xg7+
Capablanca had luck with such knight-saving intermediate moves.

28...♔h6 29 ♘gf5+ ♔h5

30 h3

White is a rook down but has plenty of pawns for it and, more importantly, far too many pieces around Black's king.

30...♘c8

If 30...♘h6 31 ♘g3 mate.

31 hxg4+ ♔xg4 32 ♗xd8 ♖xd8

Black has avoided direct loss, but he has given back the rook. Now he is absolutely constrained with his three pawn deficit.

33 g3 ♖d2 34 ♔g2 ♖e2 35 a4 ♘b6 36 ♘e3+ ♔h5 37 a5 ♘d7 38 ♘hf5 ♘f6 39 b5 ♗d4 40 ♔f3 ♖a2 41 a6 ♗a7 42 ♖c1 ♖b2 43 g4+ ♔g6 44 ♖c7 ♖xf2+ 45 ♔xf2 ♘xg4+ 46 ♔f3 1-0

This b5 sacrifice is nice indeed and I have also tried it.

G.Kasparov – J.Lautier
Euwe Memorial, Amsterdam 1995

1 e4 c5 2 ♘f3 e6 3 d4 cxd4 4 ♘xd4 ♘c6 5 ♘c3 ♕c7 6 ♗e3 a6 7 ♗d3 ♘f6 8 0-0 ♘e5 9 h3 ♗c5 10 ♔h1 d6 11 f4 ♘ed7

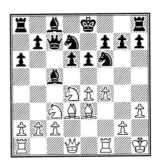

12 a3 b5

One year earlier Ivanchuk castled against me in this position. Joel obviously had time to prepare.

13 ♗xb5!?

See diagram on page 227.

I also had time to prepare and felt this sacrifice would wreak psychological damage.

13...axb5 14 ♘dxb5 ♕b6?!

After 14...♕c6 15 ♗xc5 dxc5 16 e5 ♗a6 17 a4 ♘d5 18 ♘xd5 exd5 19 ♘d6+ ♔e7 20 ♖e1 h5 21 ♕f3 Lautier evaluates his line as giving enough compensation.

15 ♗xc5 dxc5 16 ♘d6+

Also after 16 e5 ♗a6 17 a4! ♗xb5 (17...♘d5 18 ♘d6+ ♔e7 19 ♘xd5+ exd5 20 ♕xd5 wins.) 18 ♘xb5 ♘d5 (18...♘e4? 19 ♕f3) 19 c4 ♘e7 20 ♕d6 White has decent compensation for the piece.

16...♔e7

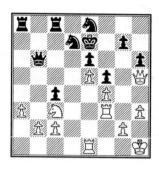

17 ♘xc8+

Capablanca captured the bishop after the d6-check. I did not do the same even though I had had the controversial experience when the computer sacrificed the bishop on h2. I still fully trusted Capablanca's way of attacking. After 17 e5 ♗a6 (17...♘e8 18 ♘c4) 18 ♖f2 ♖hd8 19 ♖d2 the position is unclear.

17...♖hxc8

It is a bit worrisome that Lautier's rook is not stuck on h8 as Bernstein's was. But I still felt relaxed.

18 e5 ♘e8 19 ♕h5 h6 20 ♖ae1

Not 20 f5? ♘xe5 21 fxe6 ♕xe6.

20...f5!

Lautier consolidates his king and now I started to realise things would not necessarily go my way. Not 20...♕xb2? 21 f5! ♕xc3 22 fxe6 fxe6 23 ♖f7+ ♔d8 24 ♖d1 and White has compensation even for the double knight deficit.

21 ♖f3

After 21 exf6+ ♘exf6 22 ♕g6 ♔f8 Black wins.

21...c4?!

Knaak's move 21...♕xb2 wins. After 22 ♖d1 (22 g4 ♖xa3) 22...♘f8 it is all over.

22 g4!

By now I had already cleared my head of the Capablanca game. I just used my own brains and made a reasonably good move, which creates chances. However, sadly, it is not enough. If 22 ♖g3 ♕f2.

22...fxg4 23 ♕xg4

After 23 hxg4 ♕c6.

23...♖a5!

Not 23...♕xb2? 24 f5.

24 ♘e4 ♕c6?!

Once again taking the b2 pawn was decisive: 24...♕xb2! 25 ♘d6 ♘xd6 26 exd6+ ♔xd6! 27 ♕xe6+ ♔c7 28 ♖d1 ♘b6 and Black is too far ahead in material.

25 ♘d6 ♘xd6?!

Impatiently and prematurely parting with the d6-knight. After 25...♖b8 26 ♔g1 ♖d5! 27 ♖f2 ♘xd6 28 exd6+ ♔d8 Black wins.

26 exd6+ ♔f8 27 ♖g1?

This move is a bad time-trouble mistake. 27 ♖xe6 was necessary. Then after 27...♖e8 (27...♘f6?? 28 d7!) 28 ♖xe8+ (28 ♖e7? ♖xe7 29 dxe7+ ♔f7) 28...♖xe8 29 ♔g1 ♕xd6 30 ♕xg7 Black has just a few pawns left and his king has no shelter. All of which makes it very hard to win with the extra knight.

27...g5!

Black saves the g-pawn which is a very important achievement for him. His queen stands well on the long diagonal.

28 ♖gg3

Defending the vulnerable f3-rook in advance. But White's king remains precariously placed. For example, after 28 fxg5+ ♖f5 29 ♖gg3 ♘e5 wins.

28...♖f5 29 ♕h5 ♘f6 30 ♕xh6+ ♔f7 31 ♔g1

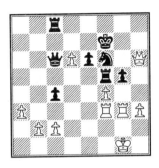

31...♖g8 0-1

Had Capablanca actually observed my position collapsing in ruins like this, he would surely have been embarrassed at his negative influence on me.

Capablanca played a very famous game where he froze his opponent's bishop on g3 with his g5 and e5 pawns.

W.Winter – J.Capablanca

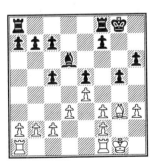

G.Kasparov – J.Timman

No doubt you have already noticed that while Winter had a frozen bishop, Timman has a knight. It's so annoying that this could happen. Go through the game and you can see why I say this!

W.Winter – J.Capablanca
Hastings Victory Congress 1919

1 e4 e5 2 ♘f3 ♘c6 3 ♘c3 ♘f6
4 ♗b5 ♗b4 5 0-0 0-0 6 ♗xc6 dxc6
7 d3 ♗d6 8 ♗g5 h6 9 ♗h4 c5

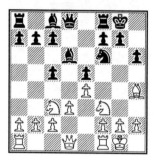

10 ♘d5? g5 11 ♘xf6+ ♕xf6 12 ♗g3
♗g4 13 h3 ♗xf3 14 ♕xf3 ♕xf3
15 gxf3

See diagram on page 231.

White's bishop on g3 is dead.
**15...f6 16 ♔g2 a5 17 a4 ♔f7 18 ♖h1
♔e6 19 h4 ♖fb8 20 hxg5 hxg5 21 b3**

21...c6
Having centralised his king,
Capablanca now opens the queenside.
He can afford a lot of things on that
side as White is virtually a piece down.
22 ♖a2 b5 23 ♖ha1

**23...c4! 24 axb5 cxb3 25 cxb3 ♖xb5
26 ♖a4 ♖xb3**

With such a frozen kingside White is
hopelessly lost.
**27 d4 ♖b5 28 ♖c4 ♖b4 29 ♖xc6
♖xd4 0-1**

G.Kasparov – J.Timman
Wereldhaven Festival, Rotterdam 1999

1 e4 e5 2 ♘f3 ♘c6 3 ♗c4 ♘f6
4 d3 ♗c5 5 c3 d6 6 ♗b3 0-0 7 ♗g5
♗e6 8 ♘bd2 a6 9 h3 ♗a7 10 ♗h4
♔h8

11 g4
When I was really young I also
gained space like this against Petrosian.
**11...♘e7 12 ♗xf6 gxf6 13 ♘h4 ♘g6
14 ♘g2**

See diagram on page 231.

In the later part of the analysis you can see why I thought Timman had a bishop on g6. But here I had some chessic doubts when a Steinitz game suddenly occurred to me.

A.Schwarz – W.Steinitz
Vienna 1873

16...♘xg3

This confused me. Steinitz captures the bishop which seems to imply that a bishop like this may not be so bad after all. Steinitz went on to win the game. On the other hand Capablanca won by saddling his opponent with this bishop. I was aware of the contradictory messages these champions were sending but thought, as the Cuban was the later champion, he must have played better than Steinitz, therefore it was his principle I followed.

17 ♖xh8 ♘xe2+ 18 ♗xe2 ♖xh8 19 dxc5 dxc5 20 ♖g1 ♖g8 21 ♔c2 ♘d8 22 ♕d5 ♕e7 23 ♖d1 c6 24 ♕b3 b5 25 c4?

Giving up the d4-square was a huge mistake of course.

25...♘e6 26 ♔b1 ♘d4 27 ♕e3 ♖h8 28 ♕d2 ♖h2 29 ♗f1 b4 30 ♕e3 ♕f6 31 ♖d3 g4 32 fxg4 ♖xf2 0-1

White resigned in this lost position.

Now we return to my game:

14...c6 15 ♕f3 d5 16 ♘f1 a5 17 ♘g3 ♗c5 18 a4 ♗e7 19 ♗a2 ♖a6 20 ♘h5

20...♖b6

Timman's rook play is interesting.

21 ♕e2 ♕d6 22 0-0 ♖d8 23 ♖fd1 d4 24 ♖d2 ♕c5

Jan should have played 24...dxc3 25 bxc3 ♕a3 26 ♖ad1 ♕xc3 27 ♘e3. White has some play for the pawn but Black should be better.

25 ♖c2 ♕d6 26 ♘e1 ♖g8 27 ♘f3 ♕d7 28 ♔h1 c5 29 ♗xe6 fxe6 30 ♘d2 ♖a6

31 ♘c4

Somehow I have gained a small edge.

31...♗d8 32 ♖cc1 ♖f8 33 f3 ♗c7 34 ♖a3 ♖aa8 35 ♖b3

It is my turn to use the rook the way that Timman did.

35...♕xa4 36 ♖xb7 ♕c6 37 ♖b3 f5 38 ♘d2 ♖f7 39 c4 a4 40 ♖b5?! [40 ♖a3] **40...♗a5 41 ♘f1**

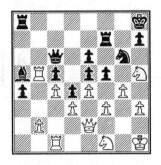

41...♗b4

Timman's bishop is very much better than Winter's as it traps the b5 rook.

42 ♘fg3 fxg4 43 fxg4 ♖af8

Black takes over the f-file.

44 ♖f1 ♕e8 45 ♖xf7 ♕xf7 46 g5?

46...♘f4

This came as a huge shock. I thought this piece was a bishop and now suddenly it moves like a knight! The piece on g6 has not moved for so long, and in my mind it remained like a slumbering bishop on g6. How could this happen? This game was an outdoor exhibition in which pieces and pawns were large steel containers moved by cranes. Their shapes were somewhat similar and I mixed them up. I was so happy that I could copy Capablanca's freeze technique. He is not solely responsible for my loss here but shares the blame with the heavy metal designer. Maybe chess events should be separated as in tennis – indoor and outdoor – so this game would not count against my indoor record.

47 ♕f3?

I was so stunned that I made a losing move, but Timman stood better anyway.

47...♘xh5 48 ♕xh5 ♕f2 49 ♘e2 ♕f3+ 50 ♕xf3

50...♖xf3

That's it.

51 ♔g2 ♖xd3 52 ♘g3 ♔g7 53 ♖b6 ♗e1 54 ♘f1 ♔f7 55 ♘h2 ♖d2+ 56 ♔h1 ♖e2 57 ♘g4 ♖xe4 58 ♘f6 ♖e2 59 ♘xh7 0-1

Alekhine praised Capablanca's talent so highly after the Cuban died and Kramnik said Leko was a tougher opponent in the final than me. I think his true thoughts lie in the fact that he never gave me a chance of a rematch.

Emanuel Lasker the 2ⁿᵈ

The second world champion beat Wilhelm Steinitz 10-5 with 4 draws in Philadelphia 1894. It was 2-2 with two draws after the sixth game, then Lasker raced away with five consecutive wins. Two years later Lasker started with four consecutive wins. In the first eleven games the ageing Steinitz made only four draws. Then Steinitz won two games in a row. In the last four games Emanuel scored three more wins, winning the match 10-2 with 5 draws. Lasker held the title for the longest period – 27 years in all. However he was the champion who played the least.

After the second Steinitz match Lasker played very little. He firstly defended his title in 1907, demolishing Marshall 11½-3½, winning 8 games and drawing 7 with no losses. One year later he beat the ageing Tarrasch 10½-5½. He won 8 games, lost 3 and drew 5.

In the famous St. Petersburg tournament Lasker and Rubinstein both scored 14½ out of 18 games, although Rubinstein beat him in their individual encounter. Rubinstein also showed his class in other tournaments. Sadly a match between the two never took place. In the same year he destroyed Janowski 8-2, winning 7 games and losing one with two draws.

In 1910 Lasker again defended his title with a 5-5 score against Schlechter.

Lasker had to win the last game to save the match. In the same year he beat Janowski again. This event was even more convincing as he dropped only 3 draws out of 11 games. In the final of the 1914 St Petersburg tournament he scored 7 out of 8 and won the tournament ahead of both Capablanca and Alekhine.

During World War I Lasker lost his wealth, so consequently he had to put his title at stake in 1921. It was here that he lost to Capablanca in Cuba. However he still scored some fine tournament results, including a victory at New York 1924 ahead of Capablanca and Alekhine. In 1935 he took third place in an extremely strong event in Moscow – at the age of 67.

The chess he played is quite different from the style of the late twentieth century. So his effect on me is less than say Smyslov's. Nevertheless, he still played games that influenced me.

He won many games with the Alekhine defence pawn structure b4-c5-d4 against Black's b7-d5-e6, but those we have discussed in the Smyslov chapter.

In the following examples we see how Lasker gained space on the kingside with g4 and then backed up his attack with the aid of his knights.

I found Lasker's pawn and knight setup rather attractive so I gave it a try.

E.Lasker – W.Steinitz

G.Kasparov – R.Hübner

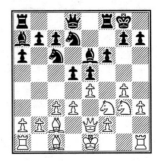

E.Lasker – W.Steinitz
Hastings 1895

1 e4 e5 2 ♘f3 ♘c6 3 ♗b5 a6 4 ♗a4 d6 5 0-0 ♘ge7 6 c3 ♗d7 7 d4 ♘g6

Though this setup is a bit passive it is steady and was still being played more than a century later. Timman won a crucial game with it against Motylev at the European Team Championship in 2005 where Holland went on to win the event!

8 ♖e1 ♗e7 9 ♘bd2 0-0 10 ♘f1 ♕e8 11 ♗c2 ♔h8 12 ♘g3

White is a slightly better.

12...♗g4 13 d5 ♘b8 14 h3 ♗c8 15 ♘f5 ♗d8 16 g4 ♘e7 17 ♘g3

See diagram above.

White's g4-pawn provides a nice space advantage on the kingside and the white knights provide proper support.

17...♘g8

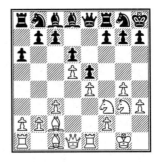

Masters still play moves like this in the King's Indian. I also played ♘g8 a few times in a King's Indian position (this game is similar). I won with this move against Korchnoi in Barcelona 1989, and Khalifman and Gelfand were my victims in the Paris Immopar rapid in 1991. The position seems to be like a Fischer Random chess position. Only three of the eight Black pieces are on their starting squares of a conventional chess game.

18 ♔g2 ♘d7 19 ♗e3 ♘b6?

Players no longer develop their queen's knight in this way.

20 b3 ♗d7 21 c4 ♘c8 22 ♕d2 ♘ce7 23 c5!

A classical manoeuvre. White cracks Black from both sides of the board. – a very effective method when it comes to exploiting a space advantage.

23...g6 24 ♕c3 f5

A desperate attempt to get some play. Waiting passively was also hopeless.

25 ♘xe5!

This takes Black apart; the rest is not very interesting.

25...dxe5 26 ♕xe5+ ♘f6 27 ♗d4 fxg4 28 hxg4 ♗xg4 29 ♕g5 ♕d7 30 ♗xf6+ ♔g8 31 ♗d1 ♗h3+ 32 ♔g1 ♘xd5 33 ♗xd8 ♘f4 34 ♗f6 ♕d2 35 ♖e2 ♘xe2+ 36 ♗xe2 ♕d7 37 ♖d1 ♕f7 38 ♗c4 ♗e6 39 e5 ♗xc4 40 ♘f5 1-0

G.Kasparov – R.Hübner
Game 4, Cologne TV blitz 1992

1 e4 e5 2 ♗c4 ♘c6 3 d3 ♗c5 4 ♘f3 d6 5 c3 ♘f6 6 ♗b3 0-0 7 h3 ♗e6 8 ♘bd2 a6 9 ♕e2 ♗a7 10 g4

I intentionally postponed castling.

10...♘d7 11 ♗c2 d5 12 ♘f1 f6 13 ♘g3

See diagram on page 236.

Hübner's position is stronger on the queenside than Steinitz's, but I was still confident because of the plus I had on the kingside.

13...d4 14 ♘f5 ♘c5 15 ♖g1 ♖f7 16 cxd4 ♗xf5 17 gxf5 ♘xd4 18 ♘xd4 ♕xd4 19 ♔f1 ♔h8 20 ♖b1

20...♖d7

I was already gaining the impression that my kingside play was possibly no stronger than Hübner's initiative on the other side of the board.

21 ♖g3 a5 22 ♗e3 ♕d6 23 ♖d1 ♘a6 24 ♗b3 ♗d4 25 ♖g4 ♘c5 26 ♗c4 ♕f8 27 ♖h4

Putting the rook on the edge doesn't achieve enough to gain an advantage.

27...♕e8 28 ♕g4 ♗xe3 29 fxe3 h6 30 ♔e2 c6 31 a3 b5 32 ♗a2 a4 33 ♖g1 ♘b3

At the end of his plan Hübner nicely cuts off the dangerous bishop.

34 ♗xb3 axb3 35 ♖c1 ♖ad8 36 ♖c3 ♕g8 37 ♕g6 ♖d6 38 ♖g4 ♖8d7 39 ♖g1 ♕d8 40 ♖xb3

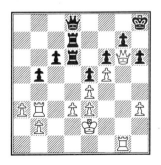

40...c5!

This was a blitz game, so I had little time to think. Nevertheless I did remember that Lasker managed to attack Steinitz's king. For a while I was hoping to do the same, but from now on I had to divide my attention between attacking and taking care of my own king.

41 ♖xb5 ♖xd3 42 ♔f3

After 42 ♖xc5 ♖xe3+? there is no perpetual, but 42...♖d2 transposes back to the game.

42...♖d2 43 ♖xc5 ♖xb2 44 ♖gc1 ♖b8 45 a4

Bringing back the queen with 45 ♕g2 was not effective. After 45...♖d2 46 ♖c8 ♖xc8 47 ♖xc8 ♕xc8 48 ♕xd2 ♕a6 49 ♕c1 ♕a4 the queen is tied to the defence of the pawn and the idea of a perpetual. White probably can't make any progress.

45...♕f8 46 a5 ♖a7 47 a6 ♖ba8!

Hübner's feel for chess doesn't let him down. He patiently takes back the pawn, or should I say *tries* to take back – as you will see. Recapturing at once with 47...♖xa6? was clearly a worse option. 48 ♖c7?! (White is a pawn up with some winning chances after 48 ♖xe5!)

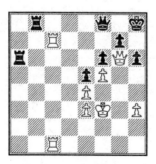

48...♖a3!! It is rather strange to analyse a blitz game, but the lines are

so nice I really want to share them. Maybe I was enjoying calculating them. 49 ♖f7 ♖xe3+! (49...♕g8 50 ♖cc7 ♖bb3) 50 ♔f2 (50 ♔xe3? ♕a3+ 51 ♔d2 ♕b2+ and Black delivers a checkmate in 8 moves.) 50...♖b2+ 51 ♔f1 ♖f3+ 52 ♔g1 ♖g3+ 53 ♕xg3 ♕xf7 54 ♖c8+ ♔h7 and it looks like Black is winning.

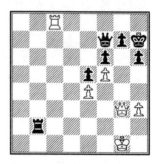

55 ♖c7!! ♖b1+ 56 ♔h2 ♕a2+ 57 ♕g2 ♕xg2+ (57...♖b2? 58 ♖xg7+!) 58 ♔xg2 ♖b4 Black can press on, but probably White holds.

48 ♖c6 0-1

In playing my move I overstepped the time limit! The position is equal as Black could take the a6-pawn.

Luckily this Lasker-affected game was only blitz, so it was not important. However the next one hit me at a crucial moment.

In the first two examples the second world champion allowed his opponents to have a strong rook on the seventh and yet he still won. Recalling his games I also allowed this – but regrettably with a different result.

Heydebreck – E.Lasker

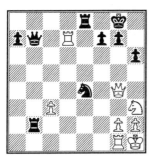

D.Janowski – E.Lasker

G.Kasparov – A.Karpov

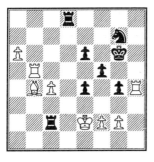

V.Topalov – G.Kasparov

Heydebreck – E.Lasker
Berlin 1889

1 ♖d7

This time the rook on the seventh is not particularly dangerous. However it looks no fun for Black either.

See diagram above.

1...♖b1!

What a nice riposte!

2 ♖dd1

Losing without much resistance. But taking the queen with 2 ♖xb7 leads to a beautiful win.

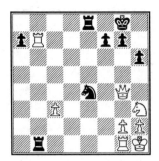

2...♘f2+!! 3 ♘xf2 ♖xg1+! 4 ♔xg1 ♖e1 mate.

2...♖xd1 3 ♖xd1 ♘xc3 0-1

White resigned.

D.Janowski – E.Lasker
Cambridge Springs 1904

1 e4 e5 2 ♘f3 ♘c6 3 ♘c3 ♘f6 4 ♗b5 ♗c5 5 ♘xe5 ♘xe5 6 d4 ♗d6 7 f4 ♘g6 8 e5 c6 9 ♗c4 ♗c7 10 exf6 ♕xf6 11 0-0 d5

12 ♗xd5

An interesting piece sacrifice.

12...cxd5 13 ♘xd5 ♕d6 14 ♕e2+ ♘e7 15 ♖e1 ♗d8 16 c4 f6

Black wants to play 17...♔f7.

17 ♗d2 a5 18 ♕h5+ g6 19 c5

19...♕a6?!

Staying closer to the centre with 19...♕c6 seems better. Then 20 ♘xe7 ♗xe7 21 ♕h6 ♗e6 22 f5 gxf5 23 ♕e3 ♖a6! and Black keeps his position together.

20 ♕h6 ♗e6 21 ♘xf6+?!

Capturing a pawn but allowing Black back into the game. Better was 21 ♘xe7! ♗xe7 22 d5 ♗f8 23 ♕h4 ♗xc5+ 24 ♔h1 and Black is in trouble.

21...♔f7 22 ♘e4 ♘f5 23 ♕h3 ♗e7 24 ♗c3

24...♗d5

After 24...♘xd4 25 ♕h6 ♖ad8 26 ♖ad1 ♘e2+ 27 ♔h1 ♘xc3 28 ♖xd8 ♖xd8 the position is equal.

25 g4 ♘h4 26 ♘d6+ ♔f8

27 ♖xe7

Janowski plays in optimistic fashion. After 27 ♔f2 the position is unclear.

27...♘f3+ 28 ♕xf3!

White sacrifices his queen based on the strength of a rook on the seventh.

28...♗xf3

29 ♖f7+?

Janowski probably misses Lasker's 32nd move. Bringing his other rook across with 29 ♖ae1! leads to some fascinating tactics. 29...♕c6 (29...♗d5 30 f5 h5! [30...g5? 31 f6 ♕c6 32 f7 ♕a4 – 32...♔g7 33 ♖1e6!! ♗xe6 34 d5+ ♔f8 35 ♖xe6 wins – 33 ♖c7 ♔g7 34 f8=♕+ ♔xf8 35 ♖f1+ ♔g8 36 ♘f5 White wins.] 31 f6 [31 fxg6? ♖h6 32 ♖7e5 ♖xg6] 31...♕c6 32 f7 ♕a4 33 ♖c7 ♔g7

34 ♘e8+ ♔h6 35 h4 g5! [35...hxg4 36 f8=♕+ ♖xf8 37 ♗d2+ ♔h5 38 ♖h7 mate] 36 hxg5+ ♔xg5 37 ♖e5+ ♔h4 38 b3 ♕xa2 39 ♗e1+ ♔h3 [39...♔xg4 40 ♘f6+] 40 ♖e3+ ♔xg4 41 ♘f6+ ♔f5 42 ♘xd5 and at the end of this long tactical line the position remains very complicated.) 30 ♖f7+ ♔g8 31 ♖ee7 ♗d5 32 ♖g7+ ♔f8

33 b3! White has compensation for the queen and the game should probably end in a draw. It looks like Black can't do anything useful in the ensuing ending. (33 f5 ♕a4!! wins. 33 ♖gf7+ ♗xf7 34 ♖xf7+ ♔g8 35 ♖g7+ ♔xg7 36 d5+ ♔g8 37 dxc6 bxc6 and Black should be a bit better.) 33...h5 (33...a4 34 ♖gf7+ ♗xf7 35 ♖xf7+ ♔g8 36 ♖g7+ ♔xg7 37 d5+ ♔g8 38 dxc6 bxc6 39 b4 White is no longer worse.) 34 f5 gxf5 (34...hxg4

35 f6 Rh3 36 Ref7+ Bxf7 37 Rxf7+
Bg8 38 Rg7+ Bf8 is equal, but not
38...Bh8?? 39 Nf7 and checkmate)
35 Rc7 fxg4 36 Rxc6 bxc6 37 Rb7 and
the position is still unclear.

**29...Bg8 30 d5 Bxd5 31 Rg7+ Bf8
32 Re1**

32...Wc6!

The only move to win. It stops
33 Rc7.

**33 b4 Rd8 34 Bd4 Rxd6 35 cxd6
Bh1 0-1**

G.Kasparov – A.Karpov
Game 18, World Championship
London/Leningrad 1986

**1 d4 Nf6 2 c4 e6 3 Nf3 b6 4 Nc3
Bb4 5 Bg5 Bb7 6 e3 h6 7 Bh4**

Lasker's spirit was alive in this game.
One game earlier I had a 4-1 lead
against Karpov and wanted to finish
him off once and for all. So even
though he had won the previous game,
I still wanted to clinch the match
with a decisive result. What does this
have to do with Lasker? Well, he was
the champion who won the most
one-sided world title matches, doing
comprehensive demolition jobs on both
Janowski and Marshall.

7...Bxc3+ 8 bxc3 d6 9 Nd2 g5

**10 Bg3 We7 11 a4 a5 12 h4 Rg8
13 hxg5 hxg5 14 Wb3 Na6**

15 Rb1!

I made sure Karpov would not castle
long.

15...Bf8

He got the message.

**16 Wd1 Bc6 17 Rh2! Bg7 18 c5
bxc5 19 Bb5 Nb8 20 dxc5 d5 21 Be5
Bf8 22 Rh6 Ne8 23 Wh5 f6 24 Rh7
Ng7 25 Wf3 Bf7 26 Wh5+ Bf8**

27 Wf3

With the help of imaginative play I
have forced him to defend doggedly.
My problem was that it took too long to
calculate and I was already short of
time.

**27...Bf7 28 Rh6 Ne8 29 e4 g4
30 Wf4 Bxb5 31 Rxb5 Nd7 32 Bxc7
Nxc5 33 We3 Nxe4 34 Nxe4 dxe4
35 Bxa5 f5 36 Bb4 Wd7**

37 ♕d4

Karpov has done well to stay in the game, but I still had the preferable position.

37...♖a7 38 ♖h7+

38 ♗c5 was strong.

38...♘g7 39 a5?

Better was 39 ♗c5!

39...♔g6?

After 39...♕xb5! 40 ♕xa7+ ♔g6 41 ♖h4 ♖d8 42 ♕e3 ♘h5 White is in trouble.

40 ♕xd7 ♖xd7 41 ♖h4

This was my sealed move.

41...♖gd8!

Karpov goes after my king.

42 c4 ♖d1+ 43 ♔e2 ♖c1!?

Karpov controls himself so well when his opponent has passed pawns. Perhaps he would play this move anyway but the must-win situation helps to prompt a move like this. After

43...♖a1 44 ♗c3! ♖c1 45 ♗e5 ♖c2+ 46 ♔e1 ♖xc4 (46...♖dd2 47 ♖h6+!! ♔g5 48 ♖h7 ♖e2+ 49 ♔d1 ♘e8 50 ♖b8 Black has no more than a perpetual.) 47 ♖b6 e3 48 fxe3 ♖e4 49 ♖d6 (49 ♗xg7? ♖xe3+ 50 ♔f2 ♖dd3!! wins.) 49...♖xe3+ 50 ♔d2 ♖xe5 51 ♖xd8 ♖xa5 White holds as I gave in my book of the match.

44 a6?

After 44 ♗c5 ♘h5 45 g3 ♖xc4 46 ♗e3 ♖a4 47 ♖b6 White is okay.

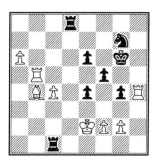

44...♖c2+!

Karpov gets his rook to the second rank but I was not worried as Lasker coped with it even when his opponent's minor pieces were backing it up. If 44...♖a1 45 ♗d2 ♖a2 46 ♖h6+ ♔f7

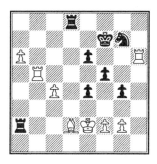

47 ♔e3!! (White's king creates sufficient counterplay. After 47 ♖b7+ ♔g8 48 ♖g6 ♖axd2+ 49 ♔e3 ♖2d7 50 c5 the subtle intermediate move

50...♔h7!! wins. [On the other hand
50...e5 is met by 51 ♖d6.] 51 ♖f6 g3
52 fxg3 ♖d3+ 53 ♔f4 e5+ 54 ♔xe5
♖e8+ 55 ♔f4 e3 56 ♖ff7 ♖e4+ 57 ♔g5
♖g4+ 58 ♔f6 ♖g6+ Black wins.)
47...♖axd2 (47...e5 48 ♖d5) 48 ♖b7+
♔g8 (48...♖2d7 49 c5) 49 ♔f4 ♖2d7
(49...♖xf2+ 50 ♔g5!) 50 c5 e5+
(50...♖f7 51 c6) 51 ♔xe5 g3 52 fxg3 e3
53 ♖xd7 ♖xd7 54 ♖h1 and White
holds.

45 ♔e1 ♖a2 46 ♖b6 ♖d3! 47 c5

After 47 ♗c5 g3! (47...f4 48 ♖b1)
48 fxg3 ♖xg3 49 ♖d6 ♖gxg2 50 a7 e3
51 ♖h1 ♘h5 52 ♖d8 ♘f4 53 a8=♕
♖xa8 54 ♖xa8 ♖e2+! 55 ♔d1 ♖d2+
56 ♔c1 ♘d3+ 57 ♔b1 ♘xc5 Black
wins.

47...♖a1+ 48 ♔e2 ♖a2+ 49 ♔e1 g3
49...♔g5! was even stronger.
50 fxg3 ♖xg3 51 ♔f1

51...♖gxg2

At this stage I was not certain
whether I should have allowed both
rooks to go to the second rank.
However, I was still relaxed. Lasker did
not mind things like this either.

52 ♗e1

As a junior Karpov liked to double
on the seventh.

52...♖gc2 53 c6 ♖a1
He gives up the idea of doubling.

However, as played, he is really hurting
the king.

**54 ♖h3 f4 55 ♖b4 ♔f5 56 ♖b5+ e5
57 ♖a5 ♖d1**

Makarychev says this squanders the
win. I was right – it makes Black find
more good moves.

58 a7?

I went down without putting up a
fight. Pushing 58 c7 would have given
me some practical chances, but in
reality it was losing as well. After
58...e3

59 ♖h2!! ♖cc1! is the simplest move.
(If 59...♖xh2 60 c8=♕+ ♘e6 61 ♕c3
♖f2+! [if 61...♘d4? 62 ♕c8+ ♔e4
63 ♕b7+ White has a perpetual check
at his disposal.] 62 ♔g1 ♘d4 63 ♕c8+
♔e4 64 ♕b7+ [64 ♖xe5+ ♔xe5]
64...♔d3 65 ♖a3+ ♔e2 and Black
wins.) 60 ♖e2 ♘e6 61 a7 ♘xc7 wins.

58...e3

I had to resign as the rooks and the knight deliver a checkmate.

59 ♖f3 ♘h5 60 a8=♕ ♘g3+ 61 ♖xg3 ♖f2+ 62 ♔g1 ♖xe1 mate

V.Topalov – G.Kasparov
Moscow Olympiad 1994

1 e4 c5 2 ♘f3 d6 3 d4 cxd4 4 ♘xd4 ♘f6 5 ♘c3 a6 6 ♗e3 e6 7 g4 h6

In those days the Perenyi variation had not yet been exhaustively analysed.

8 f4 ♘c6

In Wijk aan Zee 1999 I played 8...e5 like this game. Timman forced a perpetual after 9 ♘f5 h5 10 gxh5 exf4 11 ♗xf4 ♘xh5 12 ♘xd6+ ♗xd6 13 ♗xd6 ♕h4+ 14 ♔d2 ♕g5+ 15 ♔e1 ♕h4+ 16 ♔d2 ½-½. I did not dare to play on as I knew Steinitz liked to walk into the centre with his king. But we have one more chapter to deal with that.

9 ♗e2 e5 10 ♘f5 g6 11 ♘g3 exf4 12 ♗xf4 ♗e6 13 ♖f1 ♖c8 14 h3

14...♕b6

Since Fischer's time we Najdorf believers play this kind of move. Bönsch suggested 14...d5 as a standard kind of response.

15 ♕d2 ♗g7

Taking the b2-pawn was more consistent.

16 ♗xd6 ♘xg4

After 16...♘d4 17 e5!? ♕xb2 18 exf6 ♕xa1+ 19 ♔f2 ♕xc3 20 ♕xc3 ♖xc3 21 fxg7 ♖g8 22 ♘e4 Speelman's line is winning for White.

17 ♗xg4 ♕xb2?

If 17...♗xg4! 18 ♘a4 ♕b5 19 hxg4 ♕xa4 20 ♕d5 ♕a5+ 21 c3 White has a small edge.

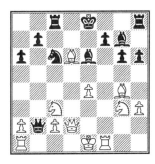

18 e5!?

This temporary rook sacrifice allows White to maintain the initiative. However 18 ♘ge2! was even better, perhaps just winning for White after 18...♕xa1+ 19 ♔f2 ♕b2 20 ♖b1.

18...♘xe5 19 ♖b1 ♕xc3

Bönsch's move 19...♘c4! underlines Lasker's play in the previous examples – and Alekhine's play in relation to batteries. 20 ♖xb2 ♘xd2 21 ♗xe6 fxe6 22 ♖xb7 ♗xc3

23 ♖ff7 (The doubled rooks on the seventh can force no more than a draw). 23...♘e4+ 24 ♔d1 ♘xd6 25 ♖be7+ and the game ends in a perpetual.

20 ♕xc3 ♖xc3 21 ♗xe6 fxe6

After 21...♖xg3 22 ♖xb7 (22 ♗xf7+ ♔d7!) 22...fxe6 Black is living dangerously, but I see no win for White.

22 ♖xb7

From what I had learned from Lasker I was confident that there is no point panicking just because one rook reaches the seventh rank.

22...♘c4

If 22...♘d7!? 23 ♖a7 ♗f6.

23 ♗b4 ♖e3+

After 23...♖xg3 24 ♖xg7 a5 (24...♘e3 25 ♖e7+ (25 ♖ff7? ♘f5) 25...♔d8 26 ♖ff7 wins.) 25 ♗c5 ♖g5 Black still resists.

24 ♘e2 ♗e5 25 ♖ff7

See diagram on page 239.

25...♖xh3?

I became too casual because of the Lasker examples. After 25...♗d6 White can keep up the pressure with 26 ♗c5!! Then 26...♖e4 (26...♗xc5? 27 ♖fc7) 27 ♖g7 ♗e5 28 ♖xg6 ♔d8 29 ♖a7 and White has an edge.

26 ♘d4!

Moving the rook away from the f-file with 26 ♖fe7+! was more precise. Then 26...♔d8 27 ♘d4 ♗g3+ 28 ♔e2 and Black can't even sacrifice the piece.

26...♖e3+

If 26...♗g3+ 27 ♔e2! ♖h2+ 28 ♔f3 ♖f2+ (28...♗h4 29 ♖fc7 ♘d2+ 30 ♔f4 ♗d8 31 ♖b8 wins.) 29 ♔xg3 ♖xf7 30 ♖b8+ ♔d7 31 ♖xh8 and Black has only two pawns for the piece.

27 ♔f1 ♖e4 28 ♖fe7+

Checkmate comes very soon.

28...♔d8 29 ♘c6+ 1-0

The last motif is not really a motif at all, more a variation. Maybe it is best to call it a defence. So far I have not paid attention to where the champions were born. In this case strangely enough it adds to the interest. I was born in Baku, no other champion was born there. The closest was Petrosian who was born in nearby Tbilisi. Emanuel Lasker was born a long way from Baku in Berlinchen, which of course sounds so similar to the German capital. My last world title match took place in London, yet thinking of the German capital generates rather painful memories.

Kramnik did not play the Russian defence (known in the West as the Petroff) in honour of his homeland. He kept playing the Berlin defence (or wall). Lasker could not have anticipated the existence of the Berlin wall. More importantly he did well against the Berlin defence and exceptionally well against the exchange Ruy Lopez where Black has a rather similar pawn structure a half a pawn down. Here is the position from which Lasker went on to win.

Now here are positions I had against Kramnik in my ill-fated World Championship match in London 2000.

G.Kasparov – V.Kramnik

G.Kasparov – V.Kramnik

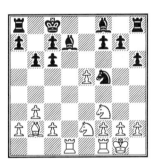

E.Lasker – Herz/Lewitt/Keidanski

E.Lasker – Herz/Lewitt/Keidanski
Consultation game, Berlin 1896

1 e4 e5 2 ♘f3 ♘c6 3 ♗b5 ♘f6 4 0-0 ♘xe4 5 d4 ♘d6 6 ♗xc6 dxc6 7 dxe5 ♘f5

The first game with this position in the database is from Leipzig 1879. Bier was White against Flechsig. But the second game was indeed played in Berlin in 1880.

8 ♕xd8+ ♔xd8 9 ♖d1+ ♔e8 10 ♘c3 h6 11 h3

11...♗e7

The next time this position occurred was in 1990 in the game Yudasin-Rogers, Manila 1990.

12 ♘e2

Lasker plays the move which is still popular.

12...♗d7

Later I played a different move in this position with Black and lost to Judit Polgar. Here are the moves. 12...♘h4 13 ♘xh4 ♗xh4 14 ♗e3 ♗f5 15 ♘d4 ♗h7 16 g4 ♗e7 17 ♔g2 h5 18 ♘f5 ♗f8 19 ♔f3 ♗g6 20 ♖d2 hxg4+ 21 hxg4 ♖h3+ 22 ♔g2 ♖h7 23 ♔g3 f6 24 ♗f4 ♗xf5 25 gxf5 fxe5 26 ♖e1 ♗d6 27 ♗xe5 ♔d7 28 c4 c5 29 ♗xd6 cxd6 30 ♖e6 ♖ah8 31 ♖exd6+ ♔c8 32 ♖2d5 ♖h3+ 33 ♔g2 ♖h2+ 34 ♔f3 ♖2h3+ 35 ♔e4 b6 36 ♖c6+ ♔b8

37 ♖d7 and again I did not mind my opponent invading on the seventh. 37...♖h2 38 ♔e3 ♖f8 39 ♖cc7 I even allow the second rook to join the first on the seventh. 39...♖xf5 40 ♖b7+ ♔c8 41 ♖dc7+ ♔d8 42 ♖xg7 ♔c8 and I was so upset I just rushed off home. 1-0 J.Polgar-Kasparov, Moscow rapid, 2002.

13 b3 ♖d8 14 ♗b2

See diagram on page 247.

14...♖g8 15 ♖d2 ♗c8 16 ♖ad1 ♖xd2 17 ♘xd2

He prepares to advance his pawns.

17...g5 18 g4 ♘g7

Black's knight has moved five times to get to g7 from g8. Chess is weird sometimes, but it didn't confuse Lasker!

19 ♘e4 ♘e6

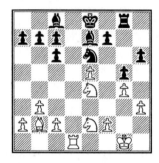

20 ♗c1!

Showing intelligent flexibility. The bishop is no longer useful on the a1-h8 diagonal.

20...♖g6

Black plays confusing moves just like Kramnik did later against me.

21 ♗e3 c5 22 ♘2g3 b6 23 ♘h5 ♘g7 24 ♘hf6+ ♔f8 25 ♘h7+ ♔g8 26 ♘ef6+ ♔h8

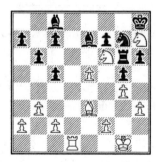

27 ♘f8

With some remarkable jumping around here and there Emanuel obtains

248

an advantage. This forces exchanges, which allow an invasion.

27...♗xf8 28 ♖d8

White invades.

28...♘e6 29 ♖xc8 ♔g7 30 ♘d5 h5 31 gxh5 ♖h6

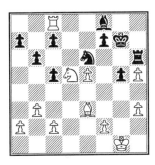

32 ♘f6!

Flexible thinking again. He returns to the queenside and wins.

32...♖h8 33 ♔g2 ♔h6 34 h4 ♗g7 35 hxg5+ ♘xg5 36 ♖xh8+ ♗xh8 37 ♘e4 1-0

Here are my first two games against the Berlin. In the first game I tried to copy Lasker's play. It contributed a lot to the loss of my title. I had a reputation for being formidable in the opening but against the Berlin the sharpness of my sword was lost for a good while.

G.Kasparov – V.Kramnik
Game 1, World Championship,
London 2000

1 e4 e5 2 ♘f3 ♘c6 3 ♗b5 ♘f6 4 0-0 ♘xe4 5 d4 ♘d6 6 ♗xc6 dxc6 7 dxe5 ♘f5

This line came as a surprise. I had had limited experience with it. I switched to 1 e4 as a main weapon only in the early 1990s.

8 ♕xd8+ ♔xd8 9 ♘c3 ♗d7 10 b3 h6 11 ♗b2 ♔c8 12 h3 b6

13 ♖ad1

At the same time I wanted to copy and improve on Lasker's play. My finesse was to use the a1-rook on the d-file. In exchange, I allowed Kramnik's king to go to the queenside. This is an idea Romanishin introduced. Incidentally, the grandmaster from Lvov defeated me a number of times, although I beat him too.

13...♘e7!?

This is a manoeuvre by Zoltan Almasi. The Hungarian grandmaster played it just a few weeks before our match so I had no time to analyse it.

14 ♘e2

See diagram on page 247.

All goes according to the Lasker plan.

14...♘g6

15 ♘e1

Lasker moved his knight to d2, so I also paved the way for my kingside pawns.

15...h5! 16 ♘d3 c5

Not 16...♚b7? 17 ♘c5+!.

17 c4

17 ♖d2!? was the right way according to Lasker.

17...a5 18 a4

I wanted to keep the a-file closed.

18...h4

This is confusing. Kramnik's last three moves were c5, a5 and h4. What is he playing for?

19 ♘c3 ♗e6! 20 ♘d5 ♚b7 21 ♘e3

21...♖h5

By means of unorthodox play Black has equalised.

22 ♗c3

If 22 f4 ♘e7.

22...♖e8 23 ♖d2 ♚c8

Going back with the king.

24 f4 ♘e7

Now he even goes back with the knight and he has a reasonable and safe position. Everything goes against logic.

25 ♘f2 ♘f5 ½-½

G.Kasparov – V.Kramnik
Game 3, World Championship,
London 2000

1 e4 e5 2 ♘f3 ♘c6 3 ♗b5 ♘f6 4 0-0 ♘xe4 5 d4 ♘d6 6 ♗xc6 dxc6 7 dxe5 ♘f5 8 ♕xd8+ ♚xd8 9 ♘c3 ♗d7

In the third Berlin game of the match Kramnik did not repeat his previous play and deviated here with 9...h6. Then 10 ♖d1+ (10 h3 was my choice in the fourth and last Berlin of the match. I also employed it in our seventh and final Berlin as well. 10...♚e8 He drew with ease in the last game of the match with 10...♗d7. Still he changed for this one. I show you an abbreviated version of Dokhoian's analysis. 11 b3 ♚e8 12 ♗b2 ♖d8 13 ♖ad1 ♘e7 14 ♖fe1 ♘g6 15 ♘e4 ♘f4 16 e6 ♘xe6

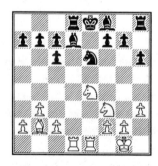

17 ♘d4?! (17 ♗e5!! This magical move would have given Kramnik a severe headache. 17...♖c8 [17...♗c8 18 ♘f6+ ♚e7 19 ♘h4 g6 20 ♘d7!] 18 ♘h4! White follows up with f4; and has a clear advantage.) 17...c5?! (17...♗c8 18 ♘f6+ gxf6 19 ♘xe6 ♖xd1 20 ♘g7+ ♚d7 21 ♖xd1+ and White is better. But 17...♖g8! should

have been played when Black can almost equalise.) 18 ♘f5 ♗c8 19 ♘xh6 ♖xd1 20 ♖xd1 ♖h8 21 ♘f5 f6) 18 ♘f5 ♖h7 19 ♗f6 ♖c8 20 ♗xg7 (20 f4!) 20...♗xg7 21 ♘xg7+ ♖xg7 22 ♘f6+ ♔e7 23 ♘xd7 ♖d8 24 ♘e5 ♖d1 25 ♖xd1 ♘f4 (25...♘d4!) 26 ♔h1! ♖g5 27 ♘g4 ♖d5 28 ♖e1+! ♔f8 29 ♘xh6 ♖d2

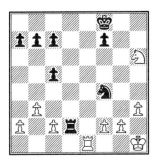

30 ♖e5! ♖xf2? This is a mistake, but he was already in time trouble. 31 ♖f5 ♔g7 32 ♘g4 ♖xg2 33 ♖xf4 ♖xc2 34 ♖f2 ♖c3 35 ♔g2 b5 36 h4 c4 37 h5 cxb3 38 axb3 ♖c5 39 h6+ ♔f8 40 ♘f6 ♖g5+ 41 ♔h1 Finally I brought down the Berlin wall. It was a last round game; I had to win to grab the first place from Kramnik. It eased my feelings about the Berlin Defence. 1-0 Kasparov-Kramnik, Astana 2001) 11 ♘e4 c5 12 c3 b6 13 ♖e1 ♗e6 14 g4 ½-½ Kasparov-Kramnik, Game 13, London 2000) 10...♔e8 11 h3 a5 12 ♗f4 ♗e6 13 g4 ♘e7 14 ♘d4 ♘d5 15 ♘ce2 ♗c5!? (New) 16 ♘xe6 fxe6 17 c4 ♘b6! 18 b3 a4 19 ♗d2 ♔f7 20 ♗c3 ♖hd8 21 ♖xd8 ♖xd8 22 ♔g2 ♖d3 23 ♖c1 g5 24 ♖c2 axb3 25 axb3 ♘d7 26 ♖a2 ♗e7 27 ♖a7 ♘c5 28 f3

♘xb3 29 ♖xb7 ♘c1 30 ♘xc1 ♖xc3 ½-½ Kasparov-Kramnik Game 9, World Championship, London 2000.

In our first Berlin after the match Vladimir played 9...♔e8, a move he did not use against me earlier. I got very close to beating him, but he escaped. 10 h3 ♗e7 11 ♗g5 ♗xg5 12 ♘xg5 h6 13 ♘ge4 b6 14 ♖fd1 ♘e7 15 f4 ♘g6 16 ♖f1 h5 17 ♖ae1 ♗f5 18 ♘g3 ♘e7 19 ♘xf5 ♘xf5 20 ♔f2 ♘d4 (20...h4 21 ♖d1 ♔e7 22 ♖d3 with a slight advantage) 21 ♖c1 ♖d8 22 ♖fd1 ♔e7 23 ♘e4 h4 24 b4 ♖h5? This is what happened in my game against Kramnik at Wijk aan Zee 2001, but better would have been 24...♘f5!?. Here I missed the opportunity to gain an almost winning advantage.

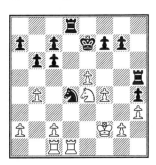

25 g4! We both overlooked this simple move. 25...♖hh8 (25...hxg3+ 26 ♘xg3 ♖xh3 27 ♖xd4!) 26 f5 and Black is in big trouble.

10 b3

In 2001 I had already played 10 ♖d1 against Kramnik, but I still could not get it right. 10...♔c8 11 ♘g5 ♗e8 12 ♘ge4 b6 13 h3 ♔b7 14 g4 ♘e7

15 ♗f4 h5 16 f3 c5 17 ♔f2 ♘c6 18 ♘d5 ♘d4 19 c3 ♘e6 20 ♗g3 ♗c6 21 ♖d2 hxg4 22 hxg4 c4 23 ♔g2 ♖d8 24 ♖ad1 ♗a4 25 ♖e1 ♗c6 26 ♖ed1 ♗a4 27 ♖e1 ♗c6 ½-½ Kasparov-Kramnik, Zurich rapid 2001.

10...h6 11 ♗b2 ♔c8 12 ♖ad1 b6 13 ♘e2!?

See diagram on page 247.

I still trust Lasker's plan, but use an improved version and hold back h3. In our last Berlin, when I finally stopped the slight embarrassment caused by this defence, I developed the knight on e4. But even in my second game with the line I followed Lasker.

13...c5 14 c4 ♗c6 15 ♘f4 ♔b7 16 ♘d5 ♘e7

16...♖e8 17 ♖d3.

17 ♖fe1 ♖g8 18 ♘f4! g5 19 ♘h5 ♖g6

20 ♘f6

The knight is jumping around just like it did in the Lasker game.

20...♗g7 21 ♖d3! ♗xf3?! 22 ♖xf3 ♗xf6

My knight will not become a hero like Lasker's, but its disappearance

doesn't mean the disappearance of Black's difficulties.

23 exf6 ♘c6 24 ♖d3 ♖f8 25 ♖e4 ♔c8

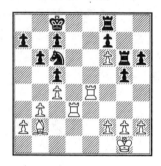

26 f4?!

More testing was 26 h4!

26...gxf4 27 ♖xf4? ♖e8 28 ♗c3?! ♖e2 29 ♖f2 ♖e4

The initiative is gradually drifting away from me.

30 ♖h3 a5! 31 ♖h5 a4 32 bxa4!? ♖xc4 33 ♗d2 ♖xa4 34 ♖xh6 ♖g8?

Black is somewhat better after 34...♖xh6! 35 ♗xh6 c4 36 g4 c3.

35 ♖h7 ♖xa2 36 ♖xf7 ♘e5 37 ♖g7 ♖f8 38 h3!?

After 38 h4 comes 34...♘d3!

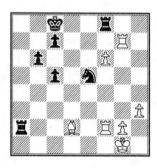

38...c4

Kramnik had little time left for the next few moves. Best was 38...♘d3! 39 f7 ♔d7! 40 ♖g8 ♖a1+ 41 ♔h2 ♘xf2 42 ♖xf8 ♔e7 and Black is safe.

39 ♖e7

According to Kramnik 39 ♗c3 would have given an edge.

39...♘d3 40 f7 ♘xf2 41 ♖e8+ ♔d7 42 ♖xf8 ♔e7 43 ♖c8 ♔xf7 44 ♖xc7+ ♔e6 45 ♗e3 ♘d1 46 ♗xb6 c3

47 h4?!

Allowing an easy draw. Better was 47 ♔h2! ♖a6! which however also draws.

47...♖a6! 48 ♗d4 ♖a4 49 ♗xc3 ♘xc3 50 ♖xc3 ♖xh4 51 ♖f3 ½-½

Probably, of all the past world champions, Lasker was the least 'professional' in his approach to chess – he had no need to be so focused – maybe my own attitude represents the modern approach of being highly professional in all aspects.

Wilhelm Steinitz the 1st

Steinitz declared himself world champion after his 12½-7½ victory over Zukertort. Before Steinitz, Morphy was the best player, but they never met. Before Morphy, Anderssen was the world's best player. Steinitz met Anderssen in a match in 1866 and beat him 8-6 with no draws.

Steinitz contributed a lot to the foundation of modern chess and also had many sacrificial games.

One might think his chess was too distant from mine, as he was born 126 years earlier than me. In a way this is true, yet I was a good pupil who was taught to respect all world champions.

My junior trainers Oleg Privorotsky and Alexander Shakharov also showed me Steinitz's games and I remembered his ideas and employed them. So let me show you how his games affected me. They may not bear such a strong resemblance as those in the previous chapters, yet Steinitz's very strong spiritual effect can still be traced back.

Here, Steinitz had a very nice riposte when his opponent tried to play on his first rank.

In the next two examples from my career, my opponents played on my back rank. I'm sure there must have been an answer to all this, but I failed to find it.

W.Steinitz – P.Meitner

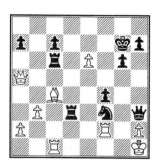

G.Kasparov – E.Magerramov

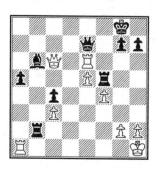

A.Karpov – G.Kasparov

J.Lautier – G.Kasparov

Once Steinitz misled me because I thought my opponent must have a defence against any ploy on the back rank. That is why I did not try to exploit White's boxed in king standing there all alone.

W.Steinitz – Ph.Meitner
Vienna 1882

1 e4 e5 2 f4 ♗c5 3 ♘f3 d6 4 ♗c4 ♗g4?

Of course my opponents never made mistakes like this.

5 fxe5 dxe5

6 ♗xf7+! ♔f8 7 ♗b3 ♘c6 8 ♘c3 g6 9 d3 ♔g7 10 ♘a4 ♗b4+ 11 c3 b5 12 cxb4 bxa4 13 ♗xa4 ♘xb4 14 ♗b5?

14 0-0 was almost winning.

14...♗xf3 15 gxf3 ♖b8 16 ♗c4 ♕h4+

Black has managed to get some compensation for the pawn.

17 ♔f1 ♘f6

Better was 17...♕h3+!

18 ♔g2 ♘h5 19 ♖f1 ♘c6

Black's knights control White's weak spots most effectively.

20 b3 ♖hf8 21 ♗e3 ♖bd8 22 ♕d2 ♘f4+ 23 ♔h1 ♖f6 24 ♖ac1 ♘d4 25 ♕a5 ♕h3 26 ♗xf4 exf4 27 ♖f2 ♘xf3

28 e5

White retains the advantage.

28...♖c6 29 e6 ♖xd3

See diagram on p.254

Black tries to take advantage of White's unprotected rook on the back rank.

30 e7! ♕e6

Black seems able to hold the passed pawn.

31 ♖e1 ♖xc4

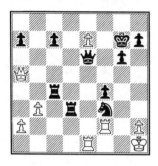

32 ♖xe6!!

White still takes the queen despite his visibly very weak back rank.

32...♖c1+ 33 ♖e1!!

A beautiful defensive move.

33...♘xe1 34 ♕e5+

This leads to checkmate.

1-0

G.Kasparov – E.Magerramov
Moscow 1976

1 e4 e5 2 ♘f3 ♘c6 3 ♗b5 a6 4 ♗a4 ♘f6 5 0-0 ♘xe4 6 d4 b5 7 ♗b3 d5 8 dxe5 ♗e6 9 c3 ♗e7 10 ♘bd2 0-0 11 ♗c2 f5 12 ♘b3 ♕d7 13 ♘bd4 ♘xd4 14 ♘xd4 c5 15 ♘xe6 ♕xe6 16 f3 ♘g5 17 ♗xg5

This is not the main line. Spassky played like this against Chekhov in USSR 1972, and I was following that game.

17...♗xg5 18 f4 ♗d8

In the above-mentioned game Black went back to e7.

19 ♔h1 ♗b6 20 a4 c4 21 axb5

21...a5

Magerramov sacrifices a pawn. He was not able to hang on the pawn with 21...axb5 because then 22 ♖xa8 ♖xa8 23 ♗xf5 wins.

22 ♕f3 ♖ac8 23 b3 ♖c5 24 bxc4 dxc4 25 ♖fd1

I felt there was no need to waste time defending the pawn. 25 ♖ab1 was also strong.

25...♖xb5 26 ♖d6 ♕e7 27 ♕c6

White is about to win.

27...♖b2

28 ♗xf5?

This is a dreadful mistake. White should just divert the queen first with 28 ♖d7! and then would win after the decisive 28...♕e8 29 ♗xf5! ♖xf5 30 ♖xg7+.

28...♖xf5 29 ♖e6?

29 ♖d7 was still good enough to stay in the game. Then 29...♕f8 is met by 30 ♕e6+ ♖f7 31 ♖b7.

29...♕a3!!

See diagram on page 254

I thought I had a riposte, just like the very first world champion.

30 ♖d1

My plan was to play on his back rank as well by 30 ♖e8+. But, after 30...♖f8 31 ♕xc4+ ♔h8

32 ♕a4, I missed 32...♗c5 which defends two pieces with one move. Then 33 ♕xa3 ♗xa3 34 ♖xf8+ ♗xf8 35 g3 ♖b5.

30...♖xf4

Black can even afford to take this pawn.

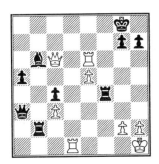

31 ♖f6

Neat but ineffective.

31...gxf6!

White not only has no mating attack, he does not even have a perpetual.

---

32 ♕e6+ ♔f8 33 ♕c8+ ♔g7
34 exf6+ ♖xf6 35 ♕g4+ ♔h8

I have run out of play.

0-1

A.Karpov – G.Kasparov
Game 17, World Championship,
Lyon/New York 1990

1 d4 ♘f6 2 c4 g6 3 ♘c3 d5 4 cxd5 ♘xd5 5 e4 ♘xc3 6 bxc3 ♗g7 7 ♗e3

Kramnik started with 7 ♘f3 in the second game of our world title match in London. I just gave him a pawn and lost. Okay, he played well, but still. 7...c5 8 ♗e3 ♕a5 9 ♕d2 ♗g4 10 ♖b1 a6 11 ♖xb7 ♗xf3 12 gxf3 ♘c6 13 ♗c4 0-0 14 0-0 cxd4 15 cxd4 ♗xd4 16 ♗d5 ♗c3 17 ♕c1 ♘d4 18 ♗xd4 ♗xd4 19 ♖xe7 ♖a7 20 ♖xa7 ♗xa7 21 f4 ♕d8 22 ♕c3 ♗b8 23 ♕f3 ♕h4 24 e5 g5 25 ♖e1 ♕xf4 26 ♕xf4 gxf4 27 e6 fxe6 28 ♖xe6 ♔g7 29 ♖xa6 ♖f5 30 ♗e4 ♖e5 31 f3 ♖e7 32 a4 ♖a7 33 ♖b6 ♗e5 34 ♖b4 ♖d7 35 ♔g2 ♖d2+ 36 ♔h3 h5 37 ♖b5 ♔f6 38 a5 ♖a2 39 ♖b6+ ♔e7 40 ♗d5 1-0 Kramnik-Kasparov, London 2000.

7...c5 8 ♕d2 0-0 9 ♘f3 ♗g4 10 ♘g5 cxd4 11 cxd4 ♘c6 12 h3 ♗d7 13 ♖b1 ♖c8

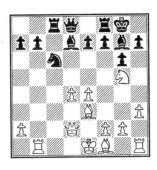

14 ♘f3

Karpov did not take the pawn with 14 ♖xb7? I thought Kramnik would not either. But Vladimir did not investigate Karpov's play. 14...♘xd4 15 ♗xd4 ♗xd4 16 ♕xd4 ♖c1+ (16...♕a5+? 17 ♕b4) 17 ♔d2

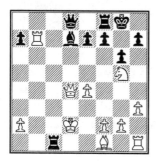

And now Black wins the queen with the lovely finesse 17...♖d1+! 18 ♔xd1 ♗a4+.

14...♘a5 15 ♗d3 ♗e6 16 0-0 ♗c4 17 ♖fd1 b5

Maybe this is a bit optimistic.

18 ♗g5! a6 19 ♖bc1 ♗xd3 20 ♖xc8 ♕xc8 21 ♕xd3

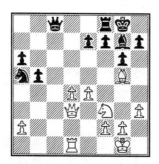

21...♖e8?

Black should defend the e7-pawn with the queen from d7 or b7.

22 ♖c1 ♕b7 23 d5 ♘c4

After 23...h6 24 ♗f4 ♘c4 25 ♘d2 g5 26 ♗g3 ♘xd2 27 ♖c7! White is better as Mikhail Gurevich pointed out.

24 ♘d2 ♘xd2

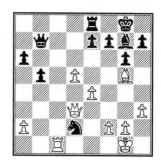

25 ♗xd2!

One can easily can miss the fact that the bishop can take back the knight.

25...♖c8

See diagram on page 254.

26 ♖c6!

Oh no! White is able to gain domination over the c-file.

26...♗e5

26...♖xc6? 27 dxc6 ♕xc6 (27...♕c7 28 ♕d7) 28 ♕d8+ Damn, unlike Steinitz I have no riposte against the back rank mate as after 28...♗f8 29 ♗h6 wins.

27 ♗c3 ♗b8

27...♗xc3 28 ♕xc3 ♖xc6 29 dxc6 (29 ♕xc6 ♕a7 30 e5 ♕d4) 29...♕c7 is no fun for Black at all.

28 ♕d4 f6 29 ♗a5 ♗d6

Black still can't take the pawn.

30 ♕c3 ♖e8

Of course with such domination White must be winning.

31 a3 ♔g7 32 g3 ♗e5 33 ♕c5 h5 34 ♗c7 ♗a1 35 ♗f4 ♕d7 36 ♖c7

This is more or less the end.

36...♕d8 37 d6 g5 38 d7 ♖f8 39 ♗d2 ♗e5 40 ♖b7 1-0

J.Lautier – G.Kasparov
Tilburg 1997

1 c4 c5 2 ♘f3 ♘f6 3 ♘c3 d5 4 cxd5 ♘xd5 5 e4 ♘b4 6 ♗b5+ ♘8c6 7 d4 cxd4

8 a3

This is the start of the so-called Dream Variation. This move occurred first in a dream of Hungarian IM Navarovszky. His friend Csom played it first and beat Stean with it in Las Palmas 1978. However for me this game proves to be not a dream but a nightmare.

8...dxc3 9 ♕xd8+ ♔xd8 10 axb4 cxb2 11 ♗xb2 e6 12 0-0 ♗d7 13 ♗xc6 ♗xc6 14 ♘e5

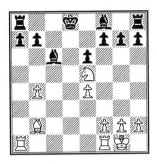

14...♔e8

I knew how to neutralise White's witty pawn sacrifice.

15 ♘xc6 bxc6 16 ♖a4 f6 17 ♖fa1 ♔f7 18 ♖xa7+ ♖xa7 19 ♖xa7+ ♗e7

20 ♖c7?? ½-½

With this bad mistake Lautier offered a draw. I accepted. I thought that had I played to exploit the back rank, the Frenchman would have a riposte just like Steinitz. But 20...c5! would win a pawn as 21 bxc5? ♖b8 wins.

As well as Botvinnik, Steinitz also contributed to my understanding of the concept of attacking on the h-file when the opponent has play on the g-file.

Here is the game I had in my mind:

Reiner – W.Steinitz
Game 4, match, Vienna 1860

1 e4 e5 2 ♘f3 ♘c6 3 d4 exd4 4 ♗c4
♗c5 5 0-0 d6 6 c3 ♗g4 7 ♕b3 ♗xf3
8 ♗xf7+ ♔f8 9 ♗xg8 ♖xg8 10 gxf3 g5
11 ♕e6 ♘e5 12 ♕f5+ ♔g7 13 ♔h1
♔h8 14 ♖g1 g4 15 f4 ♘f3 16 ♖xg4

16...♕h4!!
What a nice way to show the superiority of the h-file attack over that on the g-file!

17 ♖g2

17...♕xh2+!!
The sacrifice on the h-file provides a cute mate on the g-file. Chess is confusing isn't it? But marvellous for sure. By the way I also used the motif of having a knight on f3 and a g-file rook to beat Sunye in Graz 1981 in a sacrificial game.

18 ♖xh2 ♖g1 mate
Checkmate and what a neat one!

Steinitz's openings are no longer played in high-class tournaments, though he has left his mark on this phase of the game. Also I had a completely different repertoire. Steinitz's legacy was that the king can take a walk to the centre and several times I used this technique myself. Here are two of Steinitz's games where his king successfully took an active role.

W.Steinitz – J.Zukertort

W.Steinitz – G.Neumann

In my games, I did not mind taking risks and played with my king in the centre too. You saw my 1993 World Championship loss to Short. I selected it for the Botvinnik chapter where I pushed my g- and h- pawns. But I have plenty more examples of king play in the centre – in fact you can see this even in the very last regular game of my career.

G.Kasparov – V.Kramnik

G.Kasparov – V.Kramnik

V.Topalov – G.Kasparov

W.Steinitz – J.Zukertort
London 1872

1 e4 e5 2 ♘c3 ♘c6 3 f4 exf4 4 d4 ♛h4+

5 ♔e2

This is Steinitz's variation. White has occupied the centre and in return for the loss of castling rights his king will seek shelter behind his central pawns. Of course if Black can demolish these pawns, White's king will be exposed. Between 1900, when Chigorin played, and 1963 when Averbakh employed the opening as White there was only one game with Steinitz's line.

5...d5 6 exd5 ♗g4+ 7 ♘f3 0-0-0 8 dxc6 ♗c5

This is quite a wild line.

9 cxb7+ ♔b8 10 ♘b5 ♘f6 11 ♔d3!?

See diagram on page 260.

Steinitz continues to walk with his king in the centre.

11...♕h5

After 11...♗f5+ 12 ♔c3 ♘e4+ 13 ♔b3 ♕f6 Lasker lost to Shipley, USA 1893.

12 ♔c3 ♗xd4+?

Zukertort misses his chance to play 12...a6!

13 ♘bxd4 ♕c5+

14 ♔b3 ♕b6+ 15 ♗b5

White has enough extra material to give back some to cover his king.

15...♗xf3 16 ♕xf3 ♖xd4

Recovering one piece but he is still in arrears.

17 ♕c6 ♖a5 18 c3 ♖d6 19 ♕c4 a6 20 ♗a4 ♘d5

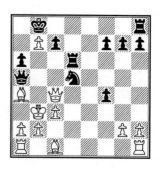

21 ♔a3

The king continues on his journey...

21...g5 22 b4 ♕b6 23 ♕d4

Zukertort keeps on playing despite having to swap queens.

23...♕xd4 24 cxd4 ♘b6 25 ♗b2 ♘c4+ 26 ♔b3

The king has to move because of the check but Steinitz liked to move his king voluntarily as well.

26...♘xb2 27 ♔xb2 ♖xd4 28 ♔c3 ♖hd8 29 ♖ad1 ♖4d6 30 ♖xd6 ♖xd6 31 ♖d1 ♖f6 32 ♗c2 ♔xb7 33 ♗xh7 ♔b6 34 h3

34...f3

Black can exchange some pawns but not all of them.

35 gxf3 ♖xf3+ 36 ♖d3 ♖f2 37 a4 a5 38 bxa5+ ♔xa5 39 ♖d5+ ♔b6 40 a5+ ♔a7 41 ♗d3 ♖f3 42 ♖xg5

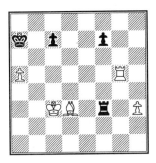

42...罩xh3

White still has one extra pawn, and that is enough.

43 罩f5 罩h7 44 罩c5 f5 45 罩xf5 罩e7 46 罩g5 罩d7 47 罩e5 罩g7 48 罩e8 罩g1 49 奧e4 罩c1+ 50 當b4 c5+ 51 當b5 1-0

It is symbolic that Black resigns in reply to a king move.

W.Steinitz – G.Neumann
Dundee 1867

1 e4 e5 2 ©c3 ©c6 3 f4 exf4 4 d4 營h4+ 5 當e2 d6 6 ©f3 奧g4 7 奧xf4 奧xf3+ 8 當xf3

See diagram on page 260.

8...©ge7 9 奧e2 0-0-0 10 奧e3 營f6+

11 當g3

Just like the previous game he moves away from the centre.

11...d5 12 奧g4+ 當b8 13 e5

White can keep the position closed.

13...營g6

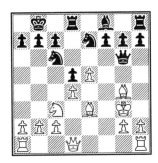

14 當f2

Returning the king to the centre.

14...h5 15 奧h3 f6 16 exf6 營xf6+ 17 營f3 營xf3+

Exchanging queens takes the pressure off the king.

18 gxf3 g6 19 ©e2 ©f5 20 奧xf5 gxf5

Black's pawns are vulnerable.

21 c3 奧d6 22 奧f4 當c8 23 罩hg1 當d7 24 罩g7+ ©e7 25 罩ag1

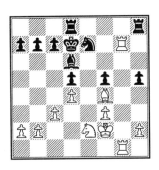

25...當e6

The king helps the pawns but Black's king becomes a target in the centre.

26 奧xd6 罩xd6 27 ©f4+ 當f6 28 ©d3 罩b6 29 b3 罩h6

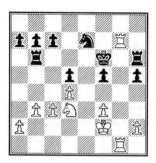

30 ♘e5

White traps the rook in a remarkable way.

30...♖b5 31 a4 ♖a5 32 b4 ♖a6 33 ♘d7+ ♔e6 34 ♘c5+ 1-0

Using the king in the centre was a technique I employed right up to my very last game. Here is the first loss from the mid-1990s.

G.Kasparov – V.Kramnik
Dos Hermanas 1996

1 d4 d5 2 c4 c6 3 ♘c3 ♘f6 4 ♘f3 e6 5 e3 ♘bd7 6 ♗d3 dxc4 7 ♗xc4 b5 8 ♗d3 ♗b7

9 0-0

Unlike Steinitz, I castled here but as you will see I did not mind returning to the centre.

9...a6 10 e4 c5 11 d5 c4 12 ♗c2 ♕c7 13 ♘d4 ♘c5 14 b4 cxb3 15 axb3 b4 16 ♘a4 ♘cxe4 17 ♗xe4 ♘xe4 18 dxe6

18...♗d6

Black's pieces look scary, but if they are not able to make any tangible threats he can have problems.

19 exf7+ ♕xf7

Kramnik prefers to retain the right to castle. There is nothing wrong with 19...♔xf7 initiating a march to the centre and meeting 20 ♕h5+ with 20...g6.

20 f3

This is one of my specialities, I like to block the b7-bishop. In my career I beat Karpov five times in the main Ruy Lopez and in each of those games I blocked his b7-bishop. I did it by playing d5 or f3. Perhaps my win in the second game of our 1990 world title match in New York, where my f2-f3 was a theoretical novelty, virtually refuted Karpov's opening. But I also scored nice victories against the Hedgehog where I reinforced e4 against a b7-bishop.

20...♕h5 21 g3

The immediate king excursion resulting from 21 fxe4 would be fatal. 21...♕xh2+ 22 ♔f2 0-0+ 23 ♘f3 ♗g3+ 24 ♔e3 ♕xg2 wins as White's king is too exposed. However an alternative is 21 h3 ♕e5 22 f4 ♕f6 23 ♗b2 with a complicated middlegame.

21...0-0

Nor can the black king take an early stroll: after 21...♘c5? 22 ♖e1+ ♔f7 23 ♘f5! ♕xf5 24 ♕xd6 White wins.

But after 21...♘xg3! 22 hxg3 (22 ♖e1+ ♘e4 23 ♖a2 0-0) 22...0-0 23 ♖a2! (23 ♔g2? ♕g4) 23...♗xg3 24 ♖g2 ♗e5 25 ♘c5 ♖ad8 26 ♗e3 ♗c8! Black is slightly better according to Kramnik.

22 fxe4 ♕h3!

On 22...♖xf1+?! I would have undertaken a glorious king-march in the centre. Had Steinitz seen it he would have loved it. 23 ♕xf1 (Recapturing with the king simply loses) 23...♗xg3 24 hxg3 ♗xe4 25 ♖a2! The most precise way of preparing the king march. (25 ♕e2!? ♕h1+ 26 ♔f2 ♕h2+ [26...♖f8+? 27 ♗f4]

27 ♔e1! [27 ♔e3 ♕xg3+ 28 ♔d2 ♕g5+ 29 ♕e3 ♕g2+ 30 ♕e2 ♕g5+ with a perpetual is given by Kramnik.] 27...♕g1+ 28 ♕f1 ♕xd4 29 ♕c4+ and Black has problems in the ending.) 25...♕h1+ 26 ♔f2 ♕h2+

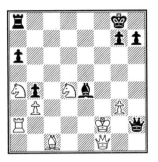

27 ♔e3 ♕xa2 28 ♔xe4 and White is winning as Black can do harm to the king in the centre.

23 ♘f3?!

Bringing the a1-rook into the defence with 23 ♖a2 was the right move. 23...♗xe4 (23...♗xg3? 24 ♘f5! ♖xf5 25 ♖xf5 ♗xe4 26 ♖g5 wins.) 24 ♖e1 ♗b7 (24...♖ae8 25 ♖e3! ♗b7 26 ♖xe8 ♖xe8 27 ♕f1 (27 ♖e2 ♖f8 28 ♘e6 ♗xg3 29 ♘xf8 ♗xh2+ 30 ♖xh2 ♕g3+ 31 ♔f1 ♕xh2 32 ♕g4 ♕h1+ White's king is too exposed, and Black holds.) 27...♕g4 (27...♕h5 28 ♘f5!) 28 ♘f5! ♕e4 29 ♕c4+ and Black is active but has only one pawn for the piece.) 25 ♕d3 (25 ♘e6 ♗xg3 26 ♖e3 ♖f3!) 25...♖ae8 26 ♖xe8 ♖xe8

...and though Black has only a pawn for the piece his bishops provide him with sufficient compensation.

23...♗xg3 24 ♘c5?

After 24 ♕e2! ♖xf3 25 ♖xf3 ♗xh2+ 26 ♔f2 (26 ♔h1 ♗xe4!) 26...♕h4+ (26...♗g3+ 27 ♖xg3 ♖f8+ 28 ♖f3 ♕h4+ 29 ♔e3 ♕xe4+

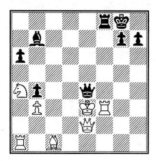

30 ♔d2 After the king march in the centre the position transposes to an equal endgame.) 27 ♔f1 ♗e5 Black has other playable moves as well (27...♗d6 28 ♗b2 ♗xe4 29 ♕c4+ ♔h8 30 ♗xg7+ and White can force a draw by 30...♔xg7 31 ♕d4+ ♔g8 32 ♕c4+ ♔h8 33 ♕d4+) but White can stay in the game. After 27...♗e5 Black can exploit the king in the centre. 28 ♕c4+ ♔h8 29 ♕f7 ♕h1+ (29...h6 30 ♕xb7 ♖d8 31 ♗e3=) 30 ♔e2 ♕g2+

31 ♔e3 ♕g5+ 32 ♔f2 ♕h4+ with a perpetual check.

24...♖xf3 25 ♖xf3

I did not want to enter a worse endgame after 25 ♖a2. Then comes

25...♖xf1+ 26 ♕xf1 ♕xf1+ 27 ♔xf1 ♖c8 28 ♗e3 ♗f4.

25...♕xh2+ 26 ♔f1

I thought Black had no more than a perpetual.

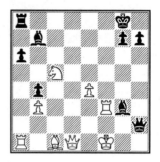

26...♗c6!

This came as a cold shower. However, I still hoped that Steinitz's method would work.

27 ♗g5!?

After 27 ♕d3 ♕h1+ 28 ♔e2 ♕e1 mate; 27 ♖a2 ♗b5+ 28 ♘d3 ♗xd3+ 29 ♖xd3 (29 ♕xd3 ♕h1+) 29...♖f8+ also leads to a checkmate.

If 27 ♖a5 ♗c7!.

27...♗b5+ 28 ♘d3 ♖e8!

Kramnik conducts the attack effectively.

29 ♖a2

Other moves also don't offer much resistance, e.g. 29 ♖c1 ♕h1+ 30 ♔e2 ♖xe4+ or 29 ♖a5 ♗xd3+! or29 ♗e3 ♖xe4 30 ♖f8+ ♔xf8 31 ♕f3+ ♖f4!.

29...♕h1+

Kramnik was already in time trouble and misses 29...♗xd3+! which is a forced checkmate. 30 ♖xd3 ♕h1+ 31 ♔e2 ♕g2+ 32 ♔e3 ♖xe4 mate.

30 ♔e2

See diagram on page 261.

I hoped that my king would survive, just like Steinitz's, especially in view of the time trouble.

30...♖xe4+ 31 ♔d2

If 31 ♗e3 ♛g2+ 32 ♖f2 ♛xf2 mate.

31...♛g2+ 32 ♔c1 ♛xa2 33 ♖xg3

Here 33 ♖f8+ ♔xf8 34 ♛f3+ ♗f4+ leads to a checkmate.

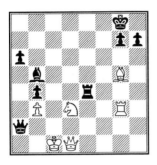

33...♛a1+ 34 ♔c2 ♛c3+ 35 ♔b1 ♖d4 0-1

I did not want to risk eventually being checkmated, therefore I resigned.

V.Kramnik – G.Kasparov
Zurich rapid 2001

1 d4 ♞f6 2 c4 e6

After losing my title in 2000, like Muhammad Ali I started to float like a butterfly and broadened my opening repertoire.

3 ♞f3 d5 4 ♞c3 dxc4

This was one of my new openings.

5 e3 a6 6 ♗xc4 b5 7 ♗d3 c5 8 a4 b4 9 ♞e4 ♞bd7 10 ♞xf6+ ♞xf6 11 0-0 ♗b7 12 dxc5 ♗xc5 13 ♛e2

13...♛d5

I had already decided not to castle.

14 ♖d1 ♛h5 15 h3

If 15 e4 ♞g4 16 ♗b5+ ♔f8.

15...♖d8! 16 ♞d4

If 16 e4 ♞xe4.

16...♛d5

Exchanging queens was safe enough but I wanted a sharper fight.

17 ♞f3 ♔e7

See diagram on page 261.

This is clearly Steinitz's influence. I intentionally did not castle and now advance with my king. I would never have lost this game if I had played safely.

18 e4

Kramnik sacrifices a pawn to get some play.

18...♞xe4 19 ♗e3 ♗xe3 20 ♛xe3 ♛c5 21 ♛e1 ♞f6

I did not feel like playing 21...f5, though it was playable. Then 22 ♖ac1 ♛b6.

22 ♖ac1 ♛b6 23 ♞e5 ♖d4?

One move leads to two different tactical motifs. I became too optimistic. I knew how many times Wilhelm won with his march in the centre. I couldn't wait to score with his brand of king play.

24 ♗xa6!!?

Kramnik sees a very deep exploitation of the risky placement of the black king. But he misses a simple win with 24 ♘c4!. Then 24...♖xc4 (24...♕c5 25 ♘e3 ♕h5 26 ♘f5+ wins.) 25 ♖xc4 a5 26 ♕e5 and Black has nothing for the exchange.

24...♖xd1

24...♖e4 would have resisted for much longer. 25 ♕d2 ♖xe5 26 ♗xb7 ♘d5 (26...♖d8 27 ♕xd8+ ♕xd8 28 ♖xd8 ♔xd8 29 ♖c4 b3 30 ♖c3 ♖e1+ 31 ♔h2 ♖e2 32 ♖xb3 ♖xf2 33 a5 wins according to Kramnik.) 27 ♗xd5 (27 ♗c6 ♖c8 28 ♗b5 and White is somewhat better.) 27...♖xd5 28 ♕f4 and with his king under pressure, Black has to fight to survive.

25 ♖xd1 ♗xa6

25...♗d5 is met by 26 ♗b5.

Alternatively 25...♕xa6 26 ♕xb4+ ♔e8 27 ♖d6 ♘d5 28 ♖xa6 ♘xb4 29 ♖b6 wins.

26 ♕xb4+!

Kramnik sees a great idea on the horizon.

26...♕xb4 27 ♘c6+ ♔f8

I had Steinitz in mind and thought I would be able to handle any back rank checkmate threat.

28 ♖d8+ ♘e8

I thought he might have missed this.

29 ♘xb4

White has only one pawn for the piece, yet Black is struggling.

29...♗e2

After 29...♗b7? 30 a5 ♔e7 31 ♖b8 ♗d5 32 a6 ♖f8 33 ♘xd5+ exd5 the lovely 34 ♖c8! wins.

Slightly better was 29...♔e7 30 ♘c6+ ♔f6 31 b4 g5 32 b5 ♗b7 33 ♘a5! ♗d5 34 b6 ♔e7 35 b7 (35 ♖b8 ♖f8) 35...♗xb7 36 ♘xb7 and the knight ending will be tough for Black.

Black's best was to divert the rook from d8 by 29...♗c4! 30 ♖c8! ♗e2 31 f3 ♔e7 (31...h5 32 ♔f2 ♗d1 33 a5) 32 ♔f2 ♔d7 33 ♖c3 and White wins back the piece, whilst retaining promising chances.

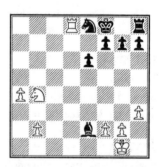

30 f3!

Kramnik's great idea is to trap the bishop. Black is paralysed because of the pin.

30...h5

After 30...♔e7 31 ♘c6+ ♔f6 32 b4 g5 33 b5 ♔g7 34 ♔f2 ♗c4 35 b6 wins.

31 b3! ♖h6

If 31...♔e7 32 ♖d2.

32 ♔f2 ♖g6 33 ♔xe2 ♖xg2+

The rook finally becomes active, but it is too late.

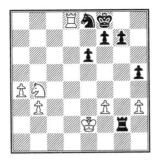

**34 ♔d3 ♖g3 35 a5 ♖xf3+ 36 ♔c4
1-0**

I resigned because White's two queenside passed pawns are too strong.

V.Topalov – G.Kasparov
Linares 2005

**1 e4 c5 2 ♘f3 ♘c6 3 ♘c3 e5 4 ♗c4
d6**

I played this line a few times against Leko, who repeatedly rejected castling even though he normally plays safe.

5 d3 ♗e7 6 0-0 ♘f6 7 ♘h4 ♘d4

After 7...♘xe4 8 dxe4 ♗xh4 9 f4 White has very nice compensation.

8 g3 ♗g4 9 f3 ♗e6 10 ♗g5 ♘g8

10 ♘b1, as Karpov played against Spassky, is a rather similar knight move.

**11 ♗xe7 ♘xe7 12 f4 exf4 13 ♗xe6
fxe6 14 ♖xf4 ♔d7**

See diagram on page 261.

Even in the last game of my career I follow the principles of a world champion. The king should be safe in the centre.

15 ♘f3

15...♖f8

After 15...♕b6 16 e5 ♘g6 17 ♖f7+ ♔e8 Black can do a lot with his king.

**16 ♖xf8 ♕xf8 17 ♘xd4 cxd4
18 ♘e2 ♕f6 19 c3**

19...♖f8

Now, in order to launch an attack first, I sacrificed a pawn. 19...dxc3 20 ♕a4+ ♘c6 21 ♖f1 ♕g5 22 ♕b3 ♘d8 23 ♘xc3 ♕e3+ 24 ♔g2 ♖c8 leads to a complicated position, as Topalov pointed out.

20 ♘xd4 ♘c6 21 ♕f1 ♕xf1+

After 21...♘xd4 22 ♕xf6 ♖xf6 23 cxd4 ♖f3 24 ♖d1 g5 25 ♔g2 (25 g4? d5!) 25...g4 Black probably holds, though once, in Game 32 of their world title match in Buenos Aires 1927, Alekhine freed a passive rook against Capablanca and managed to beat him. So who knows? But who do you trust when two world champions play against each other?

22 ♖xf1 ♖xf1+ 23 ♔xf1 ♘xd4

I knew the principle of having little chance of survival in a pawn ending, but during the game I lost faith in all champions and principles.

24 cxd4 d5

I played this instantly. Maybe playing for a fortress with 24...♔e7 was better.

25 ♔f2 ♔e7 26 ♔f3 ♔f6

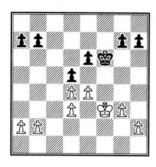

27 h4??

27 ♔g4 wins after 27...g6 (27...h6 28 ♔h5; 27...♔g6 28 ♔f4 ♔f6 29 h4 h5 30 g4 hxg4 31 ♔xg4 ♔g6 32 ♔f4 ♔f6 33 h5 wins.) 28 h3! (28 h4? h6=) 28...h6 (28...h5+ 29 ♔h4) 29 h4 as Krnic pointed out.

27...g6??

A blunder in reply. 27...h6! draws, since if 28 ♔g4 then 28...g6.

28 b4 b5 29 ♔f4 h6 30 ♔g4 1-0

I resigned here. Topalov was a point behind me before this last round game, therefore I had to share the first prize. Once I finished the game I somehow sensed that Veselin would win the next World Championship.

I suddenly understood that I could trust nobody – not even the champions. Then who could I follow? How was I to carry on playing chess? My successors Kramnik and Topalov beat me when I

used Steinitz's idea. It made me realise that somehow they were able to use the champion's legacy better than myself. At this stage, writing the Great Predecessors books was well under way. After this game I made the dramatic announcement of my retirement from professional chess.

You may joke that I retired to become an amateur in politics. But let me remind you I gained the chess crown in my second match against Karpov. Maybe I will become president after entering the race for a second time and will then rule for 15 years just as I did in chess?

Some may think I'd rather fight Putin than the new generation of chessplayers on the chessboard.

But now I'll make a sensational confession... I stopped playing chess not because of any particular interest in Russian politics, but because my last game made me lose all faith in my Predecessors.

* * * *

Now at last we take back the commentary from Garry and speak with our own voice!

Maybe these losses were hard to take, but they were a necessary part of Kasparov's career. His losses and the champions' wins were instructive and one can learn and profit considerably from studying them. Just as Kasparov himself did.

What did these losses help him to achieve? He completed a fabulous career, the best a chessplayer has ever produced. He was the dominating force in world chess for approximately two decades. He was world champion for 15 years. He was a world-class player for 25 years.

He produced the greatest number of superb creations by anyone who ever played our game. Kasparov himself estimated 250 of his games were of top quality and we are inclined to agree with him. In fact if one counts the great games he lost or drew maybe he played even more than three hundred superlative games. Furthermore no other player faced such strong opposition as him.

Very few won as many individual tournaments as him – and he must be one of the players who gained the most material rewards from chess. He also had a plus score against all his close rivals, except Kramnik – and against some of them very convincing plusses.

His contribution to the development of chess is immense, although we need still more time to form a comprehensive judgement.

He left the game in a different state from when he found it. Partly because of computers, chess culture would have developed anyway, but his unique artistry has been a telling factor.

This time we dared to joke around with his games, but we never trivialised them, nor for a single moment forgot that they will continue to bring joy to new generations of chess fans.

Kasparov's impact on chess will be felt for as long as it is played.